NUCLEAR
HOSTAGES

NUCLEAR
HOSTAGES

BERNARD J. O'KEEFE

Boston
HOUGHTON MIFFLIN COMPANY
1983

Library of Congress Cataloging in Publication Data

O'Keefe, Bernard J.
Nuclear hostages.
Includes index.
1. Atomic weapons — History.   2. Atomic weapons —
Testing.   3. Atomic weapons and disarmament.   4. O'Keefe,
Bernard J.   I. Title.
U264.O38   1983   355.8′25119   83-67
ISBN 0-395-34072-1

Printed in the United States of America

S 10 9 8 7 6 5 4 3 2 1

*To our children
and our children's children.
May we leave them
a world of peace.*

ACKNOWLEDGMENTS

While writing this book, I did not consult with any of my colleagues or associates, nor with any of the persons mentioned in the book, even though I know most of them very well. I thought it best to rely on my own memory, imperfect though it be, and on the open, unclassified literature.

The decision to rely on my own memory and open literature put a severe burden for verification and editing on my executive assistant, Theresa Kelly, who took on this task in addition to her duties in a large and growing corporation. Terry was ably assisted by her secretary, Jeanne DeFlorio, and by the research assistance of Raymond Champoux and Patricia DeMeo of our corporate staff.

At home the burden fell on my devoted wife, Madeline. It was her difficult task to maintain a healthy, happy family life with a husband who arose at four in the morning to write so that he could still be at work by eight o'clock. There were also the social duties attendant to a major corporation and in the midst of it all the added tasks of hostess to the directors of the National Association of Manufacturers. She accomplished it all with a grace and inner strength which few could muster.

CONTENTS

NUCLEAR HOSTAGES

1
THE BEGINNINGS

THE SPECTACULAR PLACE to start is with Wilhelm Roentgen, the discoverer of X-rays. Before him, scientific inquiry stretched back to the beginnings of time, building inexorably, relentlessly to an eventual revelation of the contents of the atom. Democritus coined the word in the fifth century B.C., when he taught that matter was not continuous, but was made up of small, indivisible units. Democritus's concept remained unchanged through the Dark Ages, the Renaissance, and the period of the hectic discoveries of classical physics. Throughout the eighteenth and most of the nineteenth centuries scientists were content to retain the simplified, classical version of an indivisible, indestructible atom. There was much to do and many lessons to learn without questioning it.

Classical physics moved fast. Sir Isaac Newton's laws of gravitation explained the motion of the stars and planets, opening up the opportunity for rapid advances in the science of astronomy and the practical arts. Development of the laws of thermodynamics laid bare the properties of heat and energy, forming the foundation for the industrial revolution with the development of the steam engine. Discovery of the principles of the electromagnetic theory paved the way for the invention of radio communication and the limitless applications of electric power. It seemed that scientific discovery had moved well out in front of the ability of society to assimilate its practical applications. Many people, even distinguished scientists, believed that we were approaching the day when man would completely understand the operation of the physical universe.

But classical physics with its fundamentals revealed took on the aspects of applied research, then moved into the domain of engineering. This was no theater for the visionary, the idealist, the dreamer of dreams, the investigator whose only motive was the search for knowledge. There must be new mysteries to solve, new avenues to explore, new barriers to be scaled.

Scientific discoveries do not occur in isolation. As the results of earlier discoveries are digested, practical applications are developed. New materials and components come into the marketplace, and from them new tools and techniques. One of the practical applications of thermodynamics was the development of efficient air pumps to investigate the behavior of gases at very low pressure. Another powerful tool came from improvements in photographic emulsions. Electromagnetic theory led to the development of a variety of methods for generating electric currents. The combination of these tools led the adventurous to the study of electric discharges in gases. When an electric current was passed from the positive electrode (the anode) to the negative electrode (the cathode) in a low-pressure gas, mysterious "rays" emanated from the cathode. Eugen Goldstein, a German physicist, christened them cathode rays. But what were they?

Most of the early work was done in the obscurity of physics laboratories. Roentgen brought the new phenomena to the attention of the outside world. Working with a cathode ray tube, he found that a surface covered with a special barium salt would emit light in a completely darkened room. He also found that he could expose a covered photographic plate. Conscious of the importance of his discovery, he performed one of the most famous demonstrations in scientific history before publishing his findings. He called his wife into his laboratory and placed her left hand over a photographic plate still wrapped in protective black paper. He then switched on his apparatus; when the plate was developed, he handed it to her. She saw on the plate a picture of the bones of her left hand, two rings showing clearly on her third finger. Frau Roentgen was the first person to see a picture of her own skeleton.

Roentgen quickly published his results; to emphasize the unknown nature of these strange rays he called them X-rays. The pictures were a sensation. One of the scientists intrigued by a presentation in Paris was Henri Becquerel, professor of physics at the Museum of Natural History. Becquerel set about to determine whether luminescent materials, however stimulated, would also produce X-rays. He wrapped his photographic plates in opaque paper so that only a penetrating radiation could reach the emulsion and proceeded to stimulate his fluorescent materials with bright sunlight.

For a month he had no results until he happened to choose a compound of uranium for his crystals. Sure enough, the emulsion was darkened where the crystals had lain, even through the opaque covering. It was as pretty and as misleading a piece of scientific work as you could ask for. Becquerel assumed that the crystals produced X-rays when fluorescing, but he was wrong. Excited by the results, he prepared more experiments with the uranium compound. But the weather changed and clouds came over the sun. Into a drawer went the plates, black paper, crystals, and all. There they lay the better part of a week. Becquerel knew that nothing could happen in the dark, but he processed the plates anyhow. He was dumbfounded! As they developed under the red light of his darkroom, patches darker than he had ever seen unfolded before his eyes. Radiation was emanating from the uranium without stimulation. Becquerel had discovered radioactivity. The age of modern physics had begun.

The term "modern physics" is a loose one, but the simplest distinction between it and classical physics rests on the divisibility of the atom. Classical physics was content with the idea of the indestructible atom, but Becquerel's experiments proved that with certain elements — in this case uranium — energy was released from the innermost depths of the atom itself with no outside stimulation. In the best popular tradition, this fundamental discovery was made almost by accident. In fact, for many months the importance of the findings, overshadowed by the excitement over X-rays, was not appreciated. Since they did not give pictures of bones, Becquerel's rays were not nearly as fascinating as Roentgen's, and no one else saw any profit in studying the mysterious penetrating rays from uranium. No one, that is, until the arrival on the scene of a precocious young woman from Warsaw in Russian Poland, Manya Sklodowska.

Manya, daughter of an impoverished mathematics teacher, immigrated to Paris in 1891 to further her studies in mathematics and physics. Living in a garret, subsisting on a near starvation diet of bread, butter, and tea, she obtained degrees in both subjects. The year she received her second degree, she met Pierre Curie, professor of physics at the Sorbonne, eight years her senior, the discoverer of piezoelectricity. Within a year Manya, now know as Marie, married Pierre; in 1897 their first daughter was born. In six years this remarkable woman, arriving penniless in a strange environment, had learned a new language, supported herself to obtain two degrees, met and married one of the country's most distinguished professors, and had her first child. At the age of thirty, mathematician, physicist, loving wife, and devoted mother, she looked for new worlds to conquer.

It didn't take long to find them. The fortuitous choice of Paris had kept her close to the work of Becquerel; she was fascinated by the mysterious rays that emanated from the uranium salts. Ready to embark on a doctorate, she was searching for a thesis subject and decided to find out if the property discovered in uranium could be found in other matter.

She started a systematic examination of a variety of ores, metallic compounds, and pure metals with no luck until she came to pitchblende, a natural uranium oxide ore named for its color. Pitchblende was mostly uranium, but she was surprised to find that the compound gave out rays with considerably more intensity than the pure metal. There must be impurities in the ore that were more radioactive than the uranium. The conclusion was straightforward but the proof was arduous. Pierre Curie had gradually been drawn into the experiments; soon he took his place as an equal partner. The procedure was to grind up pitchblende, dissolve it in acid, precipitate the impurities, and filter out the extraneous elements. Because of the small concentrations it became a process of boring routine to redissolve, reprecipitate, and refilter until there was a sufficient concentration to make meaningful measurements.

It is an aphorism that discovery "is 10 percent inspiration and 90 percent perspiration," but rare it is indeed to find individuals with the vision of an innovator along with the patience and perseverence of a careful experimenter. First they isolated one new element, which they called polonium for Marie's native land, and then a second, more radioactive, which they named radium for the intensity of its radiation. It was four long, painstaking years, working with tons of pitchblende, using almost primitive equipment, before they could isolate a weighable amount of radium. But they were thrilled at the result, for radium was a million times more radioactive than uranium, and they now had enough of the element so that they and others could probe more deeply into the nature of this new, densely concentrated form of energy.

During the long search, Marie, combining the duties of experimenter, wife, and mother, had not completed the requirements for her doctorate. In 1903 she presented a summary of her work as her Ph.D. dissertation. A long time in coming, it was a blockbuster when it appeared. It was certainly the greatest doctoral dissertation in scientific history, earning her not one but two Nobel Prizes. Marie, Pierre, and Becquerel received the Nobel Prize in physics in 1903 for their studies of radioactivity. Pierre died in an accident in 1906, but Marie herself received the 1911 Nobel Prize in chemistry for the discovery of polonium and radium.

It was not only the existence of two elements that the Curies had revealed to the world. Far more important was the intensity and concentration of the energy emitted. There were few, even in the scientific community, who understood the significance of this discovery, with its possible consequences to mankind. Pierre Curie, in a joint acceptance speech at the Nobel Prize ceremonies, using the example of Nobel himself, expressed the first gnawing kernels of doubt:

> One may also imagine that in criminal hands radium might become very dangerous and here we may ask ourselves if humanity had anything to gain by learning the secrets of nature, if it is ripe enough to profit by them, or if this knowledge is not harmful. The example of Nobel's discoveries is characteristic: powerful explosives have permitted men to perform admirable work. They are also a terrible means of destruction in the hands of the great criminals who lead the peoples towards war.

But the true seeker of knowledge has no time for evil, or even the contemplation of evil. The thrill of the search, not power or material gain, is the reward. The concept that aught but good will come from their revelations occurs to inquisitive minds, but it is quickly put aside as almost too sinful to contemplate. This is the rationale, the apologia, the philosophy, the fundamental faith built into the very DNA of the discoverer.

Pierre proceeded to dispel the notion in his next sentence: "I am among those who think, with Nobel, that humanity will obtain more good than evil from the new discoveries." And this was only 1903.

The next series of discoveries came from the Cavendish Laboratory of Cambridge University in England. J. J. Thomson, the director of the laboratory, plucked the first discrete particle from the billiard ball atom with the discovery of the electron. Reluctant to part with the concept of homogeneity, Thomson postulated a uniform positively charged fluid with negative electrons embedded like raisins in a cake. The next step was taken by a student of Thomson, a brash, forthright young country bumpkin from New Zealand, Ernest Rutherford.

Working with a sample of uranium furnished by Thomson,

Rutherford set about to identify the several types of radiation given off. The first he isolated was heavy, the size of a helium atom; he named it alpha. The second was lighter, the size of an electron; he named it beta. The next (naturally called gamma, the third letter of the Greek alphabet) was found later in France.

The heavy alpha particles proved to be the best atomic projectiles for further experiments. Rutherford used them to bombard various metal foils, particularly gold, which was malleable enough to be pounded into very thin sheets. The results were astonishing. Although the gold was only one fifty-thousandth of an inch thick, it contained more than two thousand layers of gold atoms. Yet most of the alpha particles sailed through the foil as though it consisted of empty space. This was remarkable enough, but he detected another, stranger phenomenon. The few particles that did not sail through seemed to bounce straight back from the target. To Rutherford this was unbelievable. That the heavy, fast-moving alpha particles could bounce straight back was "almost as incredible as if you fired a fifteen-inch shell at a piece of tissue paper and it came back and hit you." The particles must have encountered a tremendously strong electrical field, which could be produced only by an electric charge concentrated in a very small space. Thomson's atom was wrong. The atom's positive electricity could not be a fluid evenly distributed throughout the atom. It must be concentrated in a central massive core.

Rutherford's atom was mostly empty space. It contained a tiny central, positively charged nucleus, with the electrons whirling about it at a great distance, much like planets orbiting the sun. At first the theory was not well accepted. People didn't like the idea that all matter, even the atoms in their own bodies, was mostly empty space. But the planetary analogy was a soothing one, and to the general scientific community it "made sense."

Simultaneously, Rutherford was refining his theory of radioactive decay. As his picture of the atom developed, he reasoned: "If it were ever found possible to control at will

the rate of disintegration of the radioelements, an enormous
amount of energy could be obtained from a small quantity
of matter."

It wasn't clear how enormous the amount might be. He
pointed out that the energy released when one atom turned
into another was at least one hundred thousand — and it
might be one million — times more than the energy released
in the molecular change of a chemical reaction. Rutherford
was always good for a quote. To one correspondent he made
the suggestion that "could a proper detonator be found, it
was just conceivable that a wave of atomic disintegration
might be started through matter which would indeed make
this old world vanish in smoke." And this was only 1911.

Results of the new experiments did not jibe with the
theories of classical physics; new foundations were required.
Max Planck, a German physicist, provided the first. Since
the X-rays, alpha rays, and gamma rays acted very much
like light but also behaved like discrete pieces of matter, he
reconciled the two. Planck proved that we could think of
light beams as discontinuous hunks of energy, flying through
space like bullets from a gun. Strangely, the energy per bullet
varied with the frequency of the radiation. Just as the energy
of a projectile from a cannon is greater than a cork from a
popgun, so too the energy per packet of blue light is stronger
than red, white light is stronger still, ultraviolet light burns
the skin, X-rays can penetrate flesh, while gamma rays can
hurtle through steel plates. His work became the basis for
the science of quantum mechanics.

Picking up on Planck, Albert Einstein provided experimental proof by demonstrating that the energy emitted in
electrons from sensitive metals varied with the frequency or
color of the light. He verified Planck's important equation

$$E = hf$$

where Energy equals the frequency of radiation multiplied
by Planck's constant h, a very tiny number, 6.6×10^{-27}, or
boxcars preceded by twenty-seven zeros. This is the tiniest of
numbers; it explains that the individual quantum bursts of

energy are so small as to be virtually unobservable. To the senses light is continuous; to the atomic physicists it is not.

Einstein's genius was panoramic. Working in the solitude of a clerk's position in the Swiss patent office, he simultaneously turned his attention to the most cosmic of probblems, the constancy of the speed of light. Contrary to all common sense, several separate experiments had proved that light travels at a constant velocity, which nothing can exceed, whether the observer moves toward the light beam or away from it. Einstein reasoned that if this was so, since velocity is distance traveled per unit of time, then space and time must be variable. Objects would be shorter or longer, clocks would run faster or slower, depending on the position of the observer. Everything was relative, the only absolute being the speed of light. Once reaching this momentous conclusion, Einstein's imagination had a field day.

If the speed of light could not be exceeded, what if we had a very strong force that would push on a material object to accelerate it indefinitely? Wouldn't it eventually exceed the speed of light? The calculations said no. As the mass approached the speed of light, it would absorb energy and become heavier and heavier. To reach the speed of light, the mass would have to become infinitely heavy. Ergo, the experiments were correct; no object could reach the speed of light. But if this was so, another revolutionary concept must follow: It must be possible to convert force or energy into matter and vice versa. When he set about to calculate the conversion factor, not only did a very large number, the speed of light, enter the equation, but a much larger number still, the square of the speed of light. A tiny bit of mass equaled a vast amount of energy:

$$E = mc^2$$

Expressed in standard units, the value of c^2 is 10^{20}, that is, a one followed by twenty zeros. Just as Planck's constant was almost unbelievably small, the square of the speed of light was almost unbelievably large. In one mind-boggling, supernovaesque quantum burst of creativity, Einstein had united matter, radiation, and energy by verifying the quantum theory and postulating the Theory of Relativity, from the submicroscopic dimensions of the atomic nucleus to the vast reaches of the cosmos.

The conclusions staggered the imagination. They said that the energy in a pound of water could run all the steam engines in the world for two weeks or that the energy from a piece of metal as big as a fist could exceed all the explosive forces produced since gunpowder was invented. But in 1905 people could not comprehend what Einstein was saying. A great many scientists decided that the speed of light would turn out not to be constant after all and that Einstein's numbers were pure nonsense.

Back in England, Rutherford's atom was in trouble. The planetary concept, in which electrons sailed majestically around the nucleus as planets circled the sun, was excellent for conceptualizing the experimental results, but it broke all rules of electromagnetic theory. According to prevailing theory a moving charge must produce electromagnetic radiation — in this case, light. A moving electron would emit light at all times. That was only one problem; there was another, closely associated. As the circling electron emits light, it must lose energy. As it loses energy it spirals into the nucleus, much as a satellite or space shuttle, encountering the drag of air resistance, slows down, and spirals back into earth. There should be no stable planetary atom.

Enter now a new player, a young man from Copenhagen, Niels Bohr, hesitant, soft-spoken, the antithesis of Rutherford. Captivated by Rutherford's personality, Bohr joined his group to work on the problem of the planetary atom. Familiar with Planck's work and Einstein's, he applied quantum mechanics to orbiting electrons. He proved that electrons would be locked into specific orbits, moving from one to another only in specific little quantum jumps as they gained or lost energy. His theory showed that energy and mass varied like light, sometimes continuously, sometimes discontinuously, sometimes like a wave, sometimes like a particle.

Rutherford continued to probe at the nucleus. Firing his

alpha particles into nitrogen atoms, he broke off a piece and found it to be the positively charged nucleus of a hydrogen atom. He had made another fundamental discovery. The hydrogen core must be a basic particle, one of the building blocks of nature. He called it the proton (after the Greek word for "first").

As the second decade of the twentieth century drew to a close, the structure of the atom was becoming clearer. The concept of a massive nuclear core was well established. The existence of the proton as the basic positive particle was now identified. The characteristics of the tiny electron, revolving around the central nucleus, its negative charge neutralizing the positive protons, hopping from orbit to orbit when stimulated, were becoming better understood. But there was another mystery to be solved. The number of protons in a nucleus equaled the number of electrons spinning about, thus neutralizing the atom. However, something else was in there. The mass of the nucleus was heavier than the mass of all the protons. The heavier the element, the greater the discrepancy. The charged particles were in balance but the masses were not.

In 1919 the Royal Society invited Rutherford to give its annual Bakerian lecture, the highlight of the year's program in physics. Traditionally the Bakerian lecture had been used to review the state of research and the published work of the last year. No traditionalist, Rutherford decided to look into the future. He predicted that the basic hydrogen atom, the proton, would be the building block of all elements but that there would be found another building block, a particle of zero nuclear charge, which would make up the mass deficiency in the nucleus.

Concern over the possible misuse of the enormous energy of the atom was growing. Pierre Curie had given the first warning in 1903. In 1905 Einstein showed that the energy in a fistful of matter was greater than that in all the explosives manufactured to date. Rutherford, in his radioactive studies, had made repeated warnings. H. G. Wells, the prolific British historian and novelist, had read of the work on radioactivity and Einstein's equation on matter and energy. In 1914 he published a fictional account of a future world run on atomic energy, *The World Set Free*. The book predicted a world with trains, aircraft, and ships driven by this mysterious new power. Inevitably, the energy was turned into an atomic bomb, which ultimately destroyed this fictional world. In 1916 Rutherford made his own prediction about "blowing the world to bits." In the 1919 Bakerian lecture he repredicted the existence of the means for unlocking the energy of the nucleus "before men had learned to live in peace with their neighbors."

All these discoveries took place before I was born.

The early 1920s were a golden age for theoretical physics. On the cosmic scale Einstein reigned supreme. When his General Theory of Relativity, predicting that light from the stars would be bent by the sun's gravitational field, was verified by British scientists during a total eclipse, Einstein became an international sensation, made for the media. His absent-minded-professor appearance was perfect for cartoonists. Limericks, popular at the time, abounded. A typical limerick:

> There was a young speedster named Bright
> Who traveled much faster than light.
> He set out one day
> In a relative way
> And returned on the previous night.

The other side of theoretical physics, the subatomic, was ruled by Niels Bohr. The differences in approach were as different as the physical scale of the universe compared to the nucleus of the atom. Einstein worked alone, dealing majestically with planets and stars. Bohr was a team worker, laboring in obscurity with many associates. Although at least equally as important as relativity, quantum mechanics and the nucleus received very little public attention, but this suited the people involved.

Recognizing that years of work lay ahead, Bohr left England to return to his native Copenhagen. His reputation was such that he began to accumulate a small group of associates and students. In 1920 a group of Danish businessmen donated funds for a building, and the Institute for Theoretical Physics, generally known as Bohr's Institute, was born. Gradually the group built up, with George Gamow, the Cossack from Russia, Wolfgang Pauli from Austria, Werner Heisenberg from Germany.

Pauli made the first breakthrough. Known as the Pauli Exclusion Principle, it stated that no two electrons in an atom could occupy the same energy state. Two electrons could move in the first orbit because they were spinning in opposite directions. Two in the first orbit, but no more. Similar constraints limited the second orbit to eight electrons, and so on. This was an enormous improvement in the theory and led to a much fuller understanding. The relationships between physics and chemistry became clearer.

Erwin Schrödinger, Louis-Victor de Broglie, and Paul Dirac developed complex quantum and wave functions, but the goings-on inside the nucleus were elusive. They could not be pinned down with the precision that the physicists' experience demanded.

Werner Heisenberg found the answer. On the subatomic scale, events were simply not pin-downable. Interactions were so tiny that any attempt to measure them affected the measurement being taken. Calling it the Uncertainty Principle, Heisenberg demonstrated that if you knew where a particle was you couldn't tell where it was going and vice versa. It was intellectually disconcerting, but now the difference between the tiny world of the quantum and the larger world of our experience could be appreciated, if not understood. At the quantum level, if velocity is partially defined, position will be partially defined. If position is known exactly, velocity will be unknown. If velocity is defined exactly, position will be unknown. "They are," said Heisenberg, "like the boy and girl in the weather house. If one comes out, the other goes in."

The Uncertainty Principle was the final building block that allowed physics to move forward on a sound theoretical basis, but it carries with it some grave philosophical connotations. It says that we can never precisely determine what goes on in the world, but can only guess the probability of an occurrence. We must rely on statistical calculations for the answer. For most of us that makes no difference, because the number of individual atomic reactions in any event is so huge that the uncertainty is inconsequential. For some philosophers and physicists it is very significant. Einstein could not accept the concept of indeterminacy. "I shall never believe that God plays dice with the world," he stated. But for the physics of the twenties, it was just what was needed.

With theoretical physics on a sound technical and philosophic basis at the end of the twenties, experimental physics took giant steps in laboratories all over the Western Hemisphere in a free and open society. With constantly improving radio and mail communications and rail and sea transportation available and inexpensive, information passed readily from laboratory to laboratory, from nation to nation.

In France one family continued to dominate physics. After Pierre Curie's death, Marie succeeded him as professor of physics at the University of Paris. When she received the Nobel Prize for chemistry in 1911, she became the first person in history to win it twice. Her daughter Irène, born during the laborious search for radium and polonium, followed in her parents' footsteps and became an accomplished scientist. Her husband, Frédéric Joliot, had started as an assistant in her mother's laboratory. When they were married, they used the combined name of Joliot-Curie. The couple worked together, as had Pierre and Marie.

In 1930 there were reports from England and Germany of a strange phenomenon. When the light element beryllium was bombarded with alpha rays from polonium, a very penetrating radiation ensued, one that could pass through a dozen centimeters of lead. It was assumed to be a strong gamma or electromagnetic radiation. The Joliot-Curies repeated the experiments and improved on them. Not only would the radiation from the beryllium pass through lead sheets, but when it hit a substance containing hydrogen, it knocked out protons, which could be detected by Geiger counters. The Joliot-Curies, unfamiliar with Rutherford's earlier prediction of a chargeless particle, also speculated that they might be gamma rays. They published their paper in the French Academy *Journal* in February 1932, where it was read with amazement by James Chadwick at Rutherford's laboratory.

Chadwick immediately set out to determine whether this was the long-sought neutral particle; it was. Starting with the assumption that the radiation was particulate, he studied the effects of the beryllium on various other elements. Only one conclusion was possible: The radiation consisted of electrically neutral particles whose masses were equal to that of the proton. Chadwick named it the neutron.

The neutron was the final key to the basic structure of the nucleus. It explained the mass discrepancy, the fact that the heavier elements had masses much greater than the combined masses of the protons. It also explained isotopes. It had long been known that elements with the same number of protons and the same chemical properties could have a variety of masses or weights. This was caused by differing numbers of neutrons in the core, contributing to the mass but not to the electrical or chemical properties.

The year of the identification of the neutron, 1932, was christened Annus Mirabilis, the "year of wonders." Discoveries were popping up everywhere. In England, John Cockroft and Ernest Walton built a machine that accelerated protons to a high velocity and succeeded in splitting lithium atoms. It was the first of the new "atom smashers," much more powerful and convenient devices than the alpha particles emanating from radium or polonium. Gradually the Americans were coming on to the scene. Ernest Lawrence, a brilliant Californian, developed an ingenious device called the cyclotron. Instead of accelerating protons with one big push as Cockroft and Walton did, the cyclotron used magnets to force the protons into circular orbits. Each time the proton circled, it was given a little push and a little more energy until, finally, with its mass relativistically increased in accordance with Einstein's formula, it spiraled out to hit a target with the atom-smashing energy of more than one million electron volts. Also in America, Harold Urey found deuterium, the second isotope of hydrogen, followed up at Cavendish by the discovery of tritium.

Soon after Chadwick's discovery, Abram Ioffe set up a special laboratory for study of the nucleus in the Leningrad Physiotechnical Institute, and the Ukranian Physiotechnical Institute in Kharkov built a Cockroft-Walton accelerator. By 1934 four laboratories in Leningrad were working on nuclear physics under Igor Kurchatov.

One of the brightest young stars of Rutherford's laboratory was Pëtr Kapitsa, who had left his homeland at the time of the Bolshevik takeover. In 1934 the Soviet Academy of Sciences elected Kapitsa a member. He returned to Moscow to accept the nomination. Once there he was informed that he would not be allowed to return to England. Rutherford was furious. He raised every possible diplomatic protest to no avail.

In the face of this defeat, Rutherford showed a complete lack of wisdom of how the atom might be used in world politics. He shipped the entire equipment in Kapitsa's Cambridge laboratory to Russia, for which the Russians paid £30,000. The scientific Iron Curtain had begun to descend in the Soviet Union.

The exciting advances in physics brought scientists into the field from countries that had heretofore little interest or capability. Yoshio Nishina and Hideki Yakawa of Japan came into prominence. In Hungary, three of the most talented scientists surfaced. Edward Teller, Leo Szilard, and Eugene Wigner all came from Budapest but moved to Germany to continue their research. The brightest of all came out of Italy.

Enrico Fermi, born in Rome in 1901, won his doctorate at Pisa at the age of twenty-one and went on to study at Göttingen under the talented Max Born. Germany was not to his liking, and after a year he returned to Italy, where he proceeded to build up a superior school of physics at the University of Rome.

Fermi, a charismatic leader, had such a gift for seeing into the heart of problems and a paternal manner of solving them — with a piece of chalk in his hand — that his collaborators named him "The Pope." He was unique among the great physicists as an outstanding experimentalist as well as an outstanding theoretician. Others equaled him in one or the other, but none approached him in the combination.

In a time when the Cockroft-Walton accelerators and Lawrence cyclotrons were supplanting the weaker alpha rays as probes of the nucleus, Fermi decided to go in the other direction and use the chargeless neutron as his source. He reasoned that a chargeless particle, entering the nucleus easily, would be more effective than the more energetic charged particles. Furthermore, he found a method of slowing down neutrons by passing them through paraffin.

With slow neutrons, the Roman group had a powerful tool unavailable anywhere else. They set about to modify the largest nucleus of all, uranium. The results were too good. With the newer technique, they produced a bewildering array of radioactive chemicals. The natural conclusion was that neutrons were being captured and forming higher radioactive elements than uranium — transuranic elements not existing in nature. At one time they thought they had identified element 93, but the sample materials were too minute for chemical analysis. The discovery of slow neutrons was a giant step in experimental physics. Fermi and his colleagues patented the process, for which he was awarded a Nobel Prize in 1938, but they had missed the bigger game. They had split the uranium nucleus and didn't know it. Lighter elements such as barium, half the size of uranium, were in the debris but not identified. What happened? Why had the most capable theoretical and experimental team on earth not discovered the lighter elements? One reason was the minute quantities produced, too tiny for chemical analysis. Another was that they were looking for the wrong thing — for heavier elements, not lighter. It never occurred to them that a slow neutron with very little energy would split the massive uranium nucleus when no such effect had been produced with the mightiest atom smashers. Fermi's colleagues were looking in the wrong direction — up the periodic table when they should have been looking down. But maybe there was a more important, more fundamental reason. It was five long years before the correct analysis was made. By that time the world of physics had changed drastically. In 1934 the freely communicating international physics research community was intact. Rome was in touch with London, with Copenhagen, with Paris, with New York, with Berkeley, with Tokyo, with Leningrad, with Göttingen, with Berlin. The work was fully published. In hindsight, the conclusions are so apparent, so obvious, that it is hard to believe that five years would pass before the fact of uranium fission was established. On one conclusion, scientists and historians are agreed. If fission had been identified in 1934, Hitler would have had the bomb. German science was at its peak, the timetable of conquest had not been established, the Jews had not been expelled, the Allies were weak and not likely to seize the opportunity, there were enough dedicated Fascists in the scientific community to form a strong developmental cadre, and the work had been done in the home city of Hitler's puppet, Mussolini. Everything was in place. The German war machine would soon be strong enough to divert resources to new weapons as they were to do with buzz bombs and rockets. Instead of Hiroshima and Nagasaki, we might have had London and Paris.

Was some influence at work? Was some supernatural force calling the timetable for nuclear development? The Pulitzer Prize–winning science writer William L. Laurence called it "The Five Year Miracle." I can think of no better name.

Another sinister development, which was eventually to deny Hitler world scientific supremacy, began in Germany. It didn't begin with Hitler. Anti-Semitism is latent in all societies and has been for two thousand years, ready to crop out at any time. The Weimar Republic of post–World War I Germany was particularly fertile ground. A proud people, their empire torn apart, their population exhausted by war, their economy burdened by reparations, their currency destroyed by inflation, they looked for a scapegoat. Why had the kaiser, why had the empire failed? An easy answer was the lack of cooperation, the direct opposition of the Jewish merchants and industrialists. When Einstein's Theory of Relativity was verified by the British in 1919, Germany was ready for both heroes and scapegoats. Initially, the people were elated that this German citizen had risen suddenly to prominence, a prominence verified by the British themselves, that challenged the memory of the great Isaac Newton. But Einstein was his own man, not content to be a popular hero. He abhorred war and was an outspoken critic of German militarism. He became more and more committed to pacifism. With the rising tide of anti-Semitism in Berlin, Einstein was attacked for his "Bolshevism in physics"; the fury against him grew when he began publicly to support the Zionist movement. Roaming around the world during the twenties he was both loved and reviled. Soon after Adolf Hitler became chancellor, Einstein renounced his German citizenship and left the country. He accepted a full-time position at the Institute for Advanced Study in Princeton, New Jersey, where he remained for the rest of his life.

Otto Frisch was the next to go. A brilliant young physicist, he was forced out of Hamburg to England, which he left to work with Bohr at Copenhagen. The Hungarians had to move again: Wigner directly to Princeton; Szilard, after eleven years on the faculty at the University of Berlin, to England and thence to the United States; and Teller to George Washington University. At the other end of the Berlin axis, Fermi was quite comfortable in Rome. He himself was not Jewish, but his wife Laura came from a prominent Roman Jewish family. No real anti-Semitism existed in Italy; Mussolini had so declared on several occasions. But on March 12, 1938, Hitler occupied Austria without consulting or even informing his Italian ally. Mussolini was embarrassed and nonplussed. Partly to assuage his humiliation, he launched an anti-Semitic campaign for which there were no reasons, no excuses, no preparations. It was absurd, almost comic opera. In Italy there were no Jews or Aryans, only Italians. There were no Jews at all in southern Italy or in Sicily. Laura Fermi tells the story of the mayor of a remote village in Sicily who sent a telegram to Mussolini: "Re: Anti-Semitic campaign. Text: Send specimen so we can start campaign."

Joke or no joke, the Fermis decided to leave Italy as soon as possible, even though Enrico and the children were Catholics and the family could have stayed. Receiving a number of offers of positions in the United States, he chose Columbia University. Fortunately, he was awarded the Nobel Prize that year for his work on slow neutrons and was scheduled to visit Stockholm in September with his family to receive the award. The family packed up to leave for Stockholm and went directly from there to New York. Italy had lost her first Nobel Prize winner even before he received the award.

The Austrian Anschluss had another effect on Axis science. Lise Meitner was born in Vienna but had worked most of her scientific career with Otto Hahn. Meitner, who never married, had collaborated with Hahn for thirty years and had won worldwide recognition for contributions to knowledge in the field of radioactivity. For four years the team had experimented with and puzzled over the strange collection of radioactive elements created by Fermi with his slow neutrons in 1934. In 1937 they were joined by another eminent radiochemist, Fritz Strassman. The three were in the midst of pursuing new experiments in 1938 when Nazi oppression brought Meitner's scientific career in Germany to an end.

Though she had lived and worked in Berlin for thirty years, she had retained her Austrian citizenship and was allowed to continue at the Kaiser Wilhelm Institute after the advent of Hitler, despite the fact that she was Jewish. But when the Germans invaded her homeland, she became subject to the Nazi regime. She was dismissed from her post despite a personal appeal to Hitler by the dean of German science, Max Planck. Informed that the Nazis would not permit her to leave the country, her Dutch colleagues obtained permission for her to enter Holland without a passport. From there she went to Copenhagen, where her nephew Otto

Frisch had been since 1933, thence to Stockholm, where an honored position on the staff of the Physical Institute awaited her.

Otto Hahn and Fritz Strassman continued in Berlin. Poring over the radioactive debris from the slow neutron bombardment of uranium, they finally identified the presence of barium, element 56, about half the atomic weight of uranium. Alert now to the presence of the lighter elements, they soon identified traces of lanthanum, element 57, barium's neighbor on the periodic table of elements.

"How can this be?" they asked one another. It was as though they had put an ostrich egg in an incubator and seen it hatch into a chicken and a pigeon.

As chemists they were reluctant to challenge the physicists' doctrine that a uranium nucleus could not be split in half, particularly by a slow neutron of very low energy. On December 22, 1938, they published their results, replete with caveats apologetic to the physicists.

Before he told his discovery to anyone, Hahn dispatched a letter to his lifelong friend and colleague Lise Meitner, in Stockholm, telling her in detail of his experiments. Hahn's letter reached Meitner at a seaside resort where she had gone to visit friends for the holidays. Visiting with her was her nephew Otto Frisch, up from Copenhagen to be with his aunt during her first holiday in exile.

When she read Hahn's letter to him, Frisch disagreed and almost refused to listen. When his aunt persisted, he suggested that they take a walk in the snow. So they went for a walk, she on foot, he on skis. It must have been a strange sight: the diminutive sixty-year-old lady trudging alongside the thirty-four-year-old man on skis, gesticulating, trying hard to drive home a point, he indifferent, preoccupied, occasionally shaking his head in a gesture of unbelief. Suddenly, the light flashed. This was not an ordinary disintegration, in which a piece of a nucleus is knocked off by the force of an invading particle. They remembered an old concept of Bohr's in which the nucleus had been likened to a water drop. The neutron had not chipped off a piece of the nucleus, but had rather caused "the gradual deformation of the original uranium nucleus, its elongation, formation of a waist, and finally separation of the two halves . . . The most striking feature of this novel form of nuclear reaction was the large energy liberated."

The realization that the results of Hahn's experiment meant the fission of the uranium nucleus with an enormous release of energy was an overwhelming experience to Frisch. "I was excited and uncertain what to do," he wrote, "because I felt that this was a much bigger thing than I knew how to handle."

The first thing to do was to present Hahn's discovery and their interpretation of it to Niels Bohr, who was then preparing to leave for the United States. On January 6, the day the Hahn-Strassman report was published in Germany, Frisch went to Copenhagen. When he told the story to Bohr, the great physicist slapped himself on the forehead. "How could we have missed it all this time?" he exclaimed in utter astonishment. He was so excited that he almost missed the boat to Sweden, where he boarded the ship to the United States with only minutes to spare.

While Bohr was on the high seas, Frisch repeated Hahn's experiment and made further measurements that proved the interpretation of Hahn's experiment — uranium fission — was correct beyond doubt. On Monday, January 16, 1939, Meitner and Frisch sent a report to the British scientific journal *Nature*, which contained these famous lines:

> It therefore seems possible that the uranium nucleus has only small stability of form, and may, after neutron capture, divide itself into two nuclei of roughly equal size. These two nuclei will repel each other (because they both carry large positive charges) and should gain a total kinetic energy of about 200,000,000 electron volts.

In that report, Meitner and Frisch also christened the "new type of nuclear reaction" as "nuclear fission" because of "the striking similarity with the process of fission by which bacteria multiply."

When he landed in New York, Bohr was met on the dock

by Enrico Fermi, who had been in the United States only two weeks. Fermi was stunned at the news but characteristically delighted for Meitner and Frisch. They had finally found the solution that had eluded him and the other great scientists of the world for five years. Shrugging off any disappointment, Fermi went with Bohr to Washington, D.C., where they were to address the Third Annual Conference on Theoretical Physics, organized by Professors Edward Teller and George Gamow at George Washington University.

On Thursday, January 26, 1939, Niels Bohr and Enrico Fermi entered a George Washington University classroom, where the conference had already started. Word had spread around the university that the two Nobel laureates were about to report a new discovery, and the halls were packed with students and faculty, physicists, engineers, and chemists, more out of curiosity than of knowledge or interest. When Bohr told them the story, the room buzzed with excitement. Some understood completely, but others reacted with a puzzled "What did he say?"

When Fermi got up to talk, he mentioned the possibility that neutrons might be emitted in the process of nuclear fission. It was only a guess, but anything could happen at the energies involved. It was the first time the possibility of a chain reaction had been mentioned. Coming from Fermi it was interpreted as more than a guess, although there were no data to back him up. Fermi, "The Pope," had an instinct for such things.

One by one the young physicists left the room, some to go back to their laboratories to perform experiments, some to the telephone to spread the word to their colleagues. Two Associated Press reporters who covered the meeting wrote an article about what they had heard.

I was at the conference; I read the report in the *Washington Times-Herald* the next day, but it also made page two in the Sunday *New York Times*. Naturally, the story was picked up by wire services all over the world.

The secret was out!

2

NUCLEAR FISSION

I GREW UP in an Irish working-class neighborhood in Providence, Rhode Island. In high school I was very attracted to physics and mathematics, at one time considering physics as a career. There was a practical problem, however. I was also interested in business and industry; physics was considered an academic subject, with few opportunities outside of teaching. In the middle of the depression, being highly job-oriented, I compromised, choosing electrical engineering as the closest subject to physics.

Finances were a problem. My father was active in local politics; through Senator Peter G. Gerry of Rhode Island he had obtained a job running an elevator in the United States Senate for my brother, who was attending Georgetown Medical School. When my brother graduated, I inherited the job. George Washington University, located in downtown Washington close to my work, had an excellent physics department and a good engineering school. It was an obvious choice.

Washington in 1937 was a fascinating place for a seventeen-year-old college freshman.

Franklin D. Roosevelt's New Deal had hit its peak in 1936. He and his running mate, crusty old John Nance Garner of Texas, had won the most lopsided presidential victory in over a hundred years. At the same time their victory added to the Democrats' already towering majorities in Congress, leaving the Republicans fewer than one third of the votes in either chamber.

In his first term Roosevelt had put through an astounding amount of social legislation, beating back the forces of conservatism, the captains of industry, the "Economic Royalists"; simultaneously he had solidified the support of labor while making significant improvements in the lot of Southern Negroes. With strong popular support, large majorities in Congress, and a seasoned executive group, he was ready by his second inaugural to take on his only remaining domestic enemy, the Supreme Court.

Roosevelt felt he had cause to be angry at the "nine old men" in their impregnable fortress across from the Capitol. Of sixteen cases important to the New Deal, they had adjudicated against eleven, including the prime program for business recovery, the National Recovery Act, and the prime program for agricultural recovery, the Agricultural Administration Act. Confident of his power, the President proposed a "Court-packing" bill, which would allow him to add new members to the Court for any sitting justices who refused to retire at age seventy. It was a raw bid for power, and it failed miserably. In retribution he planned a purge against ten Democrats, many with impressive stature and seniority, coming up in the 1938 elections. The attempt was also a dismal failure. In a scant twenty months, Roosevelt had lost his momentum; his ability to achieve further domestic reform and recovery legislation had vanished. It was the end of the road for the New Deal.

The transition was dramatic. The Congress was full of strong personalities, chafing under the highhandedness of the "Eastern Establishment" who surrounded the President, still more than willing to step into the fray when a sign of weakness developed. Most of the important hearings took place in the Senate Caucus Room in the Senate Office Building. I ran the elevator adjacent to the Caucus Room and was often a fascinated witness to the high theater that went on, not only in the chamber, but in the halls and, yes, even in the elevators. When an exciting hearing was going on, the chamber would be crowded beyond its capacity day after day, with an atmosphere as charged with tension and drama as a criminal trial.

Prominent through his position, never compatible with his boss, Vice President Garner would walk around holding his nose in disgust but making no comment when the Court-packing bill was discussed. For color there was Tom Connolly of Texas, a large, florid man whose big black hat, shoestring tie, and long gray hair curling up at the back matched the cartoonists' image of a senator, and Howard Smith, who wore wing collars and a pince-nez. There was the courtly elegance of Henry Cabot Lodge of Massachusetts contrasting with the portly sloppiness of his colleague David I. Walsh. James Byrnes of South Carolina was a powerhouse who operated behind the scenes. Lowest on my list was Robert A. Taft, son of the former President. Taft was an iceberg. During the four years he rode in my elevator he never so much as nodded to me. My absolute favorite was Harry S Truman, junior senator from Missouri. Truman was brusque and decisive when working on a problem, but pleasant and considerate when relaxed. He often worked nights when the building was quiet. When not pressed for time he would ask me about my studies and, more often than not, would insist on walking upstairs if he saw me studying. I recall one time when Truman and James Byrnes, later to become his Secretary of State, stormed into the elevator after a particularly onerous hearing. Truman was irritated and impatient. Byrnes, the experienced, courtly Southerner, was lecturing him like a small boy. "Harry," he said, "if you're ever going to get anywhere in politics, you're going to have to learn to be patient, to roll with the punch, to take things in stride." "Bullshit!" said Truman as they walked out the door.

I ran the elevator from 5:30 to 11:00 P.M., six nights per week and every other Sunday. There wasn't much spare time except during congressional recesses, but I attended as many congressional hearings as possible and as many colloquia and seminars at the university as I could. Professors Edward Teller, the Hungarian, and George Gamow, the Russian, were

the stars of the physics faculty. Their international conferences on theoretical physics were the scientific highlight of
each year. I attended the 1938 conference even though most
of its reports were beyond the level of my training at the
time. It was a thrill to associate with the world's leading theoretical physicists even though I did not understand much
of what they were talking about.

When the Seventy-sixth Congress convened in 1939, the
Republicans recaptured the House. Roosevelt's New Deal was
dead; the Congress was still conservative and domestically
oriented. In 1934 Senator Gerald P. Nye, chairman of the
Special Senate Munitions Investigating Committee, had
shocked the nation with a series of disclosures, claiming that
World War I had been brought on through the connivance
of international bankers and munitions makers. There was
hard substance in many of the Nye Committee exposures,
but there was also a great deal of flimsy melodrama, which
did not bother a public eager to believe the worst about the
wicked "merchants of death." In the middle of the depression, the mood of the thirties developed into a militant paro-
chialism. Students and Gold Star mothers, unions and civic
clubs adopted resolutions proclaiming "America First." Pacifism became a cult, with isolationism its political theology.

In 1935 the Congress had passed the Neutrality Act, im-
posing on the President the duty to proclaim an embargo on
the shipment of "arms, ammunition, or implements of war"
to any nation at war, aggressor or victim alike. President
Roosevelt signed the act with misgivings. Notwithstanding
the Japanese moves into China, Germany's reoccupation of
the Rhineland, and the Italian conquest of Ethiopia, the Congress extended the Neutrality Act in 1937. In 1938 Hitler
moved into Austria, in 1939 into Czechoslovakia. In July the
isolationists still prevailed; the Senate Foreign Relations
Committee voted to postpone all consideration for repeal or
amendment of the Neutrality Act. On August 5 the Congress
adjourned without taking any action.

The Congress and the administration were marching to
different drummers. The administration, permeated with in-

tellectuals and internationalists, heard the messages from Europe and the Pacific and recognized the danger. The Congress was still provincial, dominated by older men from the South or Midwest who were concerned about domestic matters and confident of the isolation the oceans provided. Sessions were short, generally ending by midsummer. Travel was difficult; most had many months to spend with their constituents, worrying about domestic problems. Congressional staffs were small, usually consisting of two or three assistants, as likely to be relatives as not, who generally went home with the congressmen. There was no Washington press corps as later formed. Adjourning for the year on August 5, the Congress was living in another world.

On September 1, 1939, Hitler invaded Poland.

Roosevelt, sensing his opportunity, called a special session on September 21, once more requesting repeal of the arms embargo. The isolationists howled, but the President prevailed. America's defense efforts quickened. Congress authorized arms sales to Western Hemisphere nations and financed measures to spur military production. The hearings in the Senate Caucus Room now attracted fewer labor leaders and sociologists, more and more munitions makers and military men.

Hitler continued his march across Europe. Late in 1940 Great Britain, exhausted militarily and financially, informed the President that they would be unable to pay for additional arms and supplies. Roosevelt, unwilling to revive the memories of World War I by proposing a loan, came up with a daring plan to lease and lend material to England, which he explained in a fireside chat in December 1940. He invoked the concept of the Four Freedoms and called on the United States to become "the arsenal of democracy." The isolationists viewed the issue as their last stand; they waged a bitter two-month fight against the Lend-Lease Act, but it became law in March. Isolationism was finished in America. Increased defense expenditures were approved with alacrity; all resistance ended when the Japanese attacked Pearl Harbor on December 7, 1941.

The 1939 George Washington University conference occurred while isolationism was at its peak. The public, the Congress, and the scientists had not begun to awaken to the peril confronting the world. The thought of war was far away, the concept of secrecy unheard of. The news of Bohr and Fermi's announcement spread rapidly. In the Washington area uranium atoms were being split before the day was over. At the Kaiser Wilhelm Institute in Germany, the explanation of what their colleagues Hahn and Strassman had accomplished was electrifying. Nuclear research budgets were tripled by the Nazi government. In France the Joliot-Curies began the next stage of questioning. How many neutrons were produced per fission? At the Leningrad Institute Igor Tomm told his students, "Do you know what this new discovery means? It means a bomb can be built that will destroy a city out to a radius of maybe ten kilometers."

It didn't take long to discover that more than one neutron was emitted per fission. Almost simultaneously, a number of laboratories verified that the number was two or greater. That meant that two neutrons could emit four, four emit eight, and so on in a chain reaction that could produce enormous amounts of power or, alternatively, an explosion of heretofore inconceivable intensity. The scientists were elated but worried, worried about what would happen should this power come into the wrong hands. But it never occurred to anyone to stop. While they worried, they worked. A little frightened, a little bewildered, they kept on experimenting, sometimes hoping they were wrong, realizing they were playing with something far more dangerous than dynamite.

For the Americans the threat was remote; for the foreigners it was immediate. The specter of Hitler was real and tangible. They recognized the power and depth of German physics, that the crucial experiments had been carried out in Berlin, at the Kaiser Wilhelm Institute itself. I can remember them from the Washington meeting. With the exception of the blond Russian giant Gamow, most were stocky, swarthy, poorly dressed, heavily accented, clearly ill at ease away from their laboratories and their colleagues. The American people, their language, and their political system were a mystery to them. Many were recently uprooted from their homelands. Fermi had escaped the clutches of Mussolini less than a month before; Bohr was only a week out of Copenhagen. They made crude attempts to hide the secret, with the Hungarians, particularly Leo Szilard, in the forefront. Szilard proposed to Fermi that any information leading to the possibility of a chain reaction be kept secret. Fermi's typical reply was the Italian equivalent of "Nuts!" He did agree to hold up temporarily a paper submitted to the *Physical Review*, but in France Joliot-Curie was adamant. For forty years in France, Marie Curie's rule of always publishing, regardless of consequences, was considered unbreakable. In April the Paris team submitted a report to *Nature* headed "Number of Neutrons Liberated in the Nuclear Fission of Uranium." The average number was between three and four.

Realizing that the secrecy attempt was useless, Szilard threw up his hands; Fermi's paper was published and a rash of articles followed. The knowledge of the strong probability of successful nuclear weapon development was known to scientists in every civilized country and to any perceptive government official who inquired. Few did.

Lord C. P. Snow of England had a distinguished career as a scientist, statesman, and writer. He wrote a series of eleven related novels known collectively as *Strangers and Brothers*. Also a competent physicist, he is best known for his concept of the two cultures in modern society, the scientific and the liberal arts. He felt that the two cultures did not communicate with each other and that the lack of communication worked to the detriment of all. To help bridge to gap he published a magazine, *Discovery*, to acquaint the nonscientific community with scientific developments like quantum mechanics, the Uncertainty Principle, and relativity, which were modifying not only old scientific beliefs, but philosophical, cosmological, and theological beliefs as well. The magazine, respected by intellectuals of all backgrounds, published an editorial on fission in its September 1939 issue. Snow's comments on the principles, the practicality, the ethics, and the geopolitics of nuclear fission are a cogent summary of world knowledge in the months just preceding World War II. His final paragraph on the inexorability of the development is most prescient.

A New Means of Destruction

Some physicists think that, within a few months, science will have produced for military use an explosive a million times more violent than dynamite. It is no secret; laboratories in the United States, Germany, France, and England have been working on it feverishly since the spring. It may not come off. The most competent opinion is divided upon whether the idea is practicable. If it is, science for the first time will at one bound have altered the scope of warfare. The power of most scientific weapons has been consistently exaggerated; but it would be difficult to exaggerate this.

So there are two questions. Will it come off? How will the world be affected if it does?

As to the practicability, most of our opinions are worth little. The most eminent physicist with whom I have discussed it thinks it improbable; I have talked to others who think it as good as done. In America, as soon as the possibility came to light, it seemed so urgent that a representative of American physicists telephoned the White House and arranged an interview with the President. That was about three months ago. And it is in America where the thing will in all probability be done, if it is done at all.

The principle is fairly simple, and is discussed by Mr. D. W. F. Mayer in more detail on p. 459. Briefly, it is this: a slow neutron knocks a uranium nucleus into two approximately equal pieces, and two or more faster neutrons are discharged at the same time. These faster neutrons go on to disintegrate other uranium nuclei, and the process is self-accelerating. It is the old dream of the release of intra-atomic energy, suddenly made actual at a time when most scientists had long discarded it; energy is gained by the trigger action of the first neutrons.

The idea of the uranium bomb is to disintegrate in this manner an entire lump of uranium. As I have said, many physicists of sound judgement consider that the technical difficulties have already been removed; but their critics ask — if this scheme were really workable, why have not the great uranium mines (the biggest are in Canada and the Congo) blown themselves up long ago? The percentage of uranium in pitchblende is very high: and there are always enough neutrons about to set such a trigger action going.

Well, in such a scientific controversy, with some of the ablest physicists in the world on each side, it would be presumptuous to intrude. But on the result there may depend a good many lives, and perhaps more than that.

For what will happen, if a new means of destruction, far more effective than any now existing, comes into our hands? I think most of us, certainly those working day and night this summer upon the problem in New York, are pessimistic about the result. We have seen too much of human selfishness and frailty to pretend that men can be trusted with a new weapon of gigantic power. Most scientists are by temperament fairly hopeful and simple-minded about political things: but in the last eight years that hope has been drained away. In our time, at least, life has been impoverished, and not enriched, by the invention of flight. We cannot delude ourselves that this new invention will be better used.

Yet it must be made, if it really is a physical possibility. If it is not made in America this year, it may be next year in Germany. There is no ethical problem; if the invention is not prevented by physical laws, it will certainly be carried out somewhere in the world. It is better, at any rate, that America should have six months' start.

But again, we must not pretend. Such an invention will never be kept secret; the physical principles are too obvious, and within a year every big laboratory on earth would have come to the same result. For a short time, perhaps, the U.S. Government may have this power entrusted to it; but soon after it will be in less civilized hands.

Typically, Niels Bohr had already asked himself Snow's question, "If this scheme were really workable, why have not the great uranium mines . . . blown themselves up long ago?" and found the answer. For a time, it seemed likely to stop the whole program in its tracks. He noticed that the number of fissions produced when bombarding uranium with slow neutrons was less than 1 percent of the number predicted. Why was fission occurring in less than one out of one hundred occasions? Bohr knew that natural uranium consisted substantially of two isotopes, that is, two varieties of an element with the same chemical characteristics but different atomic weights. More than 99 percent of uranium atoms consisted of an isotope of atomic weight 238, and less than 1 percent of atomic weight 235. He also knew that elements of odd atomic weight tended to be less stable than those of even atomic weight. He reasoned then that only the rare uranium isotope was fissioning when its nucleus was penetrated by a neutron.

This threw a real monkey wrench into the works, because the two isotopes were chemically identical and could be separated only by mechanisms that depended on the difference in their weight. Since the weights were so close, differing by only three parts in 238, it seemed like an impossible task to separate the two in any meaningful quantities. Bohr seemed relieved to conclude that an explosive could not be constructed without separation and that the world was probably safe from destruction after all.

This not only answered Snow's question but gives rise to one of the mysteries of creation. Uranium is very plentiful in the earth's crust; if the U-238 isotope had been as fissionable as the U-235 isotope, the earth would have blown itself up long before any life started. It almost seemed that someone had deliberately planned for that not to happen.

The younger, more aggressive scientists wouldn't take no for an answer. Undaunted, they set about to find ways to separate U-235 from U-238.

An apparatus known as the mass spectrometer was designed to separate variants of the same elements by electromagnetic means. But the rate of separation was so infinitely slow that it would take twenty-seven thousand years to produce one gram of U-235 or twenty-seven million years to produce a kilogram. Or, if you will, it would take twenty-seven million spectrometers to produce one gram per year. Except for laboratory experimental purposes, the mass spectrometer was out.

Another method was the centrifuge, which spun materials

at high velocity, separating the light from the heavy just as a centrifuge in a dairy separates cream from milk. Other than the dairy application, no one had much experience with centrifuges.

A third method was gaseous diffusion, in which the uranium is converted into a gas, which is passed through a porous membrane. The lighter material, being just a little bit smaller, would pass through a little more easily and be more concentrated on the other side. The problem was that the gas would have to be passed through many thousands of membranes before usable concentrations could be produced.

Only the mass spectrometer was available in 1939. Using that tool, physicists at Columbia University concentrated two minute samples of U-235 and proved conclusively that Bohr's theory was correct. Neglecting the formidable problems of producing the isotope in any quantity, the press would not let go of the story. Having seen or heard nothing for almost a year, I was surprised to see this headline on page one of the *New York Times* on Sunday, May 5, 1940, over the by-line of William L. Laurence.

VAST POWER SOURCE

IN ATOMIC ENERGY

OPENED BY SCIENCE

———

RELATIVE OF URANIUM FOUND TO

YIELD FORCE 5 MILLION TIMES

AS POTENT AS COAL

———

GERMANY IS SEEKING IT

———

SCIENTISTS ORDERED TO DEVOTE

ALL TIME TO RESEARCH — TESTS

MADE AT COLUMBIA

Disappointed by their futile attempts to impose security and alarmed by reports of stepped-up activities at the Kaiser Wilhelm Institute, the foreign scientists took it upon themselves to alert the U.S. government to the danger of falling behind the Nazis. No better example of Snow's two cultures could be found than their flounderings. Enrico Fermi took the first step. Through George Pegram, dean of the graduate schools at Columbia, he arranged a meeting with Admiral S. C. Hooper, Chief of Naval Operations. He was accompanied by Merle Tuve, head of the Carnegie Foundation. When Fermi reported to Admiral Hooper the possibility of using uranium as an explosive a million times more power than TNT, the Navy's reaction was, in Fermi's words, "That little wop is crazy." Edward Teller's recollection is that the two scientists were "thrown out" of the admiral's office. Their rejection was not that abrupt, but clearly the Navy was not impressed. He was advised that the Navy would "keep in contact" with him, a don't-call-us-we'll-call-you routine. The Navy people had received technical training at Annapolis. Fermi was not a typical hare-brained scientist. It is hard to believe that, with a letter from the dean of Columbia University and a visit from a world-renowned Nobel Prize winner accompanied by the head of Washington's most prestigious think tank, the top command of the United States Navy could be so obtuse as to reject out of hand the possibility of a super weapon.

Szilard was becoming more alarmed, particularly at the prospect that the Nazis would capture the Belgian Congo's large stocks of uranium. He thought of Albert Einstein, whose reputation as physicist and pacifist gave him credentials in both cultures. Einstein, an amateur violinist, had once practiced the violin with Queen Elizabeth of Belgium. He suggested to Eugene Wigner that they visit Einstein to ask him to write to the queen. But they didn't know how to get to Long Island, where Einstein was vacationing. Szilard could not drive at all, but he remembered that Teller had a car and could drive. The three set out for the little town of Peconic to find the most famous scientist in the world, but nobody knew exactly where he lived.

Teller recalls: "Finally we found a little girl about ten years old, with pigtails, but she couldn't help us when we asked for Dr. Einstein. Then Szilard said, 'You know — he's the man with the long, flowing white hair.' That was enough — then she knew where he lived."

Einstein was skeptical but concerned lest the Germans get ahead. They all worried about the delicacy of the situation. Here were three Hungarians and a German-born Swiss proposing that they should, in behalf of the United States, advise a foreign government on what steps to take. Ironically, the conversation probably took place in German. The four began to get cold feet and decided that they should work through the U.S. government. Einstein agreed to sign a letter, which Szilard would write. Szilard knew Lewis Strauss, a banker, who knew a refugee Austrian economist, Gustav Stalper, who knew Alexander Sachs, an American economist who was a friend of President Roosevelt. Sachs agreed to deliver Einstein's letter to the President.

Albert Einstein
Old Grove Road
Nassau Point
Peconic, Long Island
August 2, 1939

F. D. Roosevelt
President of the United States
White House
Washington, D.C.

Sir:

Some recent work by E. Fermi and L. Szilard, which has been communicated to me in manuscript, leads me to expect that the element uranium may be turned into a new and important source of energy in the immediate future. Certain aspects of the situation which has arisen seem to call for watchfulness and, if necessary, quick action on the part of the Administration. I believe, therefore that it is my duty to bring to your attention the following facts and recommendations:

In the course of the last four months it has been made probable — through the work of Joliot in France as well as Fermi and Szilard in America — that it may become possible to set up a nuclear chain reaction in a large mass of uranium, by which vast amounts of power and large quantities of new radium-like elements would be generated. Now it appears almost certain that this could be achieved in the immediate future.

This new phenomenon would also lead to the construction of

bombs, and it is conceivable — though much less certain — that extremely powerful bombs of a new type may thus be constructed. A single bomb of this type, carried by boat and exploded in a port, might very well destroy the whole port together with some of the surrounding territory. However, such bombs might very well prove to be too heavy for transportation by air.

The United States has only very poor ores of uranium in moderate quantities. There is some good ore in Canada and the former Czechoslovakia, while the most important source of uranium is the Belgian Congo.

In view of this situation you may think it desirable to have some permanent contact maintained between the Administration and the group of physicists working on chain reaction in America. One possible way of achieving this might be for you to entrust with this task a person who has your confidence and who could perhaps serve in an unofficial capacity. His task might comprise the following:

a) to approach Government departments, keep them informed of the further development, and put forward recommendations for Government action, giving particular attention to the problem of securing a supply of uranium ore for the United States;

b) to speed up the experimental work which is at present being carried on within the limits of the budgets of university laboratories, by providing funds if such be required, through his contacts with private persons who are willing to make contributions for this cause, and perhaps also by obtaining the cooperation of industrial laboratories which have the necessary equipment.

I understand that Germany has actually stopped the sale of uranium from the Czechoslovakian mines which she has taken over. That she should have taken such early action might perhaps be understood on the ground that the son of the German Under-Secretary of State, von Weizsacker, is attached to the Kaiser-Wilhelm-Institute in Berlin where some of the American work on uranium is now being repeated.

Yours very truly,

(signed)   Albert Einstein

It took two months for Sachs to get in to see Roosevelt. In the meantime World War II had begun. On October 11, Sachs met with Roosevelt, his aide General Edwin M. Watson, and two military ordnance experts. Roosevelt was a lot more perceptive than the admiral had been. "Alex," he said, "what you are after is to see that the Nazis don't blow us up." Then he told General Watson, "This requires action."

It would be dramatic to report that this meeting got the ball rolling. But bureaucracy and the culture gap were alive in the land. The President did appoint an Advisory Committee on Uranium whose members included Lyman J. Briggs, the director of the National Bureau of Standards, Army Colonel Keith Z. Adamson, and Navy Commander Gilbert C. Hoover. The first meeting of the committee took place on October 21. Present were the ubiquitous Hungarians: Szilärd, Wigner, and Teller. They asked for $6000 to get the project going, but instead were treated to a pompous lecture by the colonel on the nature of war. It usually took two wars, he told them, before a new weapon could be fully developed, and besides, it was moral issues, not new arms, that brought victory.

The committee made a favorable report to the President on November 1, but no one wanted to go out on a limb to put up the money. Finally, after four months of diddling, the $6000 was appropriated. The money was not actually released, however, until February 1940. Further progress had to await the organization of the National Defense Research Committee. Bureaucracy had prevailed.

Meanwhile, back at the laboratories, research was proceeding on a shoestring. Recognizing the extraordinary engineering problems of separating the rare U-235 from the abundant U-238, the physicists set about to determine how much U-235 would be needed and whether or not it could be made into an explosive. The first problem was to calculate the critical mass. Neutrons injected into a mass of pure U-235, which caused fissions that emitted more than one neutron per fission, would not be sufficient. Most of the neutrons, being uncharged, would escape from the metal without being absorbed. As the amount of metal became larger and larger, the probability of a given neutron hitting a uranium nucleus became greater and greater, until at some size, the critical mass, a self-sustaining chain reaction could occur.

To make this calculation it would be necessary to determine the "cross section" of U-235, the probability of any given neutron hitting any given nucleus as it passes through a certain area. (Scientists like to give colorful names to their units. The unit for cross section is called a barn, from the description of a weak hitter in baseball who "couldn't hit a barn door with a baseball bat.") Cross-section measurements were the prime occupation of world physicists during 1939. Early crude measurements put the critical mass in terms of tons of U-235, ruling out the possibility of a weapon. Later refinements brought the most probable figure to some small number of pounds.

British scientists, stimulated by the war, began to have more concern about uranium research, spurred by their desire to beat the Nazis. The native-born Americans were still not giving it much attention, with the result that the British progressed faster than the Americans. Otto Frisch, the discoverer of fission, working with another refugee, Rudolf Peierls, again published the definitive paper. With more chemical engineering background than their colleagues, they were optimistic about isotope separation. A difficult, expensive engineering job, they felt, but quite practical. They calculated a critical mass to be a kilogram, about two pounds. To make a bomb, bring together, quite rapidly, two pieces of one pound each; the result would be an explosion with a force unequaled in human history.

The paper consisted of three typewritten pages, not more than a thousand words, but it was all there. A uranium bomb was feasible. The British realized the formidable task of separating the isotopes. They felt that they could do it but that it would take too much effort away from their primary task of survival. John Cockroft brought the Peierls-Frisch memo to the United States to talk it over with a number of American scientists. There was not the urgency in America, but as Snow had said in his *Discovery* editorial, "If it is not made in America this year, it may be next year in Germany." The Americans were still taking seven months to appropriate $6000.

Another development in California stirred up additional

interest. Edwin McMillan, working with colleagues Philip Abelson and Glenn Seaborg, achieved what Fermi thought he had done in 1934 — produced transuranic elements. Uranium was isolated in 1789, about the time the planet Uranus was discovered, so the new element was named for the planet. The first of the transuranic elements was named for the planet Neptune and the following for the planet Pluto. The California team found that when U-238 absorbed a neutron, it formed the nonstable isotope U-239. The U-239, after two and a half days, emitted an electron from its nucleus, giving it a higher positive charge and becoming neptunium, element 93. After a few more days, the neptunium emitted another electron, moving it up one more notch on the atomic scale to element 94, or plutonium. All calculations showed that Pu-239, with its odd number of particles in the nucleus, should be as fissionable as U-235. This added another whole dimension. Not only could plutonium be made in a pile from the plentiful U-238, but it was a different chemical element, not just another isotope of uranium, and should be separable by chemical means.

Now there were two roads to oblivion.

About the middle of 1940, the Americans began to get organized. The driving force was Vannevar Bush, chairman of the National Advisory Council for Aeronautics (NACA). A shrewd, spry Yankee — plainspoken, but with a disarming twinkle in his eye and a boyish grin — Bush was well known for his original work in applied mathematics and electrical engineering. Skilled in Washington politics, he brought together a group including Karl T. Compton, president of MIT, and James B. Conant, president of Harvard, to evolve a plan for a committee that would have the same relationship to the development of warfare devices that NACA had to problems of flight.

Bush's good friend Harry Hopkins persuaded President Roosevelt to place Bush at the head of a National Defense Research Committee (NDRC), whose function was to search out new opportunities to apply science to the needs of war. NDRC did not have to wait for a bequest from the Army or the Navy; it could judge what was needed and use its own funds. The uranium project was only a small part of the total scientific research spectrum, but it was foundering in a military-dominated Uranium Committee; the arrival of NDRC on the scene was a godsend.

Bush promptly reorganized the Uranium Committee, replacing the military officers with civilian scientists and appropriating funds for isotope separation and studies of the chain reaction.

Early studies on the feasibility of a chain reaction were carried out by Fermi with his team at Columbia. The basic scheme was to take some lumps of natural uranium mixed with a neutron source to cause fissions in the U-235. When the nuclei fissioned, the fission neutrons would have to be slowed down before hitting additional nuclei and causing further fissions. Neutrons could best be slowed down by hitting nuclei close to their own size. Heavy water containing the deuterium isotope of hydrogen would be best, but there were no supplies of heavy water available. Carbon was the next best choice; it was most useful in the form of graphite. Graphite was black and dirty; uranium oxide was black and dirty. Fermi and his crew looked more like coal miners than researchers as they measured the all important cross sections and scattering characteristics.

Early in 1942 chain reaction research was moved to the University of Chicago under Professor Arthur H. Compton, brother of Karl. The first chain reaction was planned to occur in a new building in the Argonne Forest near Chicago. When it became clear that the building would not be ready in time, the only available space big enough and isolated enough to handle the experiment was a squash court under the west stands of the Stagg Athletic Field. It wasn't being used, so Fermi commandeered it for his first critical experiment.

The simple concept was to build a lattice of graphite bricks, periodically interspersing cans of uranium oxide until it was big enough to capture escaping neutrons and maintain a critical reaction. Its supporting frame was made of wooden timbers. There were no plans or blueprints; just pile layer after layer of carbon bricks and uranium cans until something started to happen. As the experiment took shape it looked like a huge pile of bricks, so that's what it was called, a "pile." The bigger the pile became, the fewer neutrons escaped. When the number of neutrons absorbed equaled the number of neutrons generated, the pile would become "critical," or self-sustaining. If the number of neutrons generated became too large, the pile would heat up and melt down, so additional neutron absorbers would have to be available.

Into the slots went rods made of cadmium, known to be a good absorber of neutrons. If the neutron flux became too great, the rods could be inserted to slow down the reaction. If the flux was not large enough, the rods could be withdrawn. The emergency safety system was crudity itself. One rod was attached to a rope that ran over a pulley and was held out of the pile by a heavy weight on the other end. Standing by was a man with a heavy ax, ready to cut the rope and let the emergency rod fall back into the pile should the mechanism controlling the other rods fail. As extra special precautions, two young scientists stood tense and silent on a platform overlooking the pile, holding buckets filled with cadmium solution, ready to douse the pile with cadmium should all else fail. They were known to their colleagues as the "suicide bucket brigade."

As the pile grew larger and larger, the neutron strength became stronger and stronger, so it became easier to predict when it could be made to go critical. When the fifty-seventh layer of bricks was completed, the work was halted. All the cadmium rods but one were removed and the neutron count taken. It was clear from the count that once the remaining rod was removed, the pile would go critical. Since it was after midnight, all the rods were put back in and locked so that the team could get some sleep and be refreshed for the great day.

It was bitterly cold under the stands of the football field in Chicago on December 2, 1942. The scientists had discovered a supply of old raccoon coats used by football cheerleaders. Several donned the coats, adding to the eerie unreality. Fermi started at 9:00 A.M. At 9:45 he ordered the electrically controlled rods to be withdrawn. The clicking of the counters announced the quickening of the neutron flux. Slowly, deliberately the last rod was pulled out. Compton arrived to watch the final moments. The man with the ax stood poised, the suicide brigade tense and alert with their buckets ready. At 3:25 P.M. Chicago time, the needle on the chart recorder moved up in a straight vertical line that did not level off as before. Fermi raised his hand. "The pile has gone critical," he announced.

The atomic age was born.

For twenty-eight minutes the atomic fire was allowed to burn. Then as tension mounted, Fermi ordered "Zip in." The emergency rod was released and dropped into the pile.

"No cheer went up," said Herb Anderson, Fermi's assistant, "but everyone had a sense of excitement. They had been witness to a great moment in history. Wigner was prepared with a bottle of Chianti. We drank from paper cups and began to say things to one another. But there were no words that could express adequately just what we felt."

Compton returned to his office, telephoned Conant at Harvard, and told him the news:

COMPTON: "Jim, this is Arthur. I thought you'd want to know that the Italian navigator has just landed in the New World."

CONANT: "What, already?"

COMPTON: "Yes, the earth was smaller than estimated, and he arrived several days earlier than he had expected."

CONANT: "Were the natives friendly?"

COMPTON: "They were indeed. Everyone landed safe and happy."

The success at Stagg Field was reassuring. The basic question up to that time was whether a chain reaction could be created by nuclear fission. Once the answer was known to be yes, the pace quickened.

As the prospects for a controlled chain reaction and the

separation of U-235 became more likely, the uranium program gained stature within scientific management groups. After Pearl Harbor, President Roosevelt decided that it should have continuous high-level attention. Vice President Henry A. Wallace had a technical background; he could understand the problems to be solved better than most of the senior people in the administration, so he was appointed to head a top policy group, with Secretary of War Henry L. Stimson and Vannevar Bush. Recognizing that most of the problems would be with engineering, requiring the construction of mammoth facilities, the group decided to bring in the Army Corps of Engineers, initially to handle the construction but eventually to oversee the whole project. The officer selected to head the project was newly promoted Brigadier General Leslie R. Groves. Burly, impatient, tactless, military to the core, West Pointer Groves seemed an unlikely choice to work with the supersensitive scientists. Bush's initial reaction was negative. After their first meeting, Bush phoned Major General William D. Styer, Groves's boss.

"What do you think of him?" Styer asked.

"He looks too aggressive."

"He is, but we thought that quality of his was what we needed most. Groves is a go-getter; he gets things done."

"I'm afraid he may have trouble with the scientists," Bush explained.

"You may be right," Styer conceded, "and you and I will probably have to keep smoothing things out. But the work will move. I can assure you of that!"

Bush remained unconvinced. After his conversation with Styer, he wrote to Secretary Stimson: "Having seen Groves briefly, I doubt whether he has sufficient tact for the job. I fear we are in the soup."

Tactless or not, Groves was the man for the job. Two months after Groves's appointment, Fermi was successful with his first chain reaction; Groves was off and running. The dimensions of the problem were understood. Basic research was in good shape under Compton and Fermi at Chicago. Groves had to find a location for the uranium separation plant, another for the huge piles to produce plutonium, and a remote laboratory in which to design and fabricate the bomb. But first of all, like any good engineer, he had to be certain of a supply of raw material.

Groves decided to maintain his headquarters in Washington. His deputy, Colonel James C. Marshall, had been district engineer for the Manhattan District, so Groves decided to keep that title as a cover, naming the overall program the Manhattan Engineering District, or, for short, the Manhattan Project.

Scientists working on the program had not worried about accumulating large quantities of uranium. In late 1942, when the Manhattan District was formed, the amounts of U-235 available were in millionths of a gram, and the amounts of plutonium in millionths of a millionth of a gram. Groves had to take a longer look. In order to extract the few pounds that were needed for a weapon, tons of uranium would be needed to start with.

By far the most important source of uranium ore was the Shinkolobwe Mine in the Belgian Congo, owned by a Belgian company, Union Minière, whose managing director, Edgar Sengier, was a farsighted Belgian. During 1939 a number of people had started to worry about the adequacy of uranium ore supplies. Szilard, when he first approached Einstein for help, had intended to have Einstein write to the queen of Belgium, but they reconsidered and wrote to Roosevelt instead. In those early fumbling days of the project, large quantities of ore were the least of the problems, so the original concern was soon forgotten. Also in 1939, Sengier happened to be in England, where he was approached by Sir Henry Tizard, head of the British uranium project, who asked for an option on all the radium-uranium ore that would be extracted at the Shinkolobwe Mine. Sengier refused, but as he was leaving, Tizard took him by the arm and said, most impressively, "Be careful and never forget that you have in your hands something which may mean a catastrophe to your country and mine if this material were to fall into the hands of a possible enemy." Sengier, a thoughtful man, never forgot the remark.

Sengier left Brussels for New York, where he remained for

the rest of the war. With the invasion of Belgium imminent, his directors in Brussels allowed him to manage the company's operations, including those in the Belgian Congo, from his office on Wall Street.

Toward the end of 1940, fearing a possible German invasion of the Belgian Congo, Sengier directed his representatives in Africa to ship discreetly to New York the very large supply of previously mined uranium ore then in storage at the mine. During September and October, 1250 tons of extremely rich ore were packed into two thousand steel drums and shipped to the port of Lobito, in Portuguese Angola and on to New York, where Sengier stored them in a warehouse on Staten Island.

Coming to the end of his third winter in exile in New York, Sengier could not understand the Americans. Having read both Laurence articles, in May in the *New York Times* and September in the *Saturday Evening Post*, he knew something was going on, but as an alien and a nonscientist he had no way to find out what. In March 1942 he was called to the State Department for a meeting on nonferrous metals. Sengier tried to interest department officials in uranium, but they were interested in only one metal, cobalt. However, the sixty-year-old mining tycoon was not an easy man to distract: "Gentlemen, listen to me. Union Minière has available material far more valuable and vital than cobalt. It is uranium ores, rich in radium, and bound to be very important to your country in this present war."

The government officials were polite; they showed a little interest, but went on talking about cobalt. Sengier returned to New York, shaking his head in disbelief.

Early in April Sengier tried again, strongly emphasizing the strategic value of the ore in the two thousand steel drums stored on Staten Island, but the officials would have no part of it. On April 21 Sengier tried a third time, writing to Thomas K. Finletter, the special assistant to the State Department on economic and international affairs: "As I told you previously, these ores containing radium and uranium are very valuable." Still nothing happened.

On September 14, 1942, the first day of Groves's appointment, he sat down with his deputy, Colonel Kenneth D. Nichols, to discuss the adequacy of the ore supply. The prospects looked pretty dim, since both Belgium and the Belgian Congo were in enemy hands, and the known Canadian ores had only a small fraction of a percent of uranium oxide. Ten days later, in a casual conversation at the State Department, Nichols heard of a man named Sengier who might have access to some ores. Nichols made an appointment to see him in New York, knowing nothing of Sengier's previous futile attempts to interest the government.

The next morning, when Nichols opened the conversation, Sengier was somewhat guarded in his reply, recalling how the State Department had consistently ignored his repeated proddings. After inspecting Nichols's credentials, he said, "Colonel, will you tell me first if you have come here merely to talk, or to do business?" Nichols answered diplomatically, "I'm here to do business. How much ore do you have and of what quality?" "Twelve hundred fifty tons, hand sorted to sixty-five percent quality," came the astounding reply. Nichols almost fell off his chair. "Where is it?" asked Nichols, holding his breath. Sengier got up, and walked to the window, and pointed. "Over there, on Staten Island." Nichols could hardly believe his ears. Twelve hundred fifty tons of 65 percent quality, enough for the entire project, had been sitting in a warehouse on Staten Island for two years. It was almost too good to be true.

Within an hour, Nichols left Sengier's office with a sheet of yellow scratchpaper on which were written the essentials of an agreement to turn over at once all the ore in the Staten Island warehouse and, in addition, any ore that could be smuggled out of the Belgian Congo.

Groves's Manhattan Project had started out with a tenstrike!

Assured of a raw material supply, Groves could now turn his attention to the construction projects. In June 1940 Colonels Marshall and Nichols had selected a site for future atomic plants in Tennessee — Oak Ridge. It was eighteen

miles from Knoxville and eight miles south of the small town
of Clinton. It was an excellent choice: an isolated area with
plenty of electrical power, abundant water supply, almost no
population, good access by road and train, and a mild climate
that permitted outdoor work the year round. Marshall selected the Boston firm of Stone & Webster as architect engineers and gave the site its official name, the Clinton Engineering Works.

The prime mission of the Clinton Engineering District
was the separation of U-235 from U-238 to make the uranium
bomb. Of five methods earlier proposed to make the separation, only two survived the first round of low-level experiments: the electromagnetic and the gaseous diffusion. In the
electromagnetic method, developed from the mass spectrometer in which the first samples of U-235 were prepared, the
uranium atoms are given a positive electrical charge and accelerated by intense magnetic fields in a huge arc into a col-
lector. Because of the slightly different weights, the trajectory
of the two isotopes is slightly different; the U-235 isotope
can be collected at one location and the U-238 at another. In
the gaseous diffusion process the uranium is gasified and
pumped through a series of barriers with holes of micro-
scopic size. The lighter, slightly smaller isotope will pass
through a little more easily, and the gas on the other side
will be slightly enriched.

An indicator of the magnitude of the problems to be overcome at Oak Ridge was the enormous amount of copper and
aluminum required for electrical conductors. Even with its
high priority, the Oak Ridge project would be unduly delayed by the lack of electrical conductor material. Someone
suggested that the Treasury had plenty of silver lying around
in its vaults and that silver was a better conductor. Groves
decided to take a crack at it; he sent Colonel Nichols to the
Treasury Department on the outside chance that the metal,
a reserve currency, could be legally transferred.

At the Treasury Department the colonel was received by
Undersecretary Daniel Bell, a tall, well-dressed man in his
early fifties. The red, gold, and white flag of the Treasury

stood behind his massive walnut desk. The whole office had a solemn, impressive look of high federal authority.

"General Groves has told us that you wanted to discuss an important matter," Bell said in a friendly voice. "What can I do for you?"

"We need large amounts of silver, Mr. Secretary."

"What for?"

"It's top secret, Mr. Secretary," Nichols said. "All I can reveal is that it's for an important war project directed by the Army Engineers. It has the very highest priority."

"How much do you need, colonel?"

"Six thousand tons," Nichols answered firmly.

For a moment the friendliness disappeared from Bell's face. His eyebrows raised and his voice became icy. "Young man," he said, weighing each word, "*you* may think of silver in tons, but the U.S. Treasury will always think of silver in troy ounces."

Tons or ounces, Nichols got his silver. Bell immediately went to Secretary Henry Morgenthau, Jr., who approved the transfer after receiving a letter from Secretary Stimson. It was promptly removed from the mint, sent to the Phelps Dodge Company to be cast into billets, extruded and rolled into strips for assembly by Allis Chalmers, and ended up as magnet coil windings in the electromagnetic separation process. It was returned to the Treasury six months after the war but was carried on the Treasury's daily balance sheets all the while. The value at the time was about $300 million, but at today's prices it would be worth more than $1 billion. Only two hundred troy ounces were lost.

At the level of knowledge in 1942 the general physics of plutonium production was understood, but the chemistry was not. McMillan and Seaborg in California had identified and named the two new elements. They had also made magnificent progress in microchemistry, working out the characteristics with a sample of plutonium of less than two millionths of an ounce. Two things were known — the pile would be highly radioactive, and there would be danger that the pile would overreact, emitting large amounts of radioactive material. Groves decided that the Tennessee site was too close to Knoxville for comfort and that even a small accident might shut down both the uranium and the plutonium projects; he decided to find a new, more remote site for the plutonium piles.

A nationwide search ended in the small village of Hanford, Washington, on the west bank of the Columbia River in the midst of a vast, desertlike area of sagebrush and sand, some twenty miles north of Richland. It was near enough to good power sources such as the Bonneville and Grand Coulee dam systems. The weather was perfect; rain rarely fell in this part of Washington State, yet the abundant Columbia River water was cool and clear. The choice was obvious; construction soon began on the biggest project ever seen in the West. Because of the necessity for heavy shielding against radioactivity and for complicated, remotely controlled operations, it was a much more difficult construction job than Oak Ridge had been. The camp had 1177 separate buildings plus eight big mess halls. The trailer camp west of Richland, the largest in the world, started with 480 trailers and increased to 639. Peak population reached forty-five thousand construction workers plus six thousand wives and children. In two short years the world's largest and most complicated radioactive chemical production and separation facility was built and successfully operated, starting with only the basic chemistry from two millionths of an ounce of plutonium and the basic physics of the first small chain-reacting pile built on a squash court under the stands of a football stadium at the University of Chicago.

3

LOS ALAMOS

JULIUS ROBERT OPPENHEIMER once said that the two things he loved most were science and New Mexico. He found them both early.

Sickly as a youth, on a trip to Germany after his last year in school, he became terribly ill with dysentery. Back in New York he felt too sick to go to college and spent months alone in the family apartment. Eventually his parents sent him off with a tutor to the mountains of New Mexico to recuperate. He fell in love with the country, camping out or staying at guest ranches. The camping, horseback riding, mineral study, and the grandeur of the mountains made a strong impression on the young man and hardened him physically. By the fall he was ready to enter Harvard, where he threw himself into his studies mercilessly. He started out in chemisty but switched to physics. He finished his undergraduate four-year course in three years, graduating summa cum laude.

When he decided to continue his postgraduate work abroad, Oppenheimer worked on a project with J. J. Thomson, discoverer of the electron. He left Cambridge after six months, moving on to Göttingen in Germany. He spent time in Leipzig with Werner Heisenberg, discoverer of the Uncertainty Principle, and ended up with Erwin Schrödinger, Wolfgang Pauli, and Paul Dirac, developing the new science of wave mechanics.

Although he was at least the intellectual equal of the greatest physicists of his time, his wide range of interests worked to his disadvantage. At Göttingen, when the pace of progress was too rapid for all but the fleetest scientific minds, Oppenheimer studied Italian so that he could read Dante in the original, took time to study and write poetry, and absorbed himself in the intricacies of the Hindu religion. He was scientifically ambitious but was never able to immerse himself completely in the physics of a problem with the intensity of a Heisenberg or Pauli. He saw physics clearly, but he tended to attribute to every problem much more of the mysterious and novel than there really was. Oppenheimer had no great scientific achievement to his name, won no Nobel Prize, but the breadth of his intellect permitted him access to other cultures; he moved easily in many of them, which was his triumph as well as his tragedy.

Back in the United States, his wanderings took him to Harvard, then to the California Institute of Technology in Pasadena, where he taught and did research. He was also offered a professorship at the University of California in Berkeley; in typical Oppenheimer fashion he accepted both. He shuttled between the two California universities, his widely ranging intellect attracting students impressed not only with his abilities in theoretical physics but with his erudition in philosophy, in good food and wine, in languages, and with his European experiences and wide-ranging lifestyle. During the thirties he built up the first and best school of theoretical physics in the United States.

Along the way, he dabbled in a variety of intellectual pursuits. Through a woman friend, Jean Tatlock, he became interested in political action, involving himself in such innocuous-sounding organizations as the Friends of the Chinese People, the Western Council of the Consumers Union, and the American Committee for Democracy and Intellectual Freedom, all of which had Communist affiliations. Although he apparently did not join the Communist party, he contributed money to a number of Communist causes. Throughout the thirties, Oppenheimer continued his Communist affiliations, but whether he was a typical campus pinko attached to ideological solutions to social problems or a sincere Communist advocating the overthrow of the American government has never been established. It seems highly unlikely that he was the latter.

Through Ernest Lawrence and Arthur Compton, Oppenheimer was drawn into the problems of the physics of bomb development. In the summer of 1942, he brought together a small group of theoretical physicists, including Hans Bethe and Edward Teller, to see how far they could go in setting specifications for an actual weapon. The meetings went well and progressed to the point where they were able to specify the most likely size for a critical mass (a ten-inch-diameter sphere). Toward the end of the summer, Teller mentioned Fermi's suggestion that a fission device might be used to cause fusion in deuterium to create a much greater explosion. Bethe, the discoverer of the hydrogen-helium cycle, which explains how the sun gets its energy, was the world's expert on such fusion reactions and was interested in the concept. The group was diverted for a while, checking into the prospects for a "Super" weapon; much to Teller's dismay, Oppenheimer cut off the discussions, reasoning that there was enough to do to create a fission weapon without going beyond it at that time. This was the first time the hydrogen bomb was discussed, long before the work on the fission weapon had really started.

With the Metallurgical Laboratory humming along under Arthur Compton in Chicago, the uranium separation project started at Oak Ridge, Tennessee, and the plutonium-producing piles under construction at Hanford, Washington, General Groves could turn his attention to the construction of a weapon. Compton, in charge of the overall physics of bomb development, felt that a separate laboratory would be necessary for the development and fabrication of the actual weapon; furthermore, it should be situated in a remote location, both for safety and security purposes.

At the time, design and fabrication of the weapon was not considered a problem of major magnitude, estimates for the number of scientists required ranging from ten to one hundred. The design would be relatively straightforward, a gun-type weapon with a hollow cylindrical subcritical mass at one end of a tube and a smaller cylinder at the other end. For detonation, the smaller cylinder would be fired by gunpowder into the larger one, creating a critical mass. No source of neutrons would be required, as there would be enough stray neutrons roaming around to start the chain reaction once the two pieces became critical. Many of the scientists felt that this phase of the project could wait until more plutonium and uranium were produced for ease of experimentation.

Groves disagreed. He had discussions with Arthur Compton, James Conant, and Vannevar Bush and convinced them that the project should have the highest priority. Compton had assigned Oppenheimer overall responsibility for the physics of bomb development, but he was neither the first nor the obvious choice to head the new laboratory. Ernest Lawrence would have been the first choice. He was an outstanding experimental physicist and had gained good administrative experience developing and building his cyclotrons, but he was thoroughly committed to the electromagnetic separation process and could not be spared. Compton was an accomplished physicist with considerable administrative experience, but he was locked in to Chicago. Oppenheimer had two major disadvantages: He had no administrative experience, and he was not a Nobel Prize winner. Lawrence and Compton had both won the Nobel Prize, and Compton had several Nobel laureates working for him. There was a strong feeling among most of the scientific people that the head of the new laboratory should have won a Nobel Prize.

Groves went to Berkeley to meet Oppenheimer. Strangely enough, they hit it off well together. Oppenheimer was straightforward, did not act like a typical long-haired scientist, and seemed to be realistic about the importance of the job, particularly the requirements for security, a matter of grave concern to the general. Groves decided that Oppenheimer was his man, and set out to secure a test site.

A nationwide survey for a remote site with good transportation, water, and year-round climate favorable to construction zeroed in on the mountains of New Mexico north of
Albuquerque. Oppenheimer, who was familiar with the area,
had purchased a summer home in the Sangre de Cristo
("blood of Christ") Mountains. He led the searchers to a
site occupied by a boys' school on Los Alamos ("the pop-
lars") mesa of the Pajarito (little bird) plateau, a 7300-foot-
high, pine-forested shelf of the Jemez Mountains thirty-five
miles northwest of Santa Fe. It seemed ideal. The boys'
school was ready to close because of wartime problems
and had a number of buildings well suited to the hundred
or so scientists Oppenheimer envisioned for the laboratory,
so occupancy could begin immediately. It was remote but its
scenery, looking across to the Sangre de Cristos on the other
side of the Rio Grande Valley was spectacular. The air was
exhilarating, and the climate mild enough for year-round
outdoor work. The roads to the mesa were poor, but that
could be remedied. Water was scarce, but adequate for the
few hundred occupants expected. The site was turned over
to the government in December 1942.

In my junior year at George Washington University, a
scheduling conflict between my classes and my job led me
to transfer to Catholic University.

In the Senate the tenor of operations began to change.
Sessions lasted longer as the pressure of world events piled
up problems. Early summer adjournment was a thing of the
past; sessions were practically continuous. There were new
faces. The President, never happy with John Garner as Vice
President, insisted on a change of running mate and settled
on Henry A. Wallace, a corn geneticist who had become
Secretary of Agriculture. Wallace, considered a flaming liberal at the time, was a man of many talents; a prolific writer
and a successful businessman, he was also an accomplished
mathematician. I was surprised one night, as he passed the
table where I studied (as Vice President he had a suite on the
ground floor and didn't have to use an elevator), to have him

pick up my text on differential equations for a course in advanced calculus. He asked me why I was studying mathematics. I told him I was an engineering student. "Good," he said. "Most of these people around here are lawyers and don't know a damned thing about the real world." From that time on, he would wave to me and say, "Keep up the math, son."

The hearings in the Senate Caucus Room became more somber and businesslike; the theatrics and grandstanding faded away. Although military officers were not allowed to wear uniforms on Capitol Hill before the war (so they wouldn't appear to be dominating the place), there was no mistaking their ramrod-straight backs, polished shoes, and crew cuts as they went in and out of hearings with their overstuffed briefcases. The most businesslike and efficient-looking committee hearings of all were held by the Special Committee to Investigate the National Defense Program, chaired by the junior senator from Missouri, Harry S Truman. The senator ran a no-nonsense meeting; the staff was diligent and dedicated. It was apparent from the beginning that Truman and his committee would play a significant and constructive part as the interface between the Congress and the administration's defense effort.

Although the economy had picked up with the increase in defense spending, jobs were not yet plentiful for engineering graduates when I received my degree in 1941.

I was pleased to be offered a job by the General Electric Company in their engineering test program. It was a plum, much sought after by engineering graduates. Students were rotated in three-month stints to the various factories and labs of the company to perform final performance tests on the equipment they produced, such as motors, generators, and turbines. Graduate courses in production, marketing, and engineering were given on weekends at the various locations. The complete department was run by student engineers. A student who liked a particular product and had a good record could "sign up" as a supervisor for an additional six months. This procedure not only gave us good administrative and supervisory experience, but taught us to be careful in our management techniques, since the person who worked for you in one location might be your boss at the next.

All in all, it was a rewarding and instructive period through which I made many lifetime friends. I was not surprised when a 1981 article in *Fortune* magazine stated that more Fortune 500 chief executive officers had participated in the G.E. test program than in any other industrial training program in the country.

From time to time, recruiters seeking personnel for permanent assignment where the need was particularly urgent would visit from other divisions of the company. Several of us were interviewed by a G.E. engineer from Tennessee, who told us about a massive construction program at the Clinton Engineering Works near Knoxville, where the company was designing and building turbogenerators on a scale never before attempted. The company was desperately in need of engineers for the project, which would be technically stimulating and vastly important to the war effort. Unfortunately, he couldn't tell us anything about the project, stating frankly that he didn't know himself. This turned me off, but he was very persuasive and convinced several of my associates to cut their training short and move to Tennessee.

I hadn't heard anything about uranium fission in a couple of years. After the initial announcement in 1939, I had read the 1940 stories in the *New York Times* and the *Saturday Evening Post*, but nothing since then. I had gradually forgotten about it and didn't make the connection with the Tennessee project when I was interviewed. Had I the slightest inkling of the purpose of the crash program, I probably would have jumped at the chance and spent the rest of the war in Tennessee. I wonder how many others shied away from the program because of the tight security. It simply can't be exciting and stimulating to work on a project without knowing something of its purpose.

When I finished the test program, my first permanent assignment with G.E. was to the Bath Iron Works in Maine, where the company was installing turbogenerators on destroyers.

We worked long hours, and the work was not stimulating.

With a fair amount of dead time on my hands, waiting for equipment to be delivered, I learned all about running an engine room and soon became a trouble-shooter on overall engine room problems. I was next transferred to the Quincy Naval Shipyard to spend most of my time on sea trials. Often I would be the only civilian on the ship; it bothered me to be a twenty-three-year-old able-bodied civilian when everyone around me was in the service. Life on a small ship can be pretty confining; I felt so isolated and apart that I became somewhat depressed for the only time in my life. The pressure to join the service was intense, both on and off the job. I wanted to enlist but I had a draft deferment, which said that my job was important; I also had a wife and daughter for whom I was responsible. Madeline solved the problem, making a wifely sacrifice, which she repeated many times in the years to come. "Look," she said, "you won't be happy until you go into the service; I don't need an unhappy husband. Join the Navy. We'll manage."

I applied for a commission, confident that it would come through promptly because I was already competent to run an engine room, and the Navy was short of engineering officers. But I ran into a stumbling block I hadn't anticipated. I went to see my draft board and was informed that the company would not release me from my deferment, so I would not be allowed to accept a commission. This was a switch. Most people were trying to stay out of the military; I couldn't get in. No amount of pleading would change company policy. General Electric was convinced that the work we were doing was more important to the war effort than anything we would do in the service.

My break came by accident. A destroyer with engine room trouble was wallowing in submarine-infested waters off the coast of Nova Scotia. The crew thought the trouble was in the generator, but they could not diagnose it. They needed a trouble-shooter immediately; I was given the assignment. However, I could not leave the United States without permission from my draft board; granting of it was generally routine for such a purpose, but the draft board told me I could not leave the country because I had been reclassified into 1-A, subject to immediate call-up. They assured me that this was an administrative error and that my deferment would be reinstated within a couple of weeks, but for the time being I couldn't leave the country. I never did hear what happened to the destroyer, but off I went to the First Naval District in Boston to check on my commission, which, by good fortune, came through that week. I went back to the draft board staff, who still wouldn't release me, but I applied formally to an appeals board. The members of the appeals board were nonplussed, because this was the first case they had ever examined of someone trying to get into the service, not stay out of it. I finally convinced them that they couldn't have it both ways. If I was technically draftable and couldn't leave the country, I must be draftable enough to be able to take a commission in the Navy. The next day I became an ensign in the United States Naval Reserve.

I was sent to indoctrination school at Fort Schuyler, New York, expecting to go from there directly to the fleet, where I was sure that my engine room experience would win me early promotion. I reckoned without the Navy personnel system. God forbid they should assign me to an area in which I had experience. Instead, in its wisdom, the Navy decided to make me a radar officer. I was surprised but delighted. Radar was the newest and hottest project in electrical engineering. Since much of the work was classified, I knew very little about it, but at least I would know what I was working on.

I was sent to Bowdoin College in Maine for a semester of postgraduate electronics, then to the radar school at the Massachusetts Institute of Technology. The training was excellent, the equivalent of a master's degree. The Navy at MIT had a process whereby graduates bid for choice assignments, with scholastic achievement setting the priorities. My first choice was the Electronics Field Service Group, operating out of the Naval Research Laboratory in the Washington, D.C., area, an elite collection of radar trouble-shooters based in Washington but dispatched all over the world on temporary duty to solve unusual electronic problems in the fleet. This would give me the best of all worlds. I would get to see some of the war but would not be away from my wife and daughter. I graduated well up in my class and was delighted to see orders to the group of my choice. When I reported to the Naval Research Laboratory, the Wave ensign who looked at my orders said, "You're not going to be here long," and handed me a new set of orders:

> You will regard yourself detached from duty at the Electronic Field Service Group, Naval Research Laboratory, Washington, D.C.; will proceed to Santa Fe, New Mexico, and report to the Officer in Charge, Engineering Project "Y," for duty, reporting by letter to the Commander in Chief, United States Fleet, and to the Commandant, Eleventh Naval District.

I was confused; I couldn't believe that they would send me out on a field assignment the first day I reported for duty. "Don't I even get to look at the place before I take off on a field assignment?" I asked.

"That's not a field assignment," was the reply. "You are detached."

Still puzzled, I asked, "What's Project 'Y'?"

"Beats me," she replied airily.

At first I though it might be a mistake, but I looked at the orders again. They had been cut before I left MIT; apparently the Washington assignment had been a cover. I later found out that it had been just that. With its high priority, the Manhattan Project had decided to requisition the three top graduates from the radar school. Such an action would have been considered highly unusual, so we were each given cover orders to different locations.

The first thing I learned about New Mexico is that the Santa Fe Railroad does not go through Santa Fe. It cuts south of the Sangre de Cristo Mountains, stopping at the sleepy little town of Lamy, about forty miles from Santa Fe. I naturally assumed I was going to some naval base, although why it would be located in the middle of the New Mexico desert, I couldn't understand. I asked the bus driver on the way to Santa Fe. He knew of no naval base and had never heard of Project "Y."

Santa Fe is a beautiful town, seventy-five hundred feet up in the mountains, with a sunny and pleasant climate. By strict town ordinance all houses had to be built in Spanish adobe style, which gave it an authentic nineteenth-century western-town appearance. The surrounding mountains are rich in geological formations and archeological artifacts. The nearby Rio Grande had been the water supply for Indian civilizations over the centuries. As a pass through the mountains, the Santa Fe Trail was legendary in the development of the West; with the coming of the white men the Rio Grande Valley had been the first major cattle center. Extensive cave dwellings at nearby Laos and a climate congenial to those with respiratory ailments made it the cultural and artistic center of the Southwest. The town was dominated by the Presidio, an open, rectangular, Spanish-style square with the picturesque Hotel La Fonda at one end.

Most of this was lost on me at the time. I had to find a naval base to report to. No luck! I went into the hotel; the clerk knew nothing. He referred me to the bartender, who was big, burly, crew-cutted, and out of his element with the Spanish help in the hotel. He was a Counter-Intelligence Corps agent, but I did not suspect it at the time. He almost winced when I said Project "Y," but his eyes glazed over and he said he had never heard of the place. The police were no help; I finally located a naval recruiting station with a grizzled chief petty officer in charge. He was Navy; he must know about a naval base in the area. He didn't, but suggested that I stop in at a little office on the other side of the Presidio; the woman there might be able to help me. Sure enough, down a vine-covered corridor was a door with a simple sign:

POST OFFICE BOX 1663
SANTA FE, NEW MEXICO

I rang the buzzer. A pleasant, cheery voice answered. "Hi, I'm Dorothy McKibben, Ensign O'Keefe. I've been wondering where you were. There's a bus leaving for Los Alamos in twenty minutes."

"But I'm looking for a naval base. What's Los Alamos?"

She politely informed me that Project "Y," Post Office Box 1663, Santa Fe, New Mexico, was the mailing address for Los Alamos, a city of twelve thousand people, the third largest in New Mexico, thirty miles from Santa Fe. This was my first encounter with the pervasive, deadening security that permeated the project. Here was a community of twelve thousand people, with constant movement in and out — visitors, vendors, construction workers, maintenance help, shoppers, and all the necessary materials and supplies for the operation of a good-sized city, all funneling through the only gateway, Santa Fe, itself only three times as big — and no one in Santa Fe could admit that it existed. Ridiculous! Of course, everyone I had asked knew what I was looking for, but no one would tell me. I could not help but believe that such heavy-handed, crude attempts at secrecy could be anything but counterproductive. Everyone in the Southwest must have known about it. It would have been much better to acknowledge its existence with a simple explanation that would not call attention to the project. But such was not the security practice of the Manhattan Engineering District.

I boarded a rickety school bus with thirty Spanish-speaking maintenance people and proceeded on a spectacularly scenic but scary ride across the Rio Grande and up a precipitous dirt road to Pajarito Mesa, where the town of Los Alamos was located.

The town itself was drab. It had the typical look of a military base about it: more guards and barbed wire perhaps, but otherwise strictly GI.

The next morning I reported to another Wave ensign, this one ebullient and excited, who couldn't wait to tell me that we were a small, select contingent of scientific naval officers working on an army base operated by the Corps of Engineers. She was proud to inform me that the Army had the quantity, but the Navy had the quality. I knew better than to ask her what we were here for. She gave me a brief indoctrination tour. I met the scientific director, Dr. Oppenheimer, for a handshake; he made no particular impression on me. I had never heard of him; all I can recall is that he seemed pretty thin and fragile to be running a program as big as this, whatever it was.

I ended up with my commanding officer, Captain William S. Parsons, a balding, determined-looking regular Navy officer about forty years old. He greeted me politely, his mind obviously on some other problem, asking me how I liked the base.

I was pretty down in the dumps. I had left a wife and daughter and a good-paying job to join the Navy and get some sea duty as an engineering officer. The Navy in its wisdom had chosen to make me a radar officer instead. I had worked hard at Bowdoin and MIT and thought I had won a choice assignment at the Naval Research Laboratory. Instead, here I was, a member of an outnumbered group of naval officers at a crummy Army base in the middle of nowhere, probably working on some sort of a construction project.

I'm afraid my disappointment showed through. I should have shown more deference to a senior officer, but I blurted out that I had expected an overseas assignment when I joined the Navy and here I was, about as far away from the ocean as I could get. I startled Parsons a little bit; this wasn't the reply he had expected from a pink-cheeked ensign just reporting for duty. He looked at me intently for about thirty seconds; good or bad, at least I had gotten his attention. He then broke into a big grin, much to my relief, stood up, and said, "Come on and meet Ed Doll. I think you'll change your mind."

Dr. Ed Doll was a civilian, the associate leader of the fuzing group in the Ordnance Division Parsons headed. He took me into his office and gave me a thirty-minute briefing on the project. In a calm, quiet voice, working with the inevitable piece of chalk and the inevitable blackboard, he described the whole project to me — uranium, plutonium, fission, chain reaction, gun-type weapon, implosion weapon, the whole ball of wax. He spoke of the Trinity Test, the fuzing and firing system, and the time schedule for combat use of the "gadget." When he spoke of possible yields as high as ten thousand tons of TNT, I couldn't comprehend it. I knew that was a lot of explosive, but it was too much to wrap my head around in a thirty-minute briefing. Immediately, of course, I remembered the George Washington University conference and the three articles I had read. I flashed back to the interviewer for the Clinton Engineering Works in Tennessee, which Doll referred to as Oak Ridge. Everything became clear. What I couldn't understand was that twenty-four hours ago security was so tight that no one would admit to the existence of this city, yet in thirty minutes today I was given the complete details of the greatest secret ever known to mankind. I felt as though I'd made it to heaven. It took me a long while to understand the contradiction.

Los Alamos had come a long way from Oppenheimer's original plan of not more than a hundred scientists. His first estimate had been low simply because of inexperience and lack of ability to understand the dimensions of the problems. He had envisioned uranium coming out of Oak Ridge and plutonium from Hanford being fashioned into metal by Chicago and delivered to Los Alamos for assembly. He had visualized two subcritical pieces of metal brought together by a sort of gun assembly into a critical mass that would explode. From his experience, he had foreseen a theoretical physics laboratory whose main function would be to determine the critical mass, assure against predetonation in assembly, and perform the necessary subcritical experiments to test the theory.

He had given little thought to the engineering aspects of a weapon: the fuzing and firing systems, the ballistics, the safety problems, the necessity to design a device that could be handled by the military under combat conditions. He did not fully appreciate the experimental physics and chemical problems that still existed. The uranium separation plants had been designed when only milligrams of U-235 were available; the physical plants were being scaled up by factors of one hundred thousand from the simple laboratory equipment at Berkeley and Columbia. Plutonium chemistry had been done with samples of only micrograms of the metal, specks too small for the eye to see. The Hanford reactors were being extrapolated by a factor of ten thousand from the uncompleted pilot plant at Oak Ridge, itself five thousand times larger than the only chain-reacting pile in existence, Fermi's in Chicago. The problems as he arrived in Los Alamos, happy to be back in his beloved New Mexico, were awesome. But right at the beginning he foresaw and solved one problem that was far more important than all the others put together: security.

Leslie Groves and Robert Oppenheimer could not have been more different if they had been designed that way. Groves, son of an Army chaplain, was brought up in an austere religious family of four, strictly observing the Sabbath on Sunday, holding closely and firmly to the traditional American values of God and country. A West Point graduate, strict disciplinarian, meticulous engineer, he personified all that Oppenheimer did not. A nonsmoker, nondrinker, his only observable vice was a sweet tooth, which gave him a weight problem. His small mustache and portly bearing, his too-tight collar straining at the button, made him look to the scientists like an Oliver Hardy in uniform, the very caricature of an Army officer. But he knew his business and was confident of his destiny. From the beginning, he distrusted the scientists, particularly the foreigners with their strange accents and their tendency to break into incomprehensible languages when they talked to one another in his presence. It particularly bothered him when they spoke German, because it reminded him of the war and the problems of security. Even when he was appointed in 1942, many of the scientists had not fully grasped the requirements of wartime security. To them the only real problem was Germany; they felt that because the Germans were ahead in fission research, there really wasn't anything to hide.

Groves immediately clamped a tight lid of security on the project. The essence of his policy was compartmentalization. No one below the very top level of command should know any more about the project than he needed to do his job. With one or two exceptions, the scientists at Chicago did not know what was going on at Oak Ridge or Hanford or Berkeley or Columbia. Within Oak Ridge the gaseous diffusion development was compartmentalized from electromagnetics, and at Hanford pile design from plutonium separation. I'm sure it didn't completely work that way because scientists and engineers in confined locations do talk to one another, but Groves and his security people thought it did, and swift retribution was meted out to anyone caught breaking the rules. Many an Army officer or sergeant spent the rest of the war in Alaska or on a remote Pacific island for security indiscretions, and many a civilian had his clearance revoked without recourse on suspicion alone. The process cut at the very heart of the scientific tradition of free discourse. It was most difficult for the contractors and subcontractors working outside the facilities, most of them unable to guess what they were working on — the General Electrics, the Westinghouses, Allis Chalmers, Chrysler, all of whom had to motivate their employees by blind faith, assuring them that they were helping the war effort without knowing what they were doing. It was debilitating and counterproductive both from the standpoint of badly needed technical information exchange and motivation for men of vision who could not be innovative in a technological vacuum. But this was war and this was the system. The job did get done.

Oppenheimer recognized the situation instinctively. His early theoretical work for Compton had allowed him to observe the project without really becoming an integral part of it. It wasn't until his summer study session with Bethe and Teller and others that he began to realize the time dimensions of the security problem. Born into a wealthy, nonconformist Jewish family, Oppenheimer was the antithesis of Groves. Educated liberally, both domestically and internationally, he had no intellectual off-limits in his background and training. Always thin, often sickly, with two long, youthful sojourns in New Mexico with dysentery and tuberculosis, Oppenheimer smoked constantly and was proud of his reputation as an erudite martini mixer. As a radical university professor he had long associations with Communist causes and party members. He seemed the last one to embrace Groves's concept of security. Yet embrace it he did, with one exception.

Groves took to him immediately as the first scientist to accept the idea of a secret, isolated weapons development laboratory. Oppenheimer, however, a persuasive talker and consummate actor, convinced Groves to lay aside the plan of compartmentalization within the laboratory itself. He was willing to buy most anything, including putting scientists in uniform, to maintain the principle of free discourse within the laboratory. The other scientists rebelled against the idea of becoming military officers, but Oppenheimer talked them into everything else: the censorship of mail, the physical isolation, the code names, the bodyguards, the ban on communication with universities and other laboratories, retaining only the right of free discourse within the barbed wire of the technical area of the laboratory.

Oppenheimer was a quick study. It didn't take him long to recognize the seriousness of his original underestimate. He increased his target from one hundred to fifteen hundred personnel, dividing the scientific organization into four divisions. Hans Bethe, a brilliant, tousle-headed refugee from the University of Munich, became head of the Theoretical Division. Bethe had come from Germany to Cornell University, where he had developed the hydrogen-helium cycle to explain the thermonuclear reactions in the sun. He had gone from Cornell to MIT, where he had been working on radar when Oppenheimer recruited him. Robert Bacher of Cal Tech became head of the Experimental Physics Division. Both Bethe and Bacher had been working on radar and were disillusioned with its military control. It was they who objected most strenuously to joining the Army. Joseph Kennedy, only twenty-six and one of Glenn Seaborg's outstanding students, came to head the Chemistry Division. Captain William S. (Deke) Parsons, a studious, efficient regular Navy officer recruited from Vannevar Bush, for whom he had headed the work on the proximity fuse, became head of the Ordnance Division.

Parsons was the first Navy officer to arrive at Los Alamos; most of the Army military police had never seen a Navy man before. The difference in titles between the Army and Navy had always been confusing. A captain in the Navy is equivalent to a colonel in the Army; a commander equals a lieutenant colonel; a lieutenant commander a major; a lieutenant a captain, and so on down. Parsons had been promoted from commander to captain a few days before reporting to Los Alamos. One night the base commander, Major "Lex" Stevens, received an excited call from the sentry at the main gate.

"Major, I think I've caught a spy. There's a guy down here in a funny-looking uniform. He's wearing a colonel's eagles, his ID card says he's a commander, and he calls himself a captain. Shall I lock him up?"

A very embarrassed Stevens barreled posthaste out to the gate to apologize to the new senior naval officer.

Oppenheimer was a persuasive recruiter. By the summer of 1943 the place was overrun with scientists. They poured in from the universities of California, Minnesota, Wisconsin, Chicago, Rochester, Illinois, and Stanford, Purdue, Princeton, Columbia, Harvard, and MIT. They came from industrial firms, from the Bureau of Standards, Carnegie Institute, and from the ranks of the Army and Navy, transferred by the high priority of the Manhattan Engineering District wherever they could be found. They came from many nations. George Gamow and George B. Kistiakowsky had been born in Russia; Enrico Fermi and Emilio Segrè had worked together in Rome; Hans Bethe, Victor Weisskopf, and many others came from Germany; Edward Teller, Eugene Wigner, and John von Neumann were from Hungary.

Much of the specialized equipment was brought out by the scientists who were going to use it. The University of Wisconsin group brought two Van de Graaff generators for accelerating atomic particles; John Manley's group from Illinois brought a Cockroft-Walton accelerator; a complete cyclotron was requisitioned from Harvard.

The pace of the program accelerated for a number of reasons, the first being the lack of knowledge of the physics of fast neutrons. When a nucleus fissions, neutrons are ejected with very high velocity and are not easily captured. What Fermi did in 1934 when he almost discovered fission was to slow the neutrons down by having them collide with the nuclei of light elements. He applied the same principle in the Chicago pile using carbon as the "moderator" or slowing-down material. A lot of work on slow neutrons was still going on at Chicago and Hanford for the design of the plutonium production piles, but little had been done about fast neutrons. In an explosive device, the fast neutrons had to be used directly even though the ability to capture, or capture "cross section," was much lower. The whole reaction would take place in about a millionth of a second. Measurements had to be made to a hundredth of a millionth of a second to analyze the reactions properly. The scientists had to invent new units for measuring time. A hundred millionth of a second was known as a "shake" (of a lamb's tail). Fast neutron cross-section measurements took up a great deal of the time of the Experimental Physics Division.

The Chemistry Division had its hands full determining the chemical properties of plutonium, which proved to be quite complex. Another serious problem developed in 1943. Seaborg had noticed some small traces of plutonium 240, the nonfissionable isotope, in his early samples. As the quantities grew, the percentage of Pu-240 increased. Finally it was determined that the percentage of Pu-240 increased the longer the material was in the pile, so the amount that would come from the Hanford production piles would be quite high. It was not just that Pu-240 was difficult to fission. It also emitted alpha rays and would be a source of background neutrons which, calculations showed, would be strong enough to predetonate a gun-type weapon; that is, even at the highest possible muzzle velocities, the chain reaction would start before the two pieces of the core had come close enough together to become a critical mass. In that case the reaction would fizzle and the weapon would be a dud. It was impossible to separate the Pu-240 from the Pu-239 without massive physical separation facilities. This was a real blow. Los Alamos was counting on plutonium because the production rate of uranium was much slower. At any rate, if plutonium were not usable in the gun-type weapon, there would only be enough uranium for one bomb in 1945, with the next one not available until the following year.

The inability to use plutonium would have been good for the future of mankind but bad for the future of the war effort. Unfortunately for mankind, fortunately for the project, there was another solution. It seemed that nature or some supernatural force had predestined that nuclear explosives would be available in quantity. Every time an obstacle came along, nature was ready with an alternative.

In this case the alternative was called "implosion."

Before the problems of plutonium poisoning by the Pu-240 isotope became apparent, Seth Neddermeyer, one of the physicists at Los Alamos, had proposed a different assembly technique, which promised to be more efficient in the use of material but complex in execution. Instead of shooting two subcritical masses together, Neddermeyer proposed taking a subcritical mass and literally squeezing it as one might squeeze a sponge. If a sphere of noncritical mass could be squeezed real hard uniformly over its entire surface so that none of it could pop out, the molecules would be compressed to a higher density and the subcritical mass would become critical.

There were a lot of problems with this technique; many argued against it because of its complexity. To squeeze a heavy sphere of metal properly it would be necessary to surround it with high explosives, detonate the explosives simultaneously around the entire surface to create a shock wave that moved inward toward the center, imploding rather than exploding, until it encompassed the fissionable material in its converging grip and literally squeezed it into criticality. Since the technique promised to be more efficient, Oppenheimer fended off the critics and decided to enlarge the laboratory to tackle the new problems of implosion.

When the news of the plutonium predetonation problem hit Los Alamos, implosion became a priority program, and the size of the laboratory and town took another quantum jump into the thousands, further straining already over-stretched facilities. Scientists continued to pour in. Teller arrived from Chicago, still thinking about the Super. Oppenheimer assigned him to Hans Bethe's Theoretical Division, which did not please Teller in the slightest. After all, he was one of the most senior men in the program, having cosponsored the George Washington University conference in 1939, participated in the Berkeley study group in 1942, and helped Fermi with the first chain-reacting pile.

There was also the question of housing, extremely important to the wives. The enlisted men lived in barracks and the junior officers lived in dormitories, as did the junior civilian scientists. Senior personnel lived in apartments with black potbellied stoves for heat and showers in the single bathrooms. The very senior people had apartments with bathtubs; their street was known as Bathtub Row. When Teller arrived, there were no more houses on Bathtub Row. He had to settle for a shower, which piqued his pride no end.

Although Bethe and Teller had been good friends and visited each other several times over the years, Teller chafed under Bethe's authority, and the two had a falling out over Teller's refusal to work on a problem assigned to him. Teller was a loner, unable to work in an organization, one who must work at his own pace. Oppenheimer finally gave in and allowed him to have his own group, working primarily on the Super even though it would be far in the future, if it would work at all.

The great Niels Bohr arrived from London. The story of his escape would make a movie on its own. Early in the war, when Denmark was occupied, Bohr remained in his laboratory. Because of his eminence, he was allowed to continue his research in Copenhagen during the early years of the occupation; at one time he was visited by Heisenberg, his old associate in the development of the Uncertainty Principle, and now the reputed head of the German atomic project. Heisenberg assured him he would not be molested, but as time went on, living in Copenhagen became more and more dangerous for Bohr, whose mother was Jewish.

The Danish underground managed, with the help of the British Secret Service, to smuggle him out in a small fishing boat to Sweden one night. Several weeks later he was flown to England in the bomb bay of a Mosquito bomber. He was given a parachute and an oxygen mask for the short trip. He had an unusually large head, however, and the oxygen mask did not fit properly. When the plane landed in London, the great man was unconscious, having fainted from lack of oxygen. He recovered and spent a period of time in London before proceeding to the United States.

In the haste of leaving Copenhagen, Bohr had been advised to travel light and carry no identification. His two most cherished possessions were his Nobel Prize Medal and a bottle of heavy water (a scarce commodity, but the best moderator for slowing down neutrons), which he kept in a Carlsberg beer bottle so it would not be confiscated by the Nazis. He decided that a Nobel Prize Medal would be difficult to explain away if he were caught, so he dissolved it in nitric acid and left it stored on a shelf in the lab with other chemicals, where it remained until after the war, when it was restruck to all its pristine glory. The bottle of heavy water he took with him, realizing that he could drink it and recover it later if he had to. When he arrived in England, he discovered that in his haste, in typical absent-minded-professor fashion, he had carried with him only a bottle of good Danish beer. He explained his problem to the British secret servicemen who had freed him; not to be found wanting, the British went back through the Danish underground, recovered the bottle of heavy water, and presented it to Bohr before he left for the United States for the first time since his dramatic voyage in 1939.

His arrival in Los Alamos was a great shot in the arm for the overworked scientists. Many had been his students; all had wished to be. He was not given responsibility for any particular division but acted as a general consultant on all sorts of problems. His presence bolstered the research effort and gave the younger physicists more confidence. If Bohr was there, it would have to work, was the feeling.

Security was oppressive. Scientists' mail was censored; they were allowed to correspond only with their families. Counter-Intelligence Corps (CIC) agents were everywhere, particularly in Santa Fe and Albuquerque, principal gateways to "the Hill." For Oppenheimer it was particularly onerous. As late as the fall of 1943, he still did not have official security clearance; Lieutenant Colonel Boris Pash, the chief security officer, had recommended against it, but Groves still held the recommendation on his desk. Oppenheimer's mail was censored like everyone else's; in addition, his phone calls were monitored and he was followed everywhere he went. The local security officer, Captain Peer de Silva, was particularly opposed to the director. De Silva was incensed that not only had Oppenheimer been allowed to bring in California associates who had connections with the Communist party, but he had also brought his wife, who was formerly married to a card-carrying member. In addition, his brother Frank and Frank's wife had both joined the party.

Some of the security incidents were amusing. All the senior scientists had code names to cover their identity. Bohr was Nicholas Baker, affectionately called "Uncle Nick," but you couldn't miss him; everyone knew who he was. The mere presence of his bodyguard attested to his importance.

Arthur Compton had two aliases: In the West he was Mr. Comas, and in the East, Mr. Comstock. One night a stewardess awakened him from a deep sleep, asking his name. "Where are we?" asked Compton, not knowing which one to use. Fortunately, his bodyguard was awake in the seat behind and produced a ticket for Mr. Comas. The stewardess wondered how a man could fall into such a deep sleep that he couldn't even remember his own name. On another occasion, Compton and his wife of twenty-five years were joined by their Army lieutenant son at a resort where they had registered under the name of Comstock. The son was reluctant to use an assumed name. His mother came to his rescue. "This is my son from my first marriage," she told the hotel staff, a statement that was technically correct.

The case of Enrico Fermi was particularly interesting.

Fermi was given the usual bodyguard and the code name of James Farmer. With his build and accent, he no more looked or sounded like a James Farmer than the man in the moon. Wigner was given the name Wagner, which was so close that he sometimes forgot. One time he handed a guard at a checkpoint a card with the name Wagner, but announced that his name was Wigner. The guard was confused and suspicious. Wigner corrected himself. "I'm sorry, my name is Wagner."

"Will you certify that his name is Wagner, Mr. Farmer?" the guard asked Fermi. With a big grin, Fermi answered, "His name is Wagner just as sure as my name is Farmer."

One of the things that fazed security, not only at Los Alamos but even more so at Hanford and Oak Ridge, was the fact that carloads of material went in and nothing came out. The standard jokes were that they were making homes for pregnant WACs, or wheels for miscarriages. A typical reply was that they were making front ends for horses — to be shipped to Washington for assembly. One rancher in the Rio Grande Valley, observing the one-way flow of material for months on end, sagely opined, "Whatever they're making, I'm sure it would be cheaper if they went out and bought it." For us Navy types on the Hill, who stood out more prominently because of our small numbers and our distance from the ocean, the reply was always the same: "We're making windshield wipers for submarines."

When the British decided they could not muster the resources for an all-out nuclear weapon project, there were numerous visits across the Atlantic, primarily the British transferring information to the Americans, who had fallen far behind in the fumbling days of 1941. When the Los Alamos laboratory was organized, the British were invited to send a delegation in accordance with the Quebec agreements worked out between Franklin D. Roosevelt and Winston Churchill. A star-studded delegation it was. Headed by James Chadwick, the discoverer of the neutron, it included Otto Frisch, who had first identified nuclear fission; Sir Rudolf Peierls, whose short paper with Frisch had first set forth the principles for an explosive design in 1941; Mark Oliphant, the Australian who discovered tritium; and some twenty others.

All the Europeans, including Klaus Fuchs, a German-born theoretical physicist who worked with Rudolf Peierls, had been granted British citizenship. Fuchs's family had been persecuted by the Nazis and left Germany for England in 1934. In 1940 he was classified as an enemy alien and sent to an internment camp in Canada, where he felt he was badly treated. While in Canada he had joined a Communist cell; by the time he returned to England to work with Peierls, he had developed a hatred for both England and Germany and was thoroughly dedicated to the concept of Russian communism. Working with Peierls, he concentrated on calculating the size of the nuclear bomb. He learned everything about the gaseous diffusion process, in which the British were far ahead of the Americans. Within a month he had contacted the Soviet embassy in London and offered his services as a spy.

By the end of 1942, Fuchs had met four times with his Soviet contact in London and turned over to him reports of his work on atomic energy. On arriving in America, he spent four months working with the Kellex Corporation, designing the uranium separation plant. He met five times with Harry Gold, the Russian agent who had also been working with Julius and Ethel Rosenberg. In August Fuchs failed to show up for a meeting; Gold learned that he had "gone off somewhere in the Southwest." Fuchs contacted Gold six months later on a visit to Cambridge, Massachusetts, and told Gold the name of the laboratory and its location, the theory of implosion, and the progress that had been made on the plutonium bomb. Before they parted, Gold and Fuchs agreed to meet six months later in Albuquerque. Arriving in New Mexico, Gold had two contacts in Los Alamos — two, that is, that we know of. The second was David Greenglass, an Army technician — brother of Ethel Rosenberg; he was working on explosives in X Division, where I was assigned. I knew Greenglass slightly, but I don't recall ever meeting Fuchs, who was very shy and retiring. Fuchs passed on virtually everything there was to be known at Los Alamos; Greenglass's contribution was relatively minor, serving primarily to authenticate the information given by Fuchs.

All this time the security people hounded Oppenheimer to implicate his friends and associates in the Communist conspiracy. Although they never mentioned it to their superiors, they knew that the Communists had infiltrated. In one conversation with Oppenheimer, Major John Lansdale, General Groves's security aide, talked about the Soviet Union's efforts to penetrate the secrecy around the Manhattan Project.

"They know — we know they know — about Tennessee, about Los Alamos and Chicago," Lansdale said. "They know that the ... uh ... spectrographic method — I may state it wrong — is being used at Berkeley. They know that you would be in a position to start practical production in about six months from, say, February, and that perhaps six months thereafter you would be in a position to go into mass production. It is essential that we know the channels of communication."

Why weren't the security barriers eased a little now that they had been breached? Why weren't the President and Secretary Stimson notified about what the Russians knew? Probably just the innate secretiveness of security people, the refusal to admit error, but the omission paved the way for some serious policy errors on the part of the United States government. Groves must have known; perhaps that is the reason he signed Oppenheimer's security clearance against the bitter opposition of his security aides. They never forgave him or Oppenheimer for that act, and continued to harass the director at every opportunity.

About the beginning of 1945 the tasks and the options for the laboratory began to become clear. There would be enough U-235 available for one gun-type weapon in 1945 and a second in 1946. Plutonium would not work in a gun-type weapon, but would in an implosion device. If the implosion device worked, there would be enough plutonium for three critical masses prior to the invasion of Japan, scheduled for November 1, 1945. The design of the implosion weapon was so uncertain that Secretary Stimson decided to plan for a full-scale test, hoping that if it did not work, the design could be corrected befcre it was too late. If it did work, there would still be enough material for three devices, one gun-type and two implosion-type, to be used to end the war before the scheduled invasion. The area selected for the test was appropriately named. It was the desert of Jornada del Muerto ("Journey of Death"), part of the Alamogordo bombing range in southern New Mexico.

The code name for the operation was Project Trinity.

Since the work on the gun-type weapon had been proceeding for years and was simplified by the deletion of the requirement for the plutonium gun, it began to take shape rapidly in late 1944. The high priority item became the implosion device.

There were two major problems with implosion. One was the design of the initiator, the polonium-beryllium device about the size of a golf ball in the exact center of the sphere, which would provide the first flood of neutrons when the shock wave reached center. It was straightforward to design a neutron source, but there was no good way of simulating the pressures at the center of an imploding sphere until the device was developed, or of calculating neutron capture cross sections under these conditions.

The second was the design of the implosion itself, which soon became problem number one at the laboratory. A new Explosives Division was organized and placed under the direction of the able Russian-born chemist, George B. Kistiakowsky. In order to get a symmetrical imploding shock wave, different types of explosives were required. Even if the explosives were detonated at multiple points around the sphere, the shock wave close to the detonator would reach the center more quickly than the other waves because it would have the shortest distance to travel. To allow the rest of the wave to "catch up" and reach the center at the exact same time, it would be necessary to have slow-burning explosives under the detonator and fast-burning explosives at other points. Such a mixture of explosives is called a lens, but because no one had had experience with explosive lenses Kistiakowsky's group had to start from scratch.

The logistical problems of designing and testing lenses were very severe, requiring many more people and facilities than the gun weapon. As the design took shape, there were thirty-two separate lenses to be detonated around a five-foot sphere, with about two tons of explosives in the assembly. Because the gun-type weapon was long and narrow, it was named "Thin Man" or "Little Boy." Because of the large diameter of the imploding sphere, with the plutonium core and the initiator at the center, the implosion device came to be called the "Fat Man."

Another severe problem was the simultaneous detonation within a fraction of a millionth of a second of thirty-two detonators around a five-foot sphere. The original design called for thirty-two lengths of explosive cord (such as the fuse on a firecracker) all to be ignited from a single point. Quite late in the game it was realized that this method could not achieve the required simultaneity, and it was abandoned in favor of an electrical system that would ignite thirty-two separate detonators electrically from a high-voltage bank of electrical capacitors through a single switch. This too was very tricky because even at the speed of light, electricity travels less than one half inch in a hundred millionth of a second, the required simultaneity.

In an actual implosion weapon the firing of the detonators could only occur after certain conditions were met. There would first be a series of safety switches extending out through the casing of the device to render all circuits inoperative until airborne. This was for the safety of the island from which the weapon-carrying aircraft would take off. Once airborne, the aircraft commander would crawl out into the bomb bay, remove the safety switches, called "the red plugs," and plug in two "green plugs," which allowed the automatic circuits to operate. When the bomb was released at thirty thousand feet, a series of atmospheric pressure or barometric switches would disarm the firing circuits until the bomb had fallen away to a safe level of about fifteen thousand feet, at which height the capacitors for the detonators would be charged. Then a series of radars took over.

In order to obtain the maximum blast effect and the minimum radioactive effect, it would be desirable not to have the fireball touch the ground. The radars would sense the distance to the ground from the free-falling weapon, and at a predetermined level, which varied with the expected yield, would send a signal to the firing set to discharge the electrical capacitors into the detonators, starting the imploding shock wave that would squeeze the subcritical plutonium core and rupture the initiator at the very center, releasing a flood of neutrons that would start the fast chain reaction. After the release of the go-ahead signal from the radars, the complete reaction would occur in millionths of a second.

There was considerable redundancy or backup in the control and arming circuits. No single component failure could be allowed to abort the mission. There would be four barometric switches, any two of which could activate the radars. There were also four radars, any two of which could send the signal to the firing unit. Even the detonators were duplicated, with sixty-four separate cables emanating from the capacitors to the thirty-two detonators.

I had been selected from the MIT radar school to work on the design of the arming radars, four of which were crammed into a tiny space in the tail of the gadget. However, identical designs of radars were used in the Little Boy and the Fat Man; since the Little Boy design was far ahead of the Fat Man, the radars were in the final stage of development when I arrived at Los Alamos and did not provide sufficient challenge for me. I soon heard of the fascinating technical problems of designing the detonator firing units. It wasn't radar, but it was electronics. After I learned my way around, I managed to get transferred to Kistiakowsky's Explosives Division, which contained the firing group X-5.

Since the time was so short for design and production of the firing sets, it was not possible to set up a new factory for their manufacture. Using the high priority of the Manhattan District, procurement experts set out to find an existing facility they could commandeer. They found a factory in Boston, Massachusetts, used for assembling high-voltage electrical capacitors for night aerial photography — sort of a giant electrical strobe — an advanced version of the strobe lights used in photography. Production of the photographic units was stopped, and the factory was converted to the manufacture of bomb firing sets. There was no time to clear factory workers or set up proper security; the workers and their supervisors were told that the product was an advanced version of equipment for night aerial photography, and the factory was operated as an uncleared facility. The area was soon swarming with Army intelligence people, who were infiltrated into the factory and surrounding stores and restaurants. But here was an ostensibly wide-open facility, just outside Kenmore Square, developing and assembling what was now the key critical component in the whole atomic bomb program.

Our group leader, Lewis Fussell, spent most of his time in the spring of 1945 setting up the factory in Boston. For indoctrination into the group I was put under the tutelage of a competent husband and wife team of physical chemists, Donald and Lilli Hornig. The Hornigs had been working at the Woods Hole Oceanographic Institute, where Don had become expert in underwater demolitions. They had come to the Hill in 1944 and were considered early settlers. They were very helpful to me, both technically and socially, in finding my way around in the turmoil of the time.

I worked on two sets of problems, the first the development of high-speed rotating mirror camera techniques and oscilloscopic techniques for measuring detonator simultaneity. No one had ever made measurements to a hundredth of a millionth of a second accuracy before, but the job was done in a few short months. As the measurement techniques were developed, I turned my attention to the electronic controls that would arm and fire the device in the field. Since I was already familiar with the radars and the firing sets, I spent my time working on the design of the circuits controlling the interactions of the two.

Life was exhilarating at Los Alamos that spring. The climate was superb, with sunny, dry days and cool, clear nights. We worked most every night, particularly the junior people without families. I found time to visit the cave dwellings in nearby canyons and go on climbing sorties into the nearby spectacular mountains. Once or twice we visited Santa Fe on Saturday nights, but the city was terribly crowded and the few bars were swarming with security agents from Army intelligence, immediately recognizable by their snap-brimmed felt hats and poorly fitting civilian clothes. They might just as well have worn neon signs. I was content most of the time to stay on the Hill.

The technical work was fascinating. I was proud of my own small contribution to the overall effort, but for a twenty-four-year-old the associations were the main attraction. Oppenheimer had held Groves to his bargain: The town would be isolated, but within the technical area communication would be free. He held weekly symposia on the pressing technical problems of the moment, inviting solutions not only from the groups working on the problems, but from the important cross-fertilization of agile minds from other disciplines with novel approaches and solutions. There was an intellectual critical mass in that small area; just as in the gadget itself, one small suggestion could set off a chain reaction of ideas at a rapid rate, resulting in the greatest technological outpouring that had ever occurred in one location in such a short time. Listening to Bohr, Fermi, Teller, Oppenheimer, Bethe, von Neumann, Frisch, Peierls, and Chadwick was sheer ecstasy, even though I could not always follow their rapid pace and wasn't sure what they were talking about a good deal of the time.

There were two worlds on the Hill, one civilian and one military; I managed to live in both. As a naval officer I lived with the military and moved freely in their circles, but for the most part, the military were not accepted by the civilians. General Groves was hated with a passion. He was typically penny-wise and pound-foolish, spending $2 billion on the overall projects but refusing to pave the streets. He insisted on retaining cantankerous, smelly, coal-burning stoves called "Black Beauties" in the middle of the living rooms as the main heat in the apartments; they drove the wives crazy. And

there was never enough water. Since the eventual size of the
town had been badly underestimated, the water supply never
caught up. Water was brought in by trucks from Santa Fe, but
the pumps were always breaking down. When Groves was in
town, he stayed in the "Big House," the picturesque log-
covered headquarters left by the old ranch school. Whenever
he arrived, water shortage or not, one of the engineers managed to turn off the water to the Big House so that "Gee-Gee"
would suffer from his parsimony like the rest of us.

My Navy uniform immediately identified me on the Hill.
The Navy contingent was quite small, fewer than a dozen
officers; Captain Parsons was an associate director of the laboratory; some of the others, like Lieutenant Commander Norris Bradbury, were respected scientists in their own right; the
civilians considered us to be scientists in uniform, not military like Groves and his Corps of Engineers. Through the
Hornigs and other colleagues, I was able to mix comfortably
with the younger civilians; through Parsons I was able to
meet the more senior people. Deke and Martha Parsons were
the social leaders on the Hill. They lived on Bathtub Row
(where the water was never shut off) across the street from
Kitty and Robert Oppenheimer. Although the Oppenheimers
drank and went to cocktail parties, Kitty never assumed the
social position expected of the wife of a laboratory director.
The Parsonses, on the other hand, were regular Navy, comfortable and gracious in a social setting and experienced in
maintaining the social niceties in the austere atmosphere of a
military base. Whenever there was a visiting dignitary on the
Hill, the Parsonses would host the reception, and the small
naval contingent was always invited. There I managed to
meet Groves, Nichols, Arthur Compton, and other dignitaries
who would not normally cross the path of an ensign.

With my work on the interface between the radars and the
firing sets, I became involved with field operations. The staging point for overseas operations was Wendover, Utah, a small
town on the Nevada-Utah border, on the sand flats of Great
Salt Lake, about 125 miles due east of Salt Lake City. I have
been in desolate places in my life, but this one took the cake.

It was the flattest place I had ever seen. There was no vegetation; even the birds walked around on the ground. But it was a good place to fly airplanes off of. With miles of salt flat and no trees or obstructions, pilots did not have to be too concerned with gaining altitude rapidly as they cleared the runway. The location, chosen primarily for its isolation, was the headquarters for the 509th Composite Bombing Group, commanded by Colonel Paul W. Tibbets, United States Army Air Force.

Everything about the group was specially selected under the personal guidance of Commanding General of the Army Air Force Henry H. (Hap) Arnold. General Arnold had been briefed on the program in early 1944 by Vice President Wallace and Secretary Stimson. When Groves called on him in the spring, he was one officer who instantly realized that we were on the brink of a revolution in warfare. His Air Force was going to do everything possible to make that revolution come about. At the time of the visit no one was sure of the size and weight of the implosion bomb, although all were quite certain of those factors for the gun type. The Fat Man would probably fit into the bomb bay of the newest and largest bomber in the United States arsenal, the B-29, but no one was sure. Because the bomber was designed for the long-range missions of the Pacific theater, its payload was not as large as that of the British Lancaster, older but designed for the shorter ranges of the European theater.

When Groves told Arnold that they might have to use the Lancaster, Arnold replied there was no way they were going to deliver the American atom bomb in a British plane; tell him what to do, and he would see that it was done. Fifteen B-29s were released for special modification. There was considerable reluctance in the Air Force to carry out this order, for B-29s were the most precious commodity in the Pacific arsenal. But Arnold prevailed. The group was set up in September, its core being the 393rd Heavy Bombardment Squadron, selected because of its outstanding record in Europe. There was also a special troop carrier squadron with a dozen C-54s, the largest passenger transport in existence. Later, the

First Ordnance Squadron, consisting of the most skilled welders, machinists, and explosives experts in the service, was activated. Arnold personally selected the commanding officer with the best combat and administrative record he could find. Colonel Tibbets was given carte blanche to select the pilots, navigators, bombardiers, and support personnel. It was truly a crackerjack outfit.

Strict security separation between Los Alamos and Wendover was maintained. I agreed with this type of security. It always seemed ridiculous to me to try to hide a city of twelve thousand or to try to keep a secret by classifying an article already published in the Saturday Evening Post, but the establishment of a connection between the laboratory and an active operational bombing group was a secret well worth hiding and quite hidable. So far as I know, none of the spies, at least two of whom were on the Hill, ever established that connection.

There was no telephone line or radio link. Phone calls from either direction went to two special switchboards in Denver, where connections were made by a single intelligence officer. When flying to Wendover, we drove in an unmarked car to Albuquerque, boarded a plane with commercial markings, and flew to the Mojave Desert in California, out of range of any ground flight controllers. There we turned and flew northeast to the Utah base. Officers traveled in uniform with no distinguishable insignia; enlisted men traveled in civilian clothes.

There were many amusing and some not so amusing aspects of the enlisted men in civilian clothes. Both the Los Alamos and the Wendover people were a pretty select lot; the Los Alamos men were from the Special Engineering Detachment (SED), a bright, very young group of soldiers, many with advanced degrees in science, who had been requisitioned from posts throughout the Army for their technical expertise; the Wendover people, many with combat experience, were also selected from all over the world. The Wendover soldiers resented the young, obviously able-bodied civilians and were quite disdainful of them. The SEDs, able to throw their weight around for the first time since being drafted, often stepped out of bounds. I had to reprimand one young corporal who harassed a Wendover major for weeks. Later on, when the major was cleared into the program and visited the Hill, he ran into the corporal in uniform. They tell me the dressing down could have been heard in Santa Fe.

The test drop area was in the Salton Sea, a fifteen-mile-long brackish lake in the Imperial Desert of California, near the Mexican border, six hundred miles from Wendover. I flew a goodly number of these test missions, generally with Major Charles Sweeney, Tibbets's executive officer, considered one of the best bomber pilots in the Army Air Force. After a while, I began to consider myself a part of Sweeney's crew; my biggest complaint was that I was unable to collect flight pay because of security requirements. The security people would never allow a Naval ensign assigned to Los Alamos to log flying time in a B-29.

During the latter part of May and most of June, my time was about evenly divided between Wendover and Los Alamos. At Wendover, it was easy to see that the end was near. During May most of the ground support crew had cleared the base for overseas. Families were departing; husbands were leaving for an undisclosed location in the Pacific. For the wives and children of the European combat veterans, this was the second time that husbands and fathers had gone off to war, perhaps never to be seen again. For us it was an exciting time; for the wives it was back to the home town, generally to live with parents, with nothing to do but worry and wait, perplexed and bewildered as to what their husbands were doing and why.

At Los Alamos the contrast was marked. Excitement was building because here also was the feeling that the end was near, although nothing looked any different. Plutonium was arriving from Hanford to be shaped into its hollow spheres for the implosion weapons; uranium was arriving from Oak Ridge to be formed into the two-part projectile for the gun; explosive lenses were being shaped and machined; the thump from full-scale testing on the next mesa was heard more and more frequently each day. At Alamogordo, a preliminary test using one hundred tons of explosives was set off to test instruments and measuring devices, the largest deliberate explosion ever set off up to that time.

News on the firing sets was bad. Production difficulties at the Boston factory were holding up test programs all over the Hill. For flight tests we could still use dummies, but for implosion tests the real thing was needed. Our group leader, Lew Fussell, was spending most of his time in Boston coping with production problems; the assistant group leader, Lieutenant Commander Earl P. Stevenson, Ensign George Reynolds, and Donald Hornig did yeoman duty, struggling with the problems of developmental work on the Hill, flight tests at Wendover, and preparations for the Trinity tests at Alamogordo. Because the firing sets were now the controlling item in the whole implosion program, we spent more time in meetings with Kistiakowsky, the division leader, and Oppenheimer than would normally be the case.

During this period I became more fascinated with Oppie, seeing him not only at the laboratory, but also at Parsons's home. He was painfully thin and gaunt, chain-smoking, active but not nervous looking, his porkpie hat looking bigger and bigger as his face became thinner. He seemed knowledgeable and interested in everything. He queried me in detail about the test program at Wendover, which he had not had time to visit. Coming out of a meeting with him, you always felt that somehow the problems would all be solved.

Still, Los Alamos was an island. There was a sense of great excitement, but it was self-contained. It seemed as if we were getting ready for some great scientific experiment at Trinity, unrelated to anything in the outside world. We were part of the war effort, but did not seem to be part of the war. At Wendover there was stark contrast. Watching the base being disassembled, ground crews being shipped overseas, tearful good-byes from parting families, and rehearsal flights with seasoned bomber crews preparing again for combat all gave a sense of participation in the war that was personal, tangible, material.

The first week in June I was told I would be going overseas. Fussell was immersed in production problems, and Stevenson, Hornig, and Reynolds could not be spared from the Trinity test program, so I would lead the first contingent. I spent the better part of the next three weeks scrounging equipment and supplies to be sent to the overseas base; where, I was not told. We referred to it only as "Destination." The rest of the time was spent in the last few test flights at Wendover. My last flight was on June 25; we still hadn't tested a firing set with high explosive; the Trinity test was only three weeks away.

When I returned to the Hill, my orders had been cut. I was to proceed from Albuquerque by military aircraft to Los Angeles, as a cover; then to the Eleventh Naval District Headquarters at San Diego to pick up my pay accounts; from there to San Francisco for commercial travel to Hawaii; thence to the Commander in Chief, Pacific Fleet, for temporary duty in connection with ordnance matters. The Commander in Chief of the Pacific Fleet was Admiral Chester W. Nimitz. I knew his headquarters were on the island of Guam, in the Marianas, so I knew the general location of Destination. I was scheduled to leave Albuquerque Friday morning, July 3. My orders further stipulated that "Ensign O'Keefe will sit as a member, or attend on invitation, at any meetings of committees or boards requiring a representative of X-5, and will be regarded as Officer-in-Charge of X-5 activities."

My immediate superiors, Stevenson and Reynolds, would remain at Los Alamos for the Trinity test and then proceed to the overseas base. The big plum on the Hill was attendance at the Trinity test, now only a couple of weeks away. I was being sent out because I was low man on the totem pole, but I didn't care because I would be in charge of activities for most of the preparatory period.

The overseas operation was known as Project Alberta, under the command of Captain Parsons. Our job would be to do final rehearsals and active test drops at Destination, assemble the devices, and provide weaponeers to fly the combat missions.

On Thursday I was informed that I would be carrying the final top-secret assembly drawings for the Fat Man because the lab did not want to trust anything so important to the regular military courier service. I didn't mind that, although it would be a nuisance and meant that I would not be able to go to a bar or leave my hotel room on the way. What was more important that day was that my plane would be delayed going to Los Angeles; I wouldn't be able to get to San Diego until after closing time for the payroll office. Parsons and all the senior naval personnel were traveling, so I wasn't sure what to do.

I had an appointment that afternoon with Oppenheimer. He was making it a practice to have a final talk with each person leaving for the Pacific. He greeted me warmly, shook my hand, gave me a little pep talk, and asked me if there was anything he could do for me before I left. I said: "Oppie, I have a problem. I hate to bother you with it, but all my superior officers are traveling and I don't know what to do. Because our Navy group on the Hill is so small, we get paid out of Eleventh Naval District Headquarters in San Diego. I have to get to San Diego to pick up my pay accounts so I can eat. My plane is delayed, so I won't get there until after the office is closed. Peer de Silva has given me the Fat Man assembly drawings to carry with me; I'm sure they'll be unhappy if I spend the weekend in San Diego."

Oppie grinned. "I'll take care of it."

I then realized the power of the Manhattan District's priority. He picked up the phone, dialed a number in Los Angeles, and identified himself by a code name. He told the person on the other end my problem. He then said, "Have a plane ready at the Los Angeles airport to fly Ensign O'Keefe to San Diego and wait for him while he picks up his pay accounts and fly him back to Los Angeles. Call the admiral in San Diego and tell him to keep the office open until O'Keefe gets there."

"That should do it," he said as he shook my hand. "Good luck!"

I left Los Alamos the next morning, arriving in Los An-

geles at about 5:00 P.M. A B-24 two-engine bomber was waiting to fly me to San Diego, the pilot and copilot curious about
the mysterious ensign, but no questions were asked. We flew
to San Diego, but the weather was bad and we couldn't land,
so we flew back to Los Angeles. I dismissed the B-24. "What
do I do now?" I worried. I did have a code name to contact
in Los Angeles, but as I was walking toward a phone booth
I passed the American Airlines ticket counter and noticed a
flight scheduled for San Diego. I inquired and found that the
weather was clearing; they should be able to land by 10:00
P.M. I booked a seat on the flight, and off I went. By the time
I got to the Eleventh Naval District Headquarters it was after
eleven. The admiral was so impressed by the phone call that
he kept the whole headquarters staff on duty. It was a
very provoked four-striper Navy captain, the chief disbursing
officer, who would have liked to tell off a lowly naval ensign
for being late, but he didn't dare. I picked up my pay accounts
and left; only then did I realize that the date was July 3. Not
only had I kept the whole Naval District Headquarters on
alert on a Friday night before a holiday weeekend, but it was
the night before the Fourth, San Diego's swingingest party
night of the year.

The power of the priority of the Manhattan District was
impressive, but the heavy hand of bureaucracy always waits
in the background. In the confusion of the late-night visit, I
neglected to have my orders endorsed. It took eight months
and a dozen pieces of correspondence before I could get re-
imbursed for the American Airlines flight to San Diego.

4

TINIAN

THE TOP-SECRET documents I was carrying dampened my one night in San Francisco, but the priority they gave stood me in good stead. I was able to get a seat on the Pan American Clipper, the flying boat with a dining area and bunks. I didn't rate a berth, but had a sumptuous meal in the dining area as we flew across the Pacific to Hawaii. I spent the night sleeping on a couple of parachutes with my package under my jacket. "Lots better than most junior officers do," I thought as I stepped ashore refreshed in Honolulu.

From Hawaii I took a military air transport to the Marianas. When I came on board I found my commanding officer, Captain Parsons, on the same flight. We stopped at Kwajalein Atoll to refuel and then made an unscheduled stop to pick up a sailor with a ruptured appendix on an out-of-the-way little atoll called Bikini. "Well, I sure hope I don't ever see this godforsaken island again," I said to the captain as we walked around the tiny airfield to get some exercise.

When we arrived on Guam, I accompanied Parsons to Admiral Chester W. Nimitz's headquarters. The place was teeming with admirals, but Parsons was treated with special consideration. We met the great admiral and General Curtis E. Le May, commander of the Twenty-first Bomber Command, to which we would be attached. It was then I learned we were going to Tinian, one of the northern islands in the

Marianas, 1450 miles from Tokyo. As we were riding out to the airport for our flight from Guam to Tinian, the captain turned to me with a grin. "You didn't think you were going to make it overseas, did you, O'Keefe?" he said. I remembered back to my first day in his office and guessed that he had decided then and there that I would go with him.

Tinian. Here you could feel and touch the war. The island had been secured exactly one year earlier, after a massive battle for neighboring Saipan, four miles away. Tinian was about the size of Manhattan Island, with streets named after its New York counterpart. It was flat, with precipitous cliffs breaking into the ocean on the northern end and a passable harbor to the south. In one year it had been converted by the Seabees (the Navy Construction Battallion) into one massive airfield with four parallel runways long enough to handle fully loaded B-29s on their way to the Japanese Empire. The harbor was loaded with ships landing supplies for the invasion, now only 120 days away. Night after night, hundreds of B-29s plowed down the four runways, loaded with fire bombs and high explosives, the gasoline tanks filled to take advantage of the last foot of solid earth. The 509th Composite Group Headquarters was located at the intersection of Eighth Avenue and 125th Street, just by the edge of the airfield. The planes started at 3:30 in the afternoon and took off four abreast at three-minute intervals until well into the night. The noise was continuous, the heavy bombers straining at one end of the runway, lumbering at first as they gained speed, then roaring down the last few yards as their propellers reached for the sky, their payload calculated to the pound to clear the runway with no more than six to ten feet of altitude. Each gallon of gasoline that could be added meant additional safety to maneuver and dodge flak and fighter aircraft over the target. Some pilots became so skilled that they used the island like a gigantic aircraft carrier, running right off the end of the runway, dipping down over the cliffs, almost touching the ocean breakers, before rising triumphantly into the blue to begin their three-thousand-mile journey to the Empire and back. Some never made it at all. The slightest miscalculation, the tiniest cough in one of the four engines, a sudden unexpected crosscurrent would be enough to plunge the hundred-thousand-pound vehicle into the ten-foot breakers beating at the cliffs. Navy rescue boats stood offshore at all times to rescue any crews who could escape the downed aircraft; generally they plunged like rocks with all hands aboard. Most nights three to four hundred bombers took off. On March 25, one thousand aircraft participated in a massive fire-bombing of Tokyo, which left 125,000 dead. At least once per night, sometimes two or three times, a plane would malfunction and crack up on the runway or disappear into the sea. The crews knew the odds. There was about one chance in a hundred that they would die before getting off the ground. Some had flown as many as fifty missions.

On their return in the morning, the skies looked like a Sunday afternoon traffic jam after a day at the beach. Aircraft stretched for hundreds of miles, patiently waiting their turn, willingly giving their place in line to their buddies who were damaged or low on fuel. It was not unusual to see planes stalled on the taxiways after landing, with insufficient fuel to make it back to the hangars.

The men of the 509th were not highly regarded on Tinian. First, there was the secrecy. The area was tightly guarded, with the planes under special surveillance. To the thousands of men on the island, what could be so secret? They were living from day to day, from mission to mission, under constant observation by the hundreds of uncaptured Japanese on the island and thousands more on neighboring islands that had not been taken by the Americans. Every move they made, every new outfit that came on the island, was announced the next day on the radio by Tokyo Rose. If something new would shorten the war, why not use it? Every day, every hour was important to them.

Then there were the airplanes. Late in 1944, Captain Parsons had decided that the B-29s flown by the 509th were not reliable enough. General Arnold, cooperative as usual, had requisitioned fifteen brand-new aircraft, which had reversible pitch propellers, fuel injection engines, and other improvements that made them more reliable than the older planes. To flight crews, any increase in ruggedness and reliability was the difference between life and death; they resented the newcomers.

Finally, there were the missions. The odd shape of the Fat Man would make it very conspicuous if it proved a dud. For this reason several dozen bomb casings were put together with high explosives for training missions over the Empire. They were called "pumpkins." The 509th did not fly many missions. When they did, they carried only one bomb and caused practically no damage. When the 509th wasn't being resented, it was being laughed at, which was worse. On August 4, two days before Hiroshima, this poem appeared in the *Tinian Island News*, the Air Force daily bulletin:

> Nobody Knows
>
> Into the air the secret rose,
> Where they're going, nobody knows.
> Tomorrow they'll return again,
> But we'll never know where they've been.
> Don't ask us about results or such,
> Unless you want to get in Dutch.
> But take it from one who is sure of the score,
> The 509th is winning the war.
>
> When the other Groups are ready to go,
> We have a program of the whole damned show.
> And when Halsey's 5th shells Nippon's shore,
> Why, shucks, we hear about it the day before.
> And MacArthur and Doolittle give out in advance,
> But with this new bunch we haven't a chance.
> We should have been home a month or more,
> For the 509th is winning the war.

When we arrived at our base, we worked around the clock getting our compound ready. We didn't have any operating firing sets, only dummies to be used for ballistic drops. I flew a number of missions with the dummies in the pumpkins, primarily dropping them on the Japanese island of Rota. As the month of July rolled on, operational sets began to arrive, but we were not able to test the first one until August 1.

Since the firing sets were so late and there was so little test experience with them, Captain Parsons intended me to be aboard for the first Fat Man mission. I had flown a number of times with Major Sweeney's crew for that purpose. As time grew short, however, it became apparent that I could not get the training time required by the Twenty-first Bomber Command and still run the X-5 group. Other members of the group would arrive after the Trinity shot, but that could be delayed by weather; there was no telling when I would get help. He decided to make me backup weaponeer for the second, which would be ready about August 15. As backup weaponeer I would be part of a flight crew that could fly to Iwo Jima, where there were facilities for changing aircraft if there was trouble with the first one.

On July 12 Parsons flew back to New Mexico to fly as an observer over the Trinity shot. We worked feverishly all that week, wondering how things were going in New Mexico. No one arrived from the States, so we had no inkling of what was happening. The Little Boy and Fat Man had barometric pressure switches to prevent premature activation of the radars. On July 19 we received coded telegrams instructing assembly crews for both Little Boy and Fat Man to raise the altitude settings for barometric pressure switches and for the radars. These instructions would be sent only if the yield estimates had been increased; that was how we knew that the Trinity shot was successful.

A few days later people started coming in from Los Alamos with sensational stories of the magnitude of the Trinity blast. Parsons returned and took me with him to a meeting on Guam. Admiral Nimitz was there; so was General Carl "Tooey" Spaatz, the new commander of the Twentieth Air Force, just in from the European theater to head the Army Air Force for the invasion of the Empire, now less than ninety days away. General Le May was present, as were Tibbets and some of his pilots. Here I was, a lowly ensign, listening to Spaatz and Le May talk about what Truman had said to Stimson and what Marshall had said to Eisenhower. It was very impressive. Since the senior people were aware of the success of Trinity, Parsons was treated as some sort of conquering hero, even though the test was not mentioned. Spaatz and Le May had wanted Kyoto as the primary target, but had been overruled by Secretary Stimson, who felt that Kyoto, as the former capital and the holy city, should be spared. Everyone then agreed on Hiroshima as the primary target, with Kokura as second and Nagasaki as third. All were military targets in addition to being large enough cities for effects to be widespread.

Guam was a fortress. Hundreds of ships were in the harbor, unloading supplies for the invasion. Guns, tanks, trucks, Jeeps, and supplies of all kinds were piled on the shores for miles and miles. The attitude on the island was somewhat different from Tinian, where the bomber crews were in the midst of the aerial war. Guam was packed with Navy and Marines; the mood was one of preparation and anticipation. Many, if not most, were veterans of other invasions: Guadalcanal, the Marianas, Guam itself, Saipan, Iwo Jima, Okinawa; they knew that this one would be the hardest fight of all. The Japanese had been tough all across the Pacific, but in defending their homeland they would gladly give their lives to defend every inch.

Back at Tinian the time was getting short. On July 26, the cruiser *Indianapolis* arrived with the uranium and the gun for the first weapon. She had been detached from the fleet to pick up the precious cargo at San Francisco; it had been decided that this was safer than air transport. She had an uneventful trip across to Tinian, discharged her tiny cargo promptly, and put out to sea to rejoin the fleet. The uranium was brought into the technical compound; security was redoubled. My own group had nothing to do with the assembly of the gun-type weapon, but there was an atmosphere of tension around the compound as the real thing grew closer. The gun weapon would be ready by August 1. On July 30, the *Indianapolis*, on her way to rejoin the fleet, was torpedoed by a Japanese submarine and sank with the loss of nine hundred of her crew. Things were getting pretty jittery by this time; we assumed that the Japanese were on to us and had ambushed the ship on the way back instead of on the way to Tinian. Coded cables crisscrossed the ocean; all future shipments were made by air.

On August 1, the device was ready but the weather was not. General Le May, calling the shots, announced a three-day delay. On August 4 Parsons was notified that the weather was improving over Japan. He gave special instructions to the crews on the mission. There was a total of six aircraft, including weather observation planes and photoreconnaissance and instrumentation aircraft. He explained to them the effects they could expect when the bomb exploded. By now most of them knew they were dealing with a special kind of bomb, but Parsons's statement that the force of the explosion would be the equivalent of twenty thousand tons of TNT dumbfounded them.

On the morning of August 5, the weather predictions were good for the following day; Le May gave the go-ahead, and the flight was scheduled for the sixth. Immediately after assembly, the Little Boy was placed on its trailer, enshrouded in canvas for concealment, and moved to the loading pit, from which it was raised to the bomb bay of the *Enola Gay*. The final tests were run, and the bomb was ready for takeoff by early evening of the fifth.

Parsons was the mission commander, with orders to "render final judgment in the event that an emergency required deviation from the tactical plan." He decided to complete the final assembly of the bomb after takeoff. He had been worrying about this for a week, realizing that a crash and an accidental explosion would not only wipe out the airport, including us, but all material for the implosion weapons that were to follow. After takeoff, before pressurizing the plane, he climbed out into the bomb bay, took the smaller slug of uranium from its lead casing, plugged it into the projectile, and completed the assembly. The plane took off at 2:45 A.M., August 6, Tinian time (11:45 A.M., August 5, Washington time); the bomb was released at 9:15 A.M., within half a minute of schedule.

The rest is history.

In the Fat Man assembly hangar we worked around the clock. The original date for the first combat implosion weapon was August 20. Toward the end of July the date was rescheduled to August 11. The biggest problem was still the firing sets. We knew that the basic design was sound because it had functioned properly on the tower at Tinian, but we still didn't have enough flight data. Back in the States testing was still going on at Wendover. It was not until the end of July that sufficient firing sets had been tested to confirm their safety with high explosives; the first explosive-filled Fat Man with an active firing set was tested at Wendover on August 4, and we tested the first explosive-filled Fat Man with a firing set from Tinian the day before the device was used in combat.

With the success of the Hiroshima weapon, the pressure to be ready with the much more complex implosion device became excruciating. We sliced off another day, scheduling it for August 10. Everyone felt that the sooner we could get off another mission, the more likely it was that the Japanese would feel that we had large quantities of the devices and would surrender sooner. We were certain that one day saved would mean that the war would be over one day sooner. Living on that island, with planes going out every night and people dying not only in B-29s shot down, but in naval engagements all over the Pacific, we knew the importance of one day; the *Indianapolis* sinking also had a strong effect on us.

Good weather was forecast for the ninth, with bad weather to follow for the next five days. This increased the urgency to have the first Fat Man ready still another day earlier. The scientific staff, dog-tired, met and warned Parsons that cutting two full days would prevent us from completing a number of important checkout procedures, but orders were orders.

The Fat Man had the five-foot-diameter implosion sphere in the center of the bomb. The radars were in the tail, thin antennas projecting out from the fins. The original design had not contemplated the use of an electrical firing mechanism, so it had to be crammed into the nose, with the cable that would bring the signal to detonate threaded around the sphere inside the bomb casing.

By ten o'clock on the night of August 7, the sphere was complete, the radars installed, and the firing set bolted onto the front end of the sphere. I broke out for some sleep while others did final checkup and the mechanical assembly crew put the final touches on the casing. I was to come back at midnight for final checkout and to connect the two ends of the cable between the firing set and the radars; the cable had been installed the day before. Then I would turn the device over to the mechanical crew for installation of the fins and the nose cap.

When I returned at midnight, the others in my group left to get some sleep; I was alone in the assembly room with a single Army technician to make the final connection. The building was ringed with security guards, but the assembly room was sacrosanct. No one was allowed in except those doing assembly.

I did my final checkout and reached for the cable to plug it into the firing set. It wouldn't fit!

"I must be doing something wrong," I thought. "Go slowly; you're tired and not thinking straight."

I looked again. To my horror, there was a female plug on the firing set and a female plug on the cable. I walked around the weapon and looked at the radars and the other end of the cable. Two male plugs. The cable had been put in backward. I checked and double-checked. I had the technician check; he verified my findings. I felt a chill and started to sweat in the air-conditioned room.

What had happened was obvious. In the rush to take advantage of good weather, someone had gotten careless and put the cable in backward. Worse still, the checklist had been bypassed so that it was not double-checked before assembling the casing.

"This is what happens when people rush," I said to myself.

The remedy was equally obvious. Wake up the main assembly crew, remove the radars and the firing set, bring back the large cranes, which had been removed from the building, disassemble the weapon, reverse the cable, and start all over again. The Fat Man weapon had not been designed for ease of assembly. Hundreds of bolts would have to be removed. A dozen checklists would have to be redone. It had taken the better part of a day to assemble the weapon. It would certainly take that long to take it apart and reassemble it. We would miss the good weather forecast for the ninth. The end of the war would be delayed — how long? — one day, two days, maybe a week. This would be a court-martial offense for the unlucky one who had made the error.

There was another, quite simple solution: unsolder the connectors from the two ends of the cable, reverse them, and resolder them. But this was forbidden. Nothing that could generate heat was ever allowed in an explosive assembly room. Light fixtures were recessed and shielded. There were no windows. Air-conditioner ducts were multiple-screened. Special safety shoes without nails were required. The floors were padded to prevent sparks from a dropped wrench or screwdriver. Matches or cigarette lighters must be left at the door. Even keys were forbidden since they might cause a spark. This was standard operating practice in all ordnance procedures all over the world. Penalties for infractions were severe, and, of course, the danger from an explosion was real.

I was not worried about the latent twenty thousand tons of energy in the plutonium core. If I had an accident, it would certainly be a single-point detonation and no implosion wave would occur. I was worried about the two thousand pounds of high explosive surrounding the core and the thirty-two ultrasensitive detonators placed symmetrically around it, now connected to the firing set.

I sat down on an old crate we were using for a bench and began to think. Should I wake up some of my associates and consult them? Should I ask for instructions from my commanding officer? That would just be passing the buck. I had lived with this weapon for months. I knew as much about it as anyone else. Why shift the burden of the decision to others? Besides, they might give me the wrong advice. The choice was clear. Take a chance and break the rules or cause a delay.

The technician left the room while I was thinking. Suddenly I felt a whack on my shoulder. The major in charge of the final assembly had come in; deep in my thoughts, I hadn't heard him approach.

"Get off your ass, O'Keefe," he said. "You're holding up the war."

The expression was so hackneyed it wasn't considered funny anymore. But all of a sudden it hit me. I *was* holding up the war. I had it in my power to break the rules, take a chance on an accident, or call for help and delay the end of the war for a day or a week. There was no doubt in anyone's mind that the second bomb would cause the Japanese to surrender.

I stood up. "Sorry," I said, "I was just resting. I'll be finished in about fifteen minutes."

"Good," he replied. "I'm going over to the mess hall for some coffee with the gang. We'll be back in a few minutes and button this baby up."

There was no point in consulting with the major. He was a career ordnance officer who had never broken a rule in his life. He had no electrical experience and would almost certainly decide to disassemble the weapon.

My mind was made up. I was going to change the plugs without talking to anyone, rules or no rules. I called in the technician. There were no electrical outlets in the assembly room. We went out to the electronics lab and found two long extension cords and a soldering iron. We plugged the extension cords into an outlet outside the fire door to the assembly room and propped the door open so it wouldn't pinch the extension cords (another safety violation). I carefully removed the backs of the connectors and unsoldered the wires. I resoldered the plugs onto the other ends of the cable, keeping as much distance between the soldering iron and the detonators as I could as I walked around the weapon. The technician inspected the soldered joints and nodded his approval. I then reassembled the connectors as he took the soldering iron and extension cords back to the electronics lab and took the prop out of the door. I worked carefully but rapidly because I didn't want the major and his crew to come back and catch me. We must have checked the cable continuity five times before plugging the connectors into the radars and the firing set and tightening up the joints. I was finished.

As I carried away my meters after the final checks, the major came breezing into the room.

"Decided to get to work, did you, O'Keefe?" he asked, smiling.

"Yes, sir, it's all yours." I was afraid to say anything more as I was sure my voice was quaking. I went back to my tent, where I slept soundly until daylight.

The next morning I went to the assembly room. The fins had been assembled and the nose cap put on. Nothing looked any different than it was supposed to look, but I kept worrying about that cable, enclosed now deep in the bowels of the device. There was nothing for me to do. Final checks were made during the day and the device was ready by late evening. I spoke to no one about what I had done.

The X-5 group went back to the compound to work on the next Fat Man, the one I would fly with. The plutonium was already on the island; the mechanical and explosive components had been there for a week. We should have it ready in about three days, if necessary. The assembly crew of the Little Boy was closing up shop, preparing to go back to Los Alamos. There would not be enough uranium for another gun-type weapon until sometime in December. We were all certain that the war would be over by then.

The mission itself was bedeviled from the beginning. Sweeney's plane, *The Great Artiste*, had been converted into an instrumentation plane for the Hiroshima flight and would play the same role on this mission. Sweeney borrowed Captain Frederick Bock's aircraft, *Bock's Car*. At the last minute it was discovered that an auxiliary gas tank containing six hundred gallons of gasoline was leaking and had to be discarded. This cut down the fuel safety factor in case they were delayed. One of the observation planes missed the rendezvous over Iwo Jima; Sweeney decided to go forward after waiting forty minutes. Kokura, the primary target, was socked in. They made three passes, but the aiming point remained obscured and they were forbidden to bomb by radar. Sweeney, his fuel running low, decided to "go for Nagasaki," the secondary target. There, again, he found heavy overcast. Suddenly, bombardier Kermit Beahan, an experienced veteran of the war in Europe, yelled that he had spotted a break in the clouds. "Let's take it," said Sweeney. The bomb fell wide of the aiming point, exploding above the northwest section of the city. Although the power of the plutonium bomb was greater than that of the uranium bomb, it did less damage and caused fewer casualties because of the hilly terrain at Nagasaki. Even so, the effect was devastating.

By this time, Sweeney was almost out of fuel and had to make an emergency stop at Okinawa. The importance of the atom bomb had not yet sunk in to the ground crew at Okinawa. They were not particularly moved by the fact that Sweeney had just dropped a second bomb; they were extremely impressed that the plane had reversible pitch propellers, which they had never seen. Sweeney attracted a large crowd to watch him back into the gasoline loading pit.

Communications to Tinian were garbled that day. We had a report that the plane had dropped its bomb and landed at Okinawa, but we were not sure what had happened at the target. It wasn't until the plane returned to Tinian, twenty hours after takeoff, that we knew that the mission had been successful. My own gamble had paid off, but I didn't mention it to anyone until a year later, after I'd gotten out of the service.

By the next day, rumors of impending Japanese surrender spread everywhere on Tinian. We continued to prepare the next weapon for delivery, but General Le May, on orders from President Truman, was advised not to proceed with delivery unless he received specific instructions. By then we were sure that the rumors were true. Four days later, on August 14, the announcement came. The war was over.

At the time, we in the forward area knew little or nothing of what had gone on at the Potsdam conference and, of course, nothing of what had gone on in Tokyo. In our concentration we probably wouldn't have cared. All we wanted was for the war to be over. It was, and we were delirious.

All during the war, the major impetus to the development of the nuclear weapon had been the fear that the Germans would beat us to it. The foreign physicists, having great respect for the Germans' expertise in science, were particularly concerned. Right after the Normandy invasion, Army intelligence had set up a group called Alsos to follow on with the invading troops and interrogate German scientists as they could find them. There was always the possibility that at some secret German "Los Alamos" a group was feverishly assembling a nuclear weapon to be used to turn the tide of the invasion.

To everyone's surprise, the Germans had made very little progress; they had been no real threat right from the beginning. Nobody felt that the Japanese could have made much progress. A laboratory like Los Alamos might be hidden, but certainly nothing the size of Oak Ridge or Hanford. Furthermore, the Japanese simply did not have the industrial capacity to carry out such an effort. On the other hand, there was no sense taking any chances. Just on the remotest possibility that the surrender was a cover and the Japanese were buying time for their own weapon, the President decreed that a scientific mission proceed to Japan immediately after the signing of the surrender documents. A seasoned crew of investigators was dispatched from Germany to the Marianas to guide the mission, which was put under the command of Brigadier General Thomas Farrell, Groves's deputy on Tinian. A group of scientists from Los Alamos was selected to search out their Japanese equivalents and determine what, if any, nuclear research had been done during the war. I was fortunate to be selected as a member of the group, which was headed by Dr. Philip Morrison.

In the two-week interval between the surrender announcement and the actual signing in Tokyo Bay, we spent time with intelligence agents on Guam going over the meager data available on Japanese scientists and laboratories. A team of Japanese interpreters was assigned to give us a crash course in Japanese and then to accompany us to what we still called the Japanese Empire. The Alsos agents briefed us on investigative techniques and filled us in on many of the actions in Germany and Italy. It was from them that I first heard of the horrors of the Holocaust, since many of the Jewish scientists who had remained in Germany were traced to the concentration camps at Dachau and Auschwitz. They weren't sure how many had been executed, but were sure it was in the millions. It was many months before the American public was to learn the full extent of the atrocities.

The Alsos group recommended that we take items such as cigarettes, soap, and candy as friendly gifts to the people we would interview to help them to talk to us more easily. We knew that the Navy always had the best supplies. Being Navy, I volunteered to go to the ships stores of the Construction Battalion, known as the CBs or Seabees, to pick up supplies. By this time, attitudes had changed. Anyone connected with the 509th was a hero to most of the people on the island, but not to everyone. As I was walking into the ships service store, I was stopped by a second-class seaman, an older man about thirty. "Sir," he said, "you can't come in here without no cap."

It was the custom in the Navy that officers wear caps when aboard ship or indoors ashore. I had been assigned for months to an Army organization and had grown out of the habit of wearing a cap. I explained to him that I was attached to the 509th Army Air Force group on the other end of the island, that I was collecting supplies to bring to Japan, that I had forgotten my cap and would only be in the store for a few minutes. He was not impressed in the least.

"Sir," he said, "I have a wife and two kids on a farm outside of Topeka, Kansas. I wanted to help in the war, so my wife said she'd take care of the farm. I joined the Navy. They sent me to California, then put me on a troopship and sent me five thousand miles out to this island. They sat me down at this door and said, 'Don't let nobody in without no cap.' I don't know what you're doing to help the war, but this is what they told me my job was. And, sir, believe me, nobody gets in here without no cap." This brought me down to earth with a bang. I went over to the duty office, found the duty officer, also an ensign, and explained my predicament. "Could I borrow a cap for a half-hour?" He reached into his desk drawer, pulled out a cap, and handed it to me. "We run a tight ship here, buddy," he laughed. I put it on and went back to the ships store. The seaman stood up, saluted me solemnly, and stepped aside. I didn't feel like much of a hero after that.

On the day of the signing in Tokyo Bay, we loaded a dozen Jeeps into our transport planes and took off for Japan. Tibbets decided that he would like to go, and General Farrell had no objections, so he flew the lead plane. After a stopover on Iwo Jima, we flew into Atsugi Airport on the Yokusuka Naval Base at Yokohama. From the air it was a thrilling and a depressing sight. On the one side, there was the United States Pacific fleet — battleships, aircraft carriers, cruisers, destroyers, hundreds and hundreds of support vessels — filling the harbor and patrolling out in the ocean as far as the eye could see. Close in to shore was the battleship *Missouri*, site of the surrender. It was the largest single collection of naval vessels ever assembled and stood witness to Admiral Nimitz's claim that, given time, he could have finished the war by naval blockade alone, without invasions or atom bombs. But in war, time is of the essence because no one knows what will happen tomorrow. Everything must be used to defeat the enemy.

The vista from the other side of the aircraft presented mute testimony to that doctrine: As far as the eye could see, there was destruction. Yokohama and Tokyo, twenty miles away, were virtually wiped out. On one side of the aircraft, the sun shining off the sparkling blue waters, flags and banners flying, and the gray metal of the ships of the fleet bespoke the power and glory of the victorious. On the other, the flatness, accentuated by a few skeletons of buildings still standing, the blackness of the burned and battered buildings, and the smoke still wisping up from fires unquenched bespoke the agonies of the defeated. The image, viewed in seconds only as we landed at Atsugi, stood frozen in time.

The naval base was bedlam, with bewildered Japanese sailors, unable to comprehend the events of the past few days, walking about. Aircraft were landing from all over the Pacific; landing craft were scraping ashore with Marines laughing, joking, smoking cigarettes, hardly believing their good luck to be coming ashore in this manner rather than under the barrage of enemy fire, as they had for so many months and on so many islands. No doubts about dropping the bombs here.

General Douglas MacArthur had been designated the Supreme Commander of the Allied Forces; he was preparing to come ashore to take command. Quartermaster troops had landed to prepare temporary headquarters at Yokusuka, to push on to Tokyo to prepare for permanent lodging, and to commandeer office space for permanent headquarters. We saw no point in waiting. We had our own transportation with the dozen Jeeps. We were able to requisition a couple of tents and enough food for a few days until more permanent quarters and mess facilities would be provided.

At the time, Yokohama and Tokyo were separate cities with rural farm areas in between. Leaving the destruction of Yokohama, we found ourselves in a very few minutes out in the countryside. On a soft September morning we could see rice farms being tended as they had been for centuries, with women working bare-breasted in the paddies, oblivious to the steady stream of traffic on the bomb-pitted roads heading toward the capital city. As we approached Tokyo, the fragile nature of the Japanese economy struck me. Out of the capital, coming toward us, were dozens of horse-drawn vehicles, the honey wagons carrying the heavy buckets of human sewage painstakingly collected before dawn from house to house and carried in the morning to the farms and rice fields for fertilizer. My vision of the Japanese war machine faded as I began to realize that a few small pockets of modern civilization had been created in the major cities, but the pre-ponderant population still lived in primitive agricultural conditions that would have been appropriate to the seventeenth century.

Tokyo was devastated; it appeared lifeless as we approached the metropolitan area. It was difficult to determine which buildings had been what—which had been homes, which shops, which stores. The only clues were the office buildings, where steel safes had weathered the fire raids and were scattered about in random fashion on the ground as they had fallen through the burning floors of collapsing buildings. Eighty-five square miles of the city had been totally destroyed; much of the residential area had a checkerboard look, some buildings burned to the ground, some partially occupied, some untouched.

The one oasis in the city was the Imperial Palace grounds. The preservation of the Emperor had been deemed crucial to the orderly occupation of the country even before atom bombs had appeared, so strict orders had been given to the bombing command to spare the Emperor and his palace. A small area around the complex had been preserved as a buffer zone, with the main Imperial Palace administrative buildings, which would serve as MacArthur's headquarters, untouched. The Tokyo Imperial Hotel, designed by Frank Lloyd Wright, and the Dai Ichi Hotel nearby were in good condition and would serve as primary lodging for the senior officers of the occupation. We camped out in an area near the Dai Ichi. In a few days we managed to make a deal with the quartermasters. Since we were only going to be there for a couple of weeks, we arranged to trade our dozen Jeeps, to be delivered two weeks later, for accommodations in the Dai Ichi Hotel, which was supposedly reserved for flag-rank officers.

We soon fanned out to begin our investigations. My first assignment was to the Tokyo Imperial University, where Professor Yoshio Nishina, a prominent Japanese physicist, headed the physics department. Many of the streets were impassable, with bomb holes and debris forcing frequent detours. We navigated by ordering policemen out of their little Swiss-soldier-style sentry boxes, installing them on the hoods of our Jeeps, and yelling instructions through our interpreters as we bounced through the rubble-filled streets.

The first evening I walked over to the Imperial Palace grounds. It was an eerie sight. Hundreds of Japanese soldiers, sailors, civilians, men and women, were standing at the gate, some praying, some kneeling, some turned away in the traditional gesture of respect. They stared at me in silence, some imperturbable, some curious. Although I was armed, I was well aware of the kamikaze tradition, which bedeviled our fighting forces in the latter part of the war. I stood for a few minutes watching and decided this was no place for me. I walked quietly and carefully back to our tents.

The reception by the Japanese people varied. All were slightly bewildered, unable to grasp the reality of defeat, some were servile to their new masters, and some were still hostile. Most of the people we talked to were scientists, engineers, or senior administrators. They had realized for months that the end was near and were relieved when it finally came. With hundreds of thousands killed and wounded in the fire raids, they made no distinction between the atom-bomb casualties and the fire-bomb victims. They bore no more animosity toward us, the atom-bomb scientists, than to any other Americans. Nor did they question our morality. They realized that we had had a job to do and we had done it. To many the bomb was a deliverance, a weapon that ended the war and left them among the living.

Rounding up the few scientists at the university was no problem. Professor Nishina was old and weary, anxious to get back to his laboratory. Although the Japanese scientists were familiar with the worldwide research that had gone on through 1941, they were completely ignorant of wartime developments. Japan had counted on a quick war, recognizing that she did not have the industrial capacity to outlast the United States; no one had conceived of an undertaking as vast as the Manhattan Project; even if they had, they would have recognized that they had neither the time nor the resources to implement it. On the Nagasaki mission, Luis Alvarez, Nobel Prize-winning associate of Ernest Lawrence of California, had dropped leaflets, from himself, Bob Serber, and Phil Morrison, addressed to an old colleague, Dr. Ryokichi Sagane, describing the bomb and warning that many more were to come. The information almost led to Sagane's execution, but the word spread quickly through the scientific community. The only apparatus of any significance in Tokyo was an old research cyclotron, which had not been operational for years and was of no use except for basic research and instruction. We assured the scientists that the cyclotron would be left intact at the university and gave instructions to that effect. A few weeks later, after we had gone, a jittery major from the permanent occupation force heard the word *cyclotron*, panicked, and had the whole apparatus dumped unceremoniously into Tokyo Bay.

On our trips back and forth to the university, we noticed an unobtrusive, heavily guarded mansion in the suburban embassy area. Curious, we stopped one day on the way back to the hotel and asked one of the guards, through our interpreter, what the building was. It turned out to be the Russian embassy.

Russia had declared war on Japan and invaded Manchuria, then held by the Japanese, on August 9, the day of the Nagasaki raid. The Soviets had prudently recalled their ambassador to Moscow for consultations several weeks earlier, leaving the embassy in the care of a senior foreign service employee. The Japanese, on the declaration of war, had thrown a cordon of guards around the building; in the confusion of the atomic bombings and the surrender negotiations, they had completely forgotten about the embassy staff. The chargé d'affaires of the embassy had been in radio communication with Moscow and followed the surrender ceremonies on the local radio, but knew nothing else of what was happening in the city.

The guards immediately recognized us as Americans; we had no trouble entering the building, where we were welcomed by the staff as conquering heroes. We spoke no Russian and they no English, but through our interpreters we toasted the Grand Alliance, Stalin, Roosevelt, and Churchill (even though Roosevelt was dead and Churchill out of office). None of them had ever seen Americans nor had we seen real live Russians. I have never had so much vodka and potato salad in my life. As we staggered out of the embassy back to the hotel, we instructed the guards to allow our allies complete freedom to enter and leave the compound. I'm sure they had the good sense to stay put until MacArthur's headquarters became established, but we felt that we had freed the Russians.

Neither Hiroshima nor Nagasaki was a scientific center in Japan, so the investigative team had no specific reason to go there. We did fly over the cities in the course of our duties, however; from the air they did not look much different from Tokyo or Yokohama, although the destruction was much more localized. We also had contact with the medical and radiological teams, which had been flown in from the States; their reports of the dead and wounded were much more horrible than anything we had heard in the capital city. It was not possible for me to relate these tales of death and destruction to the pieces of metal I had held in my hands a few short weeks ago on the faraway and almost forgotten island of Tinian. The human mind still cannot encompass the destructive effects of nuclear warfare.

After we were in Tokyo for a few days, the American prisoners of war began arriving from camps in China and Japan. Any compassion I might have had for the Japanese victims of war was tempered by the sight of these crippled, emaciated Americans, many of whom were captured as far back as the Philippine invasion of 1942. They were smiling and laughing, but still nervous and bewildered, finding it difficult to comprehend their new freedom. On one occasion I visited a hospital ship and saw American war victims who were in need of immediate medical attention or too sick to be transported back to Honolulu. They were a pathetic sight, young men in the prime of their lives, unwilling and unwitting victims of a tale of tragedy, which had begun on December 7, 1941, and ended on August 9, 1945.

Our mission accomplished, we turned in our reports to
Karl Compton, president of MIT and brother of Arthur
Compton. He was MacArthur's chief scientific adviser and
head of the initial investigative team. We made a short stop
back at Tinian and Guam to finish up administrative affairs
before returning to the mainland on September 24. Tibbets
received a hero's welcome at the San Francisco Airport, but
I was content to fade away to a hotel.

In the airplane on the way back to the mainland, I began
to put it all together. I had seen the weapon development,
participated in the delivery, talked at length to the Alsos
investigators who had rounded up the scientists in Europe,
seen the destruction of Japan, and interviewed dozens of
Japanese engineers, scientists, and administrators before time
and circumstances could modify their recollections of the
war.

First of all, did the atom bombs end the war? There seems
to be little doubt they did. On July 26, the Potsdam con-
ferees — Harry Truman, Joseph Stalin, Winston Churchill,
and Chiang Kai-shek — had issued a proclamation calling for
immediate surrender, promising a weapon "of unusual destructive force," but giving no details of what was to follow.
On August 6, the day of Hiroshima, the Japanese cabinet
voted to reject the demand with the ultimate Japanese insult
of *moku-satu*, literally "kill with silence." They would not
disdain to answer. True, there were peace feelers going on
in Moscow and Switzerland, but whether they were genuine
or merely an attempt to persuade the Russians not to declare
war will never be known. On August 10, the day after
Nagasaki, the Japanese cabinet voted to sue for peace on the
sole condition of the preservation of the Emperor's status.
Four days later terms were agreed to, and the surrender was
announced on August 14. It had not been easy, as I learned
in Japan. The Emperor himself had made the final statement
to the cabinet. But there was a strong element of resistance in
the Japanese military, so strong that the cabinet decided that
the Emperor could not leave his palace to make the radio
announcement. The surrender message itself referred to the
atom bombs as the final blow that led to the decision. The

message was recorded on August 13 and stored overnight in a secret hiding place. During the night a palace revolution occurred, with men searching for the recording and at one time threatening the life of the Emperor himself. The following morning the message was smuggled out of the palace to a local radio station, where it was broadcast to the world. The revolutionaries committed hara-kiri. Those are the facts.

Japan was near to surrender when the bombs were dropped. Should they have been delayed? To answer that question it is necessary to have some perspective of the times. In the quantum burst of scientific activity that characterized the first forty years of this century, there developed some basic concepts that had not only scientific application, but philosophical and geopolitical application as well. The concepts of the quantum theory, relativity, and the Uncertainty Principle. In the twenty-one short days from July 16, the date of the Trinity test, through Potsdam and Hiroshima to August 9, the date of Nagasaki, the fate of the world was changed for all time. Decisions were made in the heat of war, with little data, no time for introspection, poor communication, and an inability on the part of all concerned to grasp the magnitude of this change, which had been building inexorably for at least fifty years.

Heisenberg's Uncertainty Principle is as applicable to history as it is to physics. We cannot know where we are and where we are going at the same time. The events of those twenty-one days have been analyzed in excruciating detail. We know precisely who did what and when at New Mexico, Potsdam, Washington, London, Guam, Tinian, Hiroshima, Nagasaki, and Tokyo. But the more we know about our position at those specific moments, the less we know of our momentum, our direction at the same instant. As Heisenberg put it, we are like the boy and girl on the weather clock; when one pops in, the other pops out.

What could the B-29 bomber pilot, counting his time to live by hours, the Marine, training for beach landings eighty days away, the *Indianapolis* survivor, bobbing in the waters of the Pacific, the PT boat captain, under fire from Japanese shore batteries, the kamikaze pilot preparing for his last glorious flight into eternity, the Japanese prime minister, readying to group his five million men under arms for a final defense of his homeland, a bomb delivery group on the island of Tinian, fighting for time against weather delays, what could any of these people think about the longer-range implications to the fate of mankind? There was no way that any individual or group of individuals could have materially changed the course of history during those twenty-one days. President Truman had the constitutional power, but he had also the constitutional duty to end the war as quickly and humanely as possible. Events were clearly in the saddle riding mankind. The President and everyone connected with the decision merely responded to the momentum of developments over which they had little direct control.

Secretary Stimson put it most succinctly:

> My chief purpose was to end the war in victory with the least possible cost in the lives of the men in the armies which I had helped to raise. In the light of the alternatives which, on a fair estimate, were open to us I believe that no man, in our position and subject to our responsibilities, holding in his hands a weapon of such possibilities for accomplishing this purpose and saving those lives, could have failed to use it and afterwards looked his countrymen in the face.

What if the President had tried to delay? In many respects, a chief executive is the prisoner of his advisers; he cannot act by himself; he must have staff assistance, communication, advice, and counsel. To a man, his advisers would have opposed him and almost certainly talked him out of it. And what of the millions of men in the Pacific, fighting and dying with each hour that passed? After Trinity, the secret was too big to hide. Outraged scientists and engineers, civilian and military, everyone connected with the project would have contacted congressmen and news media, crying for impeachment and disgrace. What war widow or fatherless child or Gold Star mother of a son killed after August 6 would ever have forgiven the participants in such a decision?

What good would it have done? Would it have saved lives? One hundred thousand people were killed at Hiroshima and Nagasaki; 125,000 people were killed in a single fire-bomb raid on Tokyo on March 25. Who can evaluate the difference between death from nuclear vaporization and death from fire-bombing, or drowning from a ship sunk in Pearl Harbor, or malnutrition in a prison camp, or gunfire on Iwo Jima, or a gas chamber at Auschwitz? For moralists or professors sitting in a quiet laboratory, distinctions can be made, but for decision makers there are no absolutes, only alternatives. Why not wait a few more days from the first to the second bomb to give the Japanese time to react? We were looking at a week, maybe two weeks of bad weather. Furthermore, we were convinced, and that conviction was verified when we talked to people in Japan, that a quick follow-up would give them the impression that we had great quantities of such weapons, which we had not. The people in Tokyo and Yokohama were certain that they would be next and that there was no place to hide. The invasion was scheduled for November 1. With the European war over, that date was more likely to be advanced than delayed.

The Japanese still had five million men under arms; President Truman estimated that millions of Japanese and hundreds of thousands of Americans would have died in the battle for the home islands. Why not wait until the invasion was imminent to give the enemy time to sue for peace? Diplomatic peace negotiations can move awfully slowly; with the rate of bombing raids escalating from the Marianas, several hundred thousand more victims would have died in the intervening eighty days. Why not try a test on a remote island? That was debated in detail in Washington but rejected as impractical. Even after the Trinity test we knew only that a plutonium bomb would work under static conditions. A gun-type weapon had never been detonated. We only had one anyhow. Neither type had been tested in an air drop. The firing set for the implosion device had its final airborne test off Tinian the day before it was used in combat. Besides, the logistics of transporting enemy observers and convincing them that the test was not a trick were insurmountable. None of the scientists who later deplored the bombings ever suggested inviting the Japanese to the Trinity test. Finally, we were under constant observation at Tinian, and our compound was small. If the enemy had found out what we were doing, they would have wiped us out with a single kamikaze raid.

What about the morality of developing nuclear weapons and using them at all? Was it immoral to have worked on the Manhattan Project? Was it immoral to be the first to use these most horrible inventions of mankind? It is not sufficient justification to say that if we had not done it, someone else would have, but that is true. It might be moral justification if mankind would have been worse off had they fallen into other hands. This was the moral justification that accelerated the program in the first place, the fear that they would have been developed by the Nazis. That they would have been developed if they could have is a given. From Becquerel to Roentgen to Thomson to Rutherford to Planck to Einstein to Bohr to Chadwick to Fermi to Hahn and Strassman, to Frisch and Meitner, the pace of theory and inquiry and experiment was inexorable.

By 1939, after the George Washington University conference, the world knew the secret, if there had ever been one. By 1940 fission experiments had been carried out in the United States, Great Britain, France, Sweden, Italy, Germany, Japan, and Russia. The only reason the other major powers did not pursue the program vigorously was lack of resources for a longer program and the necessity to concentrate those resources on the more immediate problems of fighting a war. What if the inexorable march of inquiry had uncovered the secret sooner?

History has taken some peculiar turns. At any stage of development, an advance could have been made that would have speeded things up. Planck's quantum theory languished until Einstein picked it up. Some of Britain's best scientists were killed in World War I. Rutherford spent two years in Canada that would have been more productive at Cavendish.

Bohr could have stayed in England with superior facilities instead of going home to Copenhagen and taking the time to set up his own laboratory. The Joliot-Curies had the neutron under their noses for many months before it was discovered by Chadwick. Bohr and Heisenberg agonized for a year before producing the Uncertainty Principle. The most puzzling delay was Fermi's. The great developer of the slow neutron technique had actually caused nuclear fission but didn't know it. He was looking for elements heavier than uranium, ignoring the residue of lighter elements. Perhaps the quantities were too small, perhaps the measurement techniques not far enough advanced. For whatever reason, he missed it.

It was five long years before Hahn and Strassman published their findings and started the wartime atomic race. If the world had known of fission earlier, Hitler would have had the bomb, and the world would have been a different place. But why did not someone else discover it? In fact, a German-Jewish chemist, Ida Noddack, published a paper in a chemistry magazine suggesting that "under neutron bombardment, heavy nuclei, like uranium, break into several large fragments," but she was ignored.

I believe that a good part of the reason was the turmoil in science caused by Hitler's anti-Semitism. Many of the most prominent scientists and the secondary physicists and chemists were Jewish. Hitler had used anti-Semitism as a mechanism to bring himself to power. By then he had achieved his objective; had he reduced his anti-Semitism to rhetoric, recognizing the talent in the Jewish population, using the talents toward his ultimate goal of world domination, how many of those talented men and women — due to play such a dominant role in the American bomb project — would have been able to resist the challenge of harnessing the atom until it was too late to stop? No, the irony of fate is that Hitler, by his persecutions, removed the one group of people who would have been able to provide him with the tool for the world dominance he so eagerly sought.

What if the development had taken longer? At any stage during the Manhattan Project a six-month delay would not have been unlikely. What if the Trinity shot had been a dud? Everything had to work perfectly for the test to be successful. A mistake in calculation, a defective initiator, a poorly assembled detonator, any number of mishaps could have occurred; some of them usually do. Would we have used the gun-type weapon, knowing we would not have another for months? Or suppose the Japanese had surrendered sooner, in June or July perhaps? By all dictates of common sense, they should have, but they didn't. If the bombs had not been ready before the war was over, a congressional investigation to end all congressional investigations would have taken place. It would certainly have lasted for months — imagine $2 billion expended in complete disregard of all proper procurement procedures for a couple of grapefruit-sized hunks of metal. Would the bomb have been tested after the war was over? Eventually, yes, but not until the investigation had run its course — not for months certainly, more likely a year or more. The American people would have abhorred the testing of a new, superdevastating weapon in the revulsion for destruction that followed the Japanese surrender. If we had not tested when we did, the first atomic explosion could well have taken place in the Soviet Union.

But what of the ultimate morality question? Should a nuclear weapon have been used anywhere, ever? It is not enough to ask whether it should have been used against a weak nation near to surrender. What if the United States had developed the weapons in 1943 or 1944, when Nazi Germany was strong? That too could have happened very easily. After the 1939 conference announcement it took six months for Einstein to sign his famous letter to the President and two more for Sachs to deliver it. It was February 1940 before the first $6000 was appropriated and late 1940 before Vannevar Bush coaled up the NDRC. One to two years could have been lopped off the schedule if someone had picked up the ball and run with it early in 1939. What if the bomb had been ready before the Normandy invasion? Would it have been moral to use it to prevent the loss of life and destruction that followed? Would it have been moral to preserve the six mil-

lion lives that were lost in the Holocaust? No one would
have known because no one would have dreamed that the
executions were about to occur. Nor do we know what would
have happened had the bombs not been used in Japan. Primary staging for the invasion would have been made from
Okinawa. There was a great storm off the Okinawa coast in
October 1945, which could have severely damaged the United
States fleet, crippled the troopships, and prolonged the war
by delaying the invasion.

Yes, by any method of analysis, dropping the bombs on
Japan was appropriate to the times. I certainly had no doubts
then or now. As an ensign in the United States Navy I did
my duty and I am proud of it.

That's the easy part. That's the rational part. But through
the thirty-eight years that have passed since 1945, there
comes always the unanalyzable question: Why me, why us,
why now? Why, after the countless generations that have
passed since the beginnings of life, why, after the progress of
science and civilization which, through the centuries of
recorded history have continually improved the lot of mankind, why, when through the marvels of production and
communication we finally have the tools to end world hun-
ger and deprivation, why, in this single generation, have we
suddenly found the power, as in some imploding backward
big bang, to reverse the process of eons of progress and destroy
civilization as we know it? Why does U-235 fission with slow
neutrons while U-238 does not? Why is plutonium, a non-
existent element fifty years ago, so easily bred in such large
quantities? Why was this generation chosen, or fated, to be
unique in the history of mankind, the potential agent of self-
destruction? I had no doubts, then or now, but the questions
I had, and they are with me still.

Los Alamos was a shambles when I returned. More than a
month had gone by since Trinity, Hiroshima, and Nagasaki;
all the excitement had passed. The war was over, no one else
had the bomb, the job was done; it was time to get on to
other things. There were rumors that the Los Alamos laboratory would be closed and moved to California. There were

other rumors that an international agreement would soon be reached to terminate all nuclear weapons research. Before leaving for Rhode Island and a well-deserved leave, I was able to find out much of what had happened at Trinity and Potsdam.

The story began back in 1942, when the British agreed to transfer their know-how to the Americans and proceed with the project in the United States. At the time full and free interchange was anticipated. As Groves and the Army came into the picture, pressure was put on for more secrecy. The British began to feel left out. They felt especially put upon when the Americans insisted on using their own thermal diffusion process for uranium separation over a more advanced British process. Since the Canadians had uranium and were doing some research, they were very much part of the picture. Squabbling continued into much of 1943, until Roosevelt and Churchill at a meeting in Quebec signed the "Quebec Agreement," spelling out the conditions for interchange of information. The agreement was intricate and convoluted, but basically it stated terms for wartime exchange between Britain, the United States, and Canada. No other allies were included.

During 1944, Niels Bohr, certain now that the weapon would work, began to use his status as senior scientific spokesman to consider postwar problems. He knew there was no secret, that any industrial nation could produce weapons once it was demonstrated that they could be made. He felt that we should immediately tell the Russians and our other allies what we were doing and work toward international control before the development had been completed. This is where the conflicts of C. P. Snow's two cultures were demonstrated at the highest level. The scientist, inarticulate and shy, with no knowledge whatsoever of politics or wartime strategy, tried to convince the two leaders of the Western world to disseminate freely to an already recalcitrant Russian ally the secret of the most powerful weapon of war ever devised. The two leaders, unable to understand the technical aspects of the problem, confident that their cause was just, could not conceive of forgoing an advantage that would assure the peace of the world on terms they felt deep in their hearts were best for mankind. I am sure they felt that they would be violating the duties of their office if they agreed to such a step. At the same time, Secretary Stimson, Bush, and Conant were also pushing for more consideration of postwar international control. Bohr's meeting with Roosevelt was inconclusive; Roosevelt listened politely but made no comments. The scientist also managed to see Churchill, who was infuriated. He took an immediate dislike to the Danish physicist and rejected his suggestions out of hand.

In September 1944 Churchill was in Quebec with his wife and daughter. On Sunday the seventeenth, the Churchill family left Quebec to pay a social visit to the Roosevelts at Hyde Park. In the quiet, informal atmosphere, the two leaders turned to talk of atomic energy and of the efforts to turn the project over to international control. To record their common views, Roosevelt and Churchill signed an "aide-memoire." Flatly rejecting Bohr's approach, they concurred that the project should continue under the utmost secrecy. Both men agreed on what amounted to an Anglo-American approach to the postwar world: "Full collaboration between the United States and the British Government in developing Tube Alloys [a code name] for military and commercial purposes should continue after the defeat of Japan unless and until determined by joint agreement." That settled that.

When Roosevelt died and Truman assumed the presidency in April 1945, he knew nothing about the Manhattan District program. It was scandalous that the project had been considered so secret that the Vice President of the United States was not informed about it, but it was an opportunity to reconsider international control, since Truman was not bound by Roosevelt's "aide-memoire."

Stimson prepared a memorandum for a briefing of the new President in which he expressed the fears that all scientific men shared. His memorandum was a forceful statement of their central thesis that the United States could not retain its advantage indefinitely. Although Russia was the only nation able to begin production in the next few years, there was the real danger that some nation — even a small one — might build the weapon in secret and unleash it, without warning, against its unsuspecting neighbors. The very existence of modern civilization was at stake. As American leaders approached the new world organization, they must appreciate the bomb's awful power. A primary question was whether the United States should share this weapon with other powers and, if so, when and under what terms. The memorandum concluded that a committee should be appointed to recommend early steps in anticipation of postwar problems and to deal with interim policy. For three quarters of an hour, the President listened. Stimson was convinced that he had accomplished much.

The Interim Committee was chaired by Stimson himself. It included Bush, Conant, Karl Compton, the undersecretaries of the Navy and State departments, and James F. Byrnes as personal representative of the President. Scientific advisers included Oppenheimer, Fermi, and Lawrence. Unfortunately, the committee was caught up in the momentum of the Trinity test and the policies toward Japan. They reinforced the policy of use without warning but could not agree on postwar policy. Byrnes, who had been Truman's mentor in the Senate, a Supreme Court Justice, and war mobilization director under Roosevelt, carried considerable weight as the President's personal representative. On May 31 the committee met to reconsider postwar policy. The main debate was on the troubling question, Should the United States tell Russia about the bomb? Byrnes intervened decisively. He feared that if the United States gave information to the Russians, even in general terms, Stalin would ask to come into the partnership. He felt that the best policy was to push production and research to make certain the United States stayed ahead while making every effort to improve political relations with Russia. Such a strong statement by a man of Byrnes's prestige was not to be dismissed lightly. All present indicated their concurrence.

The next week Byrnes was appointed Secretary of State. There were now only six weeks before the Potsdam conference. The momentum of events prevented further discussion of policy. The Trinity test occurred during the Potsdam meeting, at which the Russians were militant and demanding, especially with regard to Poland and the Balkan nations. At the conference, Stimson changed his mind about pushing for international control but felt that Truman should say something to Stalin, since the bomb had already been tested and the secret would soon be out.

Truman was cautious and devious in his approach to the Russians. On July 24 the President casually approached Stalin after one conference session and told him only that the United States had developed "a new weapon of unusual destructive force."

Stalin didn't bat an eye. He politely expressed hope that the United States would make "good use" of the weapon against the Japanese. Indeed, the dour reaction of the Russian leader led Byrnes to believe that "Stalin did not grasp the importance" of Truman's message. Nothing could be further from the truth. *Stalin knew more about the bomb than Truman did.*

According to Marshal Georgi Zhukov in his memoirs, Stalin said to him after dinner about ten o'clock that night, "It looks like we are going to have to talk to Kurchatov and get him to speed things up."

Although much is clouded in secrecy, the beginning of the nuclear arms race can be pinpointed precisely: It was 10:00 P.M. Potsdam time, July 24, 1945.

Stalin knew where he stood and he knew where we stood. That was a lot more than Truman knew. Igor Kurchatov was the foremost physicist in Russia. He had received his training at the Crimean University; in 1925 he went to the Leningrad Physiotechnical Institute as an assistant to Academician A. F. Ioffe. Kurchatov and Ioffe had been at the forefront of nuclear physics at Leningrad and had kept up with world research during the twenties and thirties. In 1939, when fission was discovered, Kurchatov publicly predicted the possibilities of a nuclear weapon. For the Soviet government of 1939, such predictions could not have gone unnoticed. When the Germans invaded Russia in 1941, all nuclear research stopped; in the siege of Leningrad the institute was demolished. But the Russians had not forgotten nuclear fission. When the tide of battle turned at Stalingrad in 1943, they lost no time in setting up a new Institute of Atomic Energy in Moscow under Kurchatov's direction. By 1944 he had the first Russian cyclotron in operation.

It is not known how much they had accomplished by the middle of 1945, but it was clear that they had decided to construct a weapon. They had the benefit of Klaus Fuchs's espionage and Greenglass's diagrams of the implosion lenses, as well as the reports of their Canadian espionage agents, and who knows how much else that has never been revealed. They knew that the Trinity device was a plutonium implosion weapon, and when they learned that it worked, they were ready for a crash program. Stalin was aware that the British and the Americans had no intention of sharing the secret. It probably never occurred to him that they would even consider such a possibility. It was clear from their actions at Potsdam that the Russians did not intend to be intimidated by the atom bomb; to the surprise and dismay of Truman and Byrnes, they pressed their points as aggressively as if it did not exist. They were confident of their ability and were going to make it on their own. I don't think that an offer to share the secret would have made any difference. They would probably have been suspicious of it as a delaying tactic and gone ahead on their own anyhow. They knew all they needed to know. Could it have been otherwise? Probably not. But the Allies missed their best chance to try. I believe that the missed opportunity was caused by the obsessive security established by Groves and the American military.

Because of the barrier of the two cultures, senior nontechnical members of the administration never understood the nature of the development. Although some were briefed, they never grasped the fact that uranium fission was common knowledge around the world, that Japan, Germany, and Russia, like Britain, had not considered a crash program because they lacked the resources in the middle of what they perceived to be a short war. The American development was primarily an engineering achievement, not a scientific one. The basic science was known by 1940.

In addition to the cultural barrier, there was the security barrier. In a democratic society matters of international policy need open debate. The fact that the Vice President of the United States and the senior members of the Congress were not cleared into the program is disgraceful. By 1944 the Russians knew all about the development while our senior officials did not. What's more, we knew that they knew. John Lansdale had admitted that to Oppenheimer in 1943. There was nothing to lose in the latter stages of the war by bringing more of the nontechnical American talents into the program. It was too late for anyone to catch up.

The only danger was sabotage, but we knew that the Japanese and Germans had no espionage network in the United States. The Russians certainly weren't going to consider sabotage because we were doing their engineering for them for free. If Truman had been cleared along with a group of advisers when he was elected Vice President, maybe we would have been able to develop an international policy that would have delayed the arms race. Maybe not. But one thing was inexcusable and can be blamed directly on obsessive security. Truman and his advisers were at a tremendous disadvantage at Potsdam. They thought they had a secret. Stalin knew they did not. The great triumph had turned into a bust.

5

TESTING

IT TOOK a couple of weeks after my arrival at Los Alamos
for my leave papers to be processed. Then home to Rhode
Island. Since I would be in the Navy for another six months
at least, I had intended to bring my family back to the Hill.
While I was on leave I received orders to report to the Massachusetts Institute of Technology for temporary duty to assist Mr. Herbert E. Grier.

He was a member of the partnership of Harold Edgerton,
Kenneth Germeshausen, and Grier, a group started in 1931
to develop electronic flash or strobe. During the war, strobo-
scopic techniques were used for night aerial photography as
an alternative to flares. The large airborne electrical capacitor banks were the closest components to the capacitor banks
needed for the electronic detonating system of the implosion
weapon. When the Manhattan District commandeered the
Boston factory manufacturing the assemblies and converted
it to weapon firing sets, they hired Grier as a consultant from
nearby MIT. Because of the urgency of the program, there
was no time to design the firing sets to good engineering
practice. At the end of the war, Grier agreed to accept a contract at MIT to redesign the firing sets. I was sent to MIT for
a few weeks to help him organize the new research group.
The few weeks stretched into months; my family stayed in

Rhode Island, and except for monthly visits to Los Alamos, I remained at the Institute until I was discharged from the Navy in the summer of 1946.

On my discharge from the service President Karl Compton of MIT offered me an appointment as a research associate in the Department of Electrical Engineering and as associate project manager for Grier's research program. I accepted, conditional on being allowed to pursue private consulting activities, one of which was for my old associate at Los Alamos, Donald Hornig. He had invented a radiation measuring device for infrared spectroscopy that was being built in Cambridge in a laboratory that was having production difficulties. I signed on as a consultant. We later formed a partnership, then a corporation — the Radiation Instruments Company. For a number of months I worked days at MIT and nights and weekends at the Radiation Instruments Company laboratory in Boston.

In the summer of 1947 I was called back from vacation to a meeting at MIT with Norris Bradbury, the new Los Alamos director, and Alvin Graves, his test division leader. They were planning a series of weapon development tests, to take place in 1948 at the atoll of Eniwetok, two hundred miles east of Bikini. Since those in our MIT group were the principal designers of the firing sets, we were asked to design a special version for the Eniwetok tests. When we agreed, they asked the next question: Would we design a system of signals to actuate unmanned instrumentation and coordinate them with the firing signal? We said we would, but pointed out that, among other things, we would have to procure several million dollars' worth of underwater signal cable to string around the atoll. Our MIT contract was funded at only $200,000 total. Money was no problem, we were told.

At the time, most of the MIT faculty was back in force, ready to resume teaching and nonmilitary research. MIT and other universities had had a gutful of military research. When the MIT director of research programs heard about the proposed tenfold expansion of our little project, he balked, saying that MIT was trying to get out of military research, not into it. He suggested to Grier that he and his partners form a corporation to take over the government business and move it off campus. Edgerton and Germeshausen didn't care much one way or the other, but Grier thought it was a great idea, so the corporation of Edgerton, Germeshausen & Grier, Inc., was formed.

Almost at the same time, Hornig and I received a good offer for our Radiation Instruments Company and decided to sell. Hornig went off to a professorship at Princeton University; I transferred from MIT to the new corporation at its founding. As 1947 progressed, our project grew, and we moved to an old garage on Brookline Avenue in Boston. We were also asked to do a neutron measurement because we were also expert in fast pulse measurements. This pulled Edgerton into the project. Since Grier was project director, he became president and chief executive officer of the new corporation; Edgerton, who wanted no business responsibilities, became the chairman of the board; and Germeshausen was vice president and treasurer.

International control of nuclear weapons means world government, nothing else. There is no possible way that the Russian police state could accommodate or even consider the loss of sovereignty implicit in international inspection and controls. The Soviet policy on this matter has been unwavering because the Russians feel that they have no choice. It is not that they are smarter than we or more foresighted but that they have fewer options. They had carried out their nuclear research since 1943 on a relatively modest scale, consciously or unconsciously pacing their efforts to the progress made in the United States. Arnold Kramish, in his book *Atomic Energy in the Soviet Union*, points to numerous indications that the Soviets knew what we were doing. When our bomb became a reality, they initiated a crash program.

Although we might have debated the subject of international controls and offered to give them the secrets under controlled conditions, I can't believe that they ever thought we would do so. Every indication they gave in the ensuing few years was that our offers to share our secrets were pure rhetoric put forth in an effort to get them to slow down their program. They had to have the bomb and they would get it. It was as simple as that. Totalitarian regimes can accomplish great things when they decide to do so. Whether it is a Kremlinski polace, or a Moscow subway, or a man in space, the Soviets have vast resources and a single-mindedness of purpose to apply to tasks such as the nuclear research effort. Other things suffer, such as the population's standard of living, but the population can do nothing about it. There is no philosophizing, no moralizing, no concern about the end justifying the means. To the Soviets, espionage is a perfectly legitimate instrument of national policy; they used it to the maximum possible extent.

In our society, consensus is difficult to obtain. The scientists knew we had a wasting asset; they tried very hard to utilize that asset before it disappeared. But they were politically naive. They could not comprehend that the other side also knew we had a wasting asset and was not prepared to sacrifice any advantage to get it. This was Stalin's trump card. He knew what he could do and he knew what we could do.

The politicians in the United States vacillated. They listened to the scientists tell them of the transitory nature of our advantages, but the scientists were "wooly headed"; maybe they really didn't know how great our advantage was. A politician instinctively could not give up a negotiating advantage without some quid pro quo. Stimson went back and forth. So did Byrnes. So did Truman.

Endless proposals were put forth with countless variations. Byrnes started out in complete opposition to giving away any secrets. In September he went eagerly to a foreign ministers' conference in London, where he ran into a stone wall. From the beginning, Vyacheslav Molotov was not prepared to negotiate on anything — Italian peace treaty, Iran, the Middle East, Eastern Europe. Although Byrnes had not expected to bring up the subject of the bomb, Molotov, on the second day of the conference, accused Byrnes of having "an atomic bomb in his side pocket." It became apparent that the Russians were quite aware of America's atomic advantage but were unwilling to be intimidated by it. As the conference continued with complete stalemate, it became obvious that America's atomic monopoly, far from being an asset at London, was a diplomatic liability. This was Byrnes's first venture into head-to-head international diplomacy; after two weeks it became a debacle. When the Council of Foreign Ministers adjourned on October 2, they could not even agree on whether or where to meet again. It was a stinging personal defeat for Byrnes. After his return, he told John Foster Dulles that he had realized at Potsdam that "we were going to have trouble with the Soviets," but it was not until London that he realized the Russians were "stubborn, obstinate, and they don't scare."

In the meantime, the President was coming to his own conclusions. Clear opposition to any concessions came up in the Cabinet. Treasury Secretary Fred M. Vinson, a longtime friend, Secretary of the Navy James V. Forrestal, a powerful national figure, and Secretary of Agriculture Clinton Anderson were adamant in their opposition. Senators Arthur Vandenberg of Michigan, Tom Connolly of Texas, and Scott Lucas of Michigan — all members of the newly formed Joint Committee on Atomic Energy — met with Truman to warn him about rumors that he intended to "share" the bomb with the Russians. Soon after, a delegation of congressmen from the same committee called on him to urge that the secret be kept. It was clear by October that any attempt to share with the Russians would be given short shrift in the Congress.

From the very beginning the American public could not comprehend the complexities of the subject. Away from Los Alamos and the military, I was extremely disappointed in my discussions with friends and in reading the press to realize how poorly equipped we were as a nation to grapple with this most important subject, this happening that had changed the world forever. Most people didn't want to think about it at all. Those who did took a completely simplistic view. This was an exclusively American development; we owned it; why give it away? To many, there was a strong moral conviction that since God had entrusted us with this secret, we should husband it and not give it away to the godless Com-

munists. Public opinion surveys in September 1945 revealed
that 70 percent of the public and 90 percent of the Congress
objected to "sharing the atomic bomb secret" with other nations. The President was also strongly influenced by that font
of all knowledge, General Groves. Although the general realized that eventually the techniques would become common
knowledge, in his heart he felt that it would be a generation
before others could do what he had done. He told Truman
that twenty years would pass before we would have a rival.

Realizing the depth of public opinion, recognizing the re-
alities of passing legislation through the Congress, listening
to the words he wanted to hear from Groves, the President
made his own announcement, not in the stately settings of
the palace in Potsdam or to a combined meeting of the House
and Senate in Washington, but in typical homespun Truman
fashion while on a trip to visit the Pemiscot County Fair in
Caruthersville, Missouri. Later, talking to reporters on the
porch of Linda Lodge at Reelfoot Lake near Tiptonville, Tennessee, the President was questioned about the bomb. He replied that there was no real secret, that the scientific knowledge to build a bomb was "worldwide knowledge already,"
but that it was the "combination of industrial capacity and
resources necessary to produce the bomb" that the United
States alone enjoyed and was not about to give up. To nail
down his point, the President went on to say that if other
nations were to "catch up" with us, "they will have to do it
on their own hook, just as we did."

This was policy at its most pungent, like it or leave it.

Byrnes was not ready to like it. Stinging from his defeat at
the Foreign Ministers Council, Byrnes proposed another
meeting in Moscow in December. His purpose was to get an
agreement — some agreement — on atomic matters with the
Soviets. Although Truman was at ease with his Secretary of
State, Byrnes, who had been one of the most powerful figures
in the Senate, could never accept Truman as his superior. I
can recall when Byrnes was courtly but patronizing to the
new senator from Missouri, instructing him in the ways of
politics, always the teacher, always the superior. He went on

to be a Supreme Court Justice, then Director of War Mobilization, so-called Assistant President under Roosevelt. In 1944 he had fully expected to be nominated for Vice President, but was shot down by the labor unions, who turned to Truman as a compromise.

Byrnes had to reestablish himself, reversing his atomic policy to do it. He put together a four-step strategy to offer the Russians: first, a broad exchange of scientists and scientific information; second, exchange of knowledge about the location and development of uranium supplies; third, a release of engineering information on atomic energy in general; and fourth, development of controls over military use of the bomb.

The proposal was completely counter to the President's October statement on policy and had never been discussed with him. To Byrnes's bitter amazement, Molotov rejected the offer out of hand. The Moscow meeting developed into another fiasco. In order to salvage something, Byrnes appealed directly to Stalin, who was not available until late in the evening. According to Ambassador Charles Bohlen, Stalin appeared "listless" and inattentive, but blunt in his replies. He would accept Byrnes's offer only if Byrnes would make other concessions on the United Nations organization and the Middle East. Byrnes was dumbfounded. Here was the atomic secret offered on a silver platter and Stalin was insisting on other conditions before he would accept it. Atomic diplomacy had come full circle. Not only was it not the trump card Byrnes had expected, he couldn't even give it away. Byrnes retreated to Washington with his tail between his legs. Word of his defeat soon reached Truman, who was furious at his old mentor. His influence gone, Byrnes quietly faded away and left the government some months later.

Private diplomacy having failed, Truman turned to the United Nations. The world organization was only a few months old, having been organized in San Francisco during the spring of 1945. Undersecretary of State Dean Acheson was appointed to head a government committee on an atomic policy to be presented to the United Nations. Acheson selected a board of consultants headed by David Lilienthal, chairman of the Tennessee Valley Authority. The two groups formulated a policy, largely drafted by Robert Oppenheimer, which was similar to the proposal Molotov and Stalin had rejected at Moscow. Known as the Acheson-Lilienthal Report, it was not well received by the Congress, the press, or the public. In order to attract more support from the conservatives, Truman appointed Bernard M. Baruch, a pompous Wall Street millionaire, as special atomic delegate to the United Nations. Baruch modified the Acheson-Lilienthal Report to call for total disarmament, not just nuclear disarmament, and wide-open, unrestricted inspection of all nations' military facilities. Never modest, Baruch named this new proposal the Baruch plan. It didn't have a chance. The American scientists withdrew from the panel, the military were skeptical, and the Russians wouldn't give it the time of day. That ended efforts to work through the United Nations.

In the midst of the United Nations debate, the Canadian spy scandal broke. Allen Nunn May, a Canadian physicist, headed a Canadian Communist cluster, which had attempted to determine information on Canadian resources of uranium and thorium and pass it on to the Soviet Union. The amount of information obtained and transferred was deemed insignificant even by General Groves, but flagged by commentator Drew Pearson on his evening radio show, it made for a first-rate scandal. The press and the American public, reasoning that there must be a secret or the Russians would not try to steal it, clamored for secrecy. By the middle of 1946, even the Baruch plan was abandoned, and all hope for action through the United Nations was lost. The atomic curtain had descended with an ominous clang.

With the failure of personal diplomacy and the rejection of the Baruch plan, international control efforts were abandoned. But there still had to be a domestic policy.

When the war ended, all nuclear research development and manufacture was under the direct control of General Groves. The Congress set out to write legislation that would put the program under civilian control. The War Department, anticipating such a move, prepared its own version of a bill, giving civilians participation but retaining basic control in the military. Named the May-Johnson Bill for its sponsors, it was introduced in the fall of 1945 and almost passed without any organized opposition. Here the scientists finally proved to be effective. A newly formed Federation of Atomic Scientists rose in opposition; although they were unable to introduce their own legislation, they managed to stall enactment of the May-Johnson Bill until more formidable opposition could be organized.

A freshman senator from Connecticut, Brien McMahon, stepped into the fray, sponsoring a resolution for a special Senate Committee on Atomic Energy and becoming chairman at its enactment. The new committee, committed to civilian control, dueled with the powerful Senate Committee on Military Affairs. McMahon's committee sponsored its own legislation, known as the McMahon Act, featuring military participation under civilian control. The battle in Congress raged for nine months, from October 1945 to July 1946, while the atomic establishment continued to disintegrate. Not only had the civilian members of the Manhattan District left Los Alamos, Oak Ridge, Hanford, Chicago, and other installations, but the reserve military officers had returned to civilian life. Most of my military associates at Los Alamos had been discharged from the active reserves by midsummer of 1946, as I had.

As the year wore on, the nation's appetite for matters military had abated considerably, and the base of support for the May-Johnson Bill began to abate. By July 1946 McMahon had won his battle; the Atomic Energy Act of 1946 was enacted, calling for a civilian commission of five members to oversee an agency of a number of divisions for military and peaceful development of atomic energy. The bill provided for one division to be under the direction of a military officer on active duty, but civilian control was clearly established. A Military Liaison Committee was established to correlate military matters between the commission and the Department of Defense.

David Lilienthal was named chairman of the new Atomic

Energy Commission. Serving with him would be Sumner T. Pike, a New England businessman; William W. Waymack, a gentleman farmer and newspaper editor from Iowa; Lewis L. Strauss, an investment banker who had served as liaison, through Sachs, between Einstein and Roosevelt in 1939; and one scientist, Robert F. Bacher, a Cornell physicist who had served as a division leader at Los Alamos.

After nine months of controversy in the Congress, it took many more months to obtain congressional confirmation of the new commissioners. Although the Atomic Energy Act was passed in July, the new commission did not take control until January 1, 1947, almost a year and a half after Hiroshima.

In December 1946, one month before the commission took charge, the Russians' first chain-reacting atomic pile went critical.

The Atomic Energy Commission inherited a confused and deteriorating atomic establishment. Things had pretty much ground to a halt after the Japanese surrender, not only because of personnel departures, but also because of lack of direction from the top. No one thought it would take sixteen months of wrangling before a decision could be made on domestic policy; no one thought that international policy would make no progress, much less move backward in that period of time. The sheer logistics of the transfer were staggering — dozens of facilities, hundreds of thousands of people, records in poor condition because of wartime haste, personnel changing rapidly — all making orderly transfer very difficult.

Los Alamos was more fortunate than most. Although the very continuance of the laboratory was in doubt for many months, Norris Bradbury, the new director, began to forge a strong organization. A reserve Navy commander during the war, he understood both the military and civilian points of view. Recognizing that the laboratory would be shorthanded for years, he placed a good deal of confidence in his contractors, such as our group at MIT. Improved weapons concepts and systems, ideas that had been around the laboratory but had not been incorporated because of time pressure, were brought out, dusted off, and put into practice. The stockpile, if you could call it that, was woefully small. New designs promised to double the efficiency of the implosion, effectively doubling the size of the stockpile at one stroke. Bradbury began planning for a series of tests on the new designs.

One series of tests had been conducted by the military in the summer of 1946. Called Operation Crossroads, it took place at Bikini Atoll, a coral formation roughly circular, twenty-five miles in diameter, located in the Marshall Islands, twenty-seven hundred miles southwest of Hawaii and two hundred miles north of Kwajalein. The inhabitants of Bikini were moved to Rongerik Atoll, 130 miles away, to become wards of the American government.

The purported purpose of the tests was to determine the ability of naval vessels to survive an atomic attack, but I think the real purpose was to convince senior military, particularly Navy, personnel that the bomb was not just another piece of ordnance. The tests were poorly conceived and inexpertly executed. Some ninety Japanese and outdated U.S. warships, including battleships, aircraft carriers, submarines, and landing craft, were anchored in the lagoon. A Nagasaki-type bomb was exploded in the air above the fleet in the first test, another detonated below the surface of the lagoon as the second. They were conducted during the height of debate in the United Nations about the Baruch plan and provided beautiful propaganda fodder for the Soviets.

On the first test, an error in the operation of the radio-controlled timing system prevented crucial instrumentation, such as high-speed cameras, from operating until fifteen seconds after the device had detonated; much valuable data were lost. Five ships were sunk, but a demonstration of this type over the open sea could not have nearly the effect of the devastation caused at Hiroshima and Nagasaki.

The second bomb, according to the Civilian Evaluation Commission created by Truman, "caused a deluge of water loaded with deadly radioactive elements over an area that embraced ninety percent of the target array. All but a few of the target ships were drenched with radioactive seawater and all within the zone of evident damage are unsafe to board." This was the first indication to the military of the problems caused by radioactivity. The ships were still afloat but uninhabitable. The contamination was so great that a scheduled third test had to be canceled. The world became aware, as it had not from the Japanese bombings, that the effects of nuclear weapons were not confined to the blast, shock, and fire.

The next series of tests, Operation Sandstone, was planned to be of an entirely different character. Because of the contamination at Bikini, they were moved to the atoll of Eniwetok, a slightly smaller coral configuration two hundred miles to the west. They were developmental in nature, planned to test the new designs, as opposed to the Crossroads effects tests. Another group of natives had to be evacuated, perhaps never to return.

The Trinity test had been instrumented with detectors and measuring equipment for neutrons, gamma rays, X-rays, visible light, and shock wave. The possible range of yields and partition of energy at Trinity required a wide dynamic range of instrumentation, with resultant loss of accuracy and sensitivity. Furthermore, precise measurements were of second order importance; the big problem was whether the implosion technique would work at all. Sandstone was different. Four implosion devices had worked remarkably well: Trinity, Nagasaki, and the two Crossroads tests. (Except for special purposes, the gun-type weapon had been abandoned.) The problem here was to test the efficiency of the new designs that had been developed since 1945. Wide varieties of instruments were used to measure the output characteristics, some up close, some on distant islands. The primary job for our company was to turn on instrumentation after the area had been evacuated and, for measuring devices with short operating times, to start them in the final seconds between the remote arming and the firing of the device. This was the task for Grier and me. Edgerton headed a small group responsible for an optical technique to measure the multiplication of neutrons. Germeshausen stayed home to "mind the store."

We had the responsibility to operate instrumentation automatically during "dry runs," to check out timing installations after the islands had been evacuated, to serve on the arming party with the test director, and to operate the equipment that armed and fired the devices.

A nuclear weapons test is a massive undertaking. Thousands of people and hundreds of ships, boats, motor vehicles, and aircraft were organized under the military command of a Joint Task Force, with Army, Navy, Air Force, and civilian scientific task groups. All equipment, to the last nail and screw, was assembled months before the test and transported thousands of miles to these remote Pacific islands. Towers, hundreds of feet high, were built as platforms for the devices to approximate air burst conditions and minimize ground contamination. Additional towers were constructed to house photographic operations on distant islands, to keep the field of view of the cameras above the salt spray of the lagoon. Heavy concrete bunkers covered with sand were needed to protect instrumentation from blast and radioactivity. Miles of underwater cable were laid to connect the various instruments to the timing and firing system. Aircraft for atmospheric measurements and cloud-following aircraft to sample the characteristics of the mushroom cloud and track its direction of travel were based on the larger atoll of Kwajalein, two hundred miles away.

On the day before the shot, all personnel other than the arming and firing party were evacuated to the ships in the lagoon. Every individual had to be accounted for — no mean task with thousands involved — before the test could proceed. Late in the evening the firing party traveled by small boat to the tower housing the device to make the final connections. Sometimes the final connections were delayed until a few hours before dawn if personnel were unaccounted for or the weather was questionable. For the first Sandstone test, Grier and I had spent the previous two days checking every screw, every wire, every connection in the crucial arming and firing circuits.

On that last evening, after all others were evacuated, we joined the test director and proceeded to the tower containing the explosive. We then rode up the construction elevator, clanging and banging, to the two-hundred-foot-high cab, swaying slightly in the twenty-knot trade winds, which blew constantly. It was an eerie feeling in the pitch-black silence where for weeks, day and night, construction workers and scientists had swarmed about the tower. Bomb assembly people had long since departed, with the device left in the custody of heavily armed Marine guards nervously peering into the blackness of the surrounding ocean.

I had not been close to an active device since we prepared the Nagasaki weapon on Tinian. I thought of the misassembled cable and my dilemma of the evening, but this time there were no radars or outer casing or tail fins. There was only the steel sphere crisscrossed by the dozens of coaxial cables leading to the multiple detonators from the firing set. As we plugged in the final cables and threw the connecting switch, I felt a little more worried than I had on Tinian. There the bomb had been self-contained. No one could set it off externally. Here it was connected to miles of underwater cable, where there was always the possibility of short circuits from the movement of the cable on the sharp coral reef, of misconnection we had not uncovered in our two days of checking, or of tampering after checkout. Finally, there was the Russian boogyman.

The cold war was at its height in the spring of 1948. All negotiations for international control had collapsed. The Russians were truculent and intransigent all over the world, particularly in Berlin. In February they had marched into Czechoslovakia. After the spy scares of 1946, the American press and public were convinced that there was an atomic secret; the price of compromise on the Atomic Energy Act had been a rigid, overcautious security provision. The atomic energy commissioners had been appalled at the condition of the stockpile of weapons and the lack of trained weapon assembly teams. At one point they considered cancellation of the Sandstone tests for fear that a Pearl Harbor–type raid on Eniwetok would wipe out our scientific group, which represented the bulk of the country's atomic bomb handling capability.

There was also the possibility that the Russians would come ashore from a submarine and literally steal the bomb. What better way to steal the secret? Security was very jittery. I was worried more about trigger-happy Marine guards than I was about the bomb.

To satisfy security, we were required to dismantle the elevator and remain at the base of the tower until the guards had made a final screen of the area and left. Then we could take our twenty-mile, small-boat ride back to the control tower on the island of Parry.

The tests were carried out thirty minutes before sunrise to have a dark background for photography on the ground and daylight at thirty thousand feet so that the cloud-tracking aircraft could navigate visually.

Time stood still in the silent control room as the lights and meters signified the operation of measuring equipment all over the atoll, the arming of the device in the final thirty seconds, and the familiar countdown of *five . . . four . . . three . . . two . . . one . . . zero.*

Although I had been working on nuclear devices for years, I had never seen one explode. Because we had to watch the control panel until the last second in the event of a malfunction, we could not wear welders' glasses to protect our eyes; we kept our backs to the windows and our eyes glued to the panels.

The flash of light coming in the small window reflecting from the gray metal panel boards was blinding as the image of the meters froze my vision for seconds, then gradually turned to motion as the lights flashed crazily on and off and meters bent their needles against their stop posts from the force of the electromagnetic pulse traveling down the submerged cables with the speed of light. The pulse was so powerful that one of our engineers, halfway around the world in Boston and knowing the scheduled time of the explosion, was able to detect it with a makeshift antenna and an oscilloscope, the world's first remote detection measurement.

Turning to the window, I watched the fireball rise from a darker stem of explosive debris to a dull blue, with some green and orange at the periphery, and finally to a variety of reds as it cooled and rose and expanded in diameter, then whitish and colorful again as it became high enough to reflect the rays of the rising sun. In ninety seconds the shock wave hit with a sharp crack, over before it would be sensed. Since we were indoors, we could feel the longer duration of the negative pulse behind the frontal shock wave sucking the air from the building with a *whoosh* that lasted several seconds. The rising plume had now reached the inversion layer in the upper atmosphere, where it flattened and spread horizontally in a mushroom shape, which seemed to cover the entire western sky. Our job was done. We merely had to wait in our tower for thirty minutes to protect against a possible water wave, which could wash over the island, but none came. Then down to the dock to be met by a small boat from the Task Force Command ship and up rope ladders to the safety of the vessel, which could steam out to sea should the radioactive cloud change direction and pass over the control island.

Twice more the scene was repeated, vaporizing towers on the islands of Biiziri and Ruunitto, each a little closer to the control island, each a little more spectacular because of its proximity. Then back to the States and a year of data analysis.

As we worked in the quiet seclusion of our laboratory, the state of the world worsened. Soon after our return, the Soviets blocked the corridors to West Berlin, forcing the United States to counter with the Berlin airlift. Tensions were growing. A substantial number of Americans saw a real danger of armed conflict.

As the year wore on, the corporation negotiated our contract with the Atomic Energy Commission, superseding a temporary agreement made in 1947, when the company was formed. By the end of the Sandstone series, our original group of six had expanded to twenty-six. Edgerton had returned to his professorship at MIT. Germeshausen and I began to plan for commercial activities; since I had already operated one commercial business, I was eager to prepare again for a future not tied completely to nuclear weapons. Grier was content with the government business; he had no interest in commercial activities. In that first full year of corporate existence we had sales of slightly over a half million dollars and earned the princely sum of six thousand dollars. A tough way to make a living, I thought, remembering the Sandstone experience and the unsettling effect of long periods away from my family. Clearly, that kind of work is not done for money.

In the latter months of 1948 and the beginning of 1949, conferences at Los Alamos began to include more and more talk about the "Super," the hydrogen bomb or thermonuclear weapon. Nobody liked the idea very much. We had heard no reports of Russian activities; there were improved versions of the implosion devices, giving greater efficiency, higher yield, and better safety through development of less sensitive detonators and implosion lenses. There was even a device on the drawing boards with a design yield of five hundred thousand tons, one-half a megaton, twenty-five times the size of Trinity. The idea of a new order of magnitude of destruction was intellectually disquieting and morally repulsive. Besides, it didn't seem necessary. Because space is three-dimensional, the radius of destruction increases only as the cube root of the explosive yield. Another factor of ten would only increase the radius by slightly more than a factor of two. Finally, nobody was sure how to make it work. But it wouldn't go away.

The nucleus of an atom is like a house with fifty rooms. For reasons not significant, it is most comfortable when there is a positive charge or proton in every room, accompanied by an appropriate number of neutrons, the chargeless particles. Elements in the middle of the range, like iron, are the most stable. The number of charges increases as we progress up the periodic table of the elements, the listing used to tabulate chemical characteristics. The house becomes more and more crowded and the nucleus becomes less stable, to the point that the heaviest elements become unstable enough to spit out particles from time to time, becoming naturally radioactive. Above uranium the nucleus becomes so unstable that no transuranic elements now exist in nature, having decayed away millions of years ago.

Under certain conditions a neutron can split the rooms in two, making two new fifty-room houses and releasing the energy contained in the overcrowded house. This is analogous to fission, where the nucleus effectively splits in two.

As we move down in the periodic table, the picture changes, with more and more rooms unoccupied, until we come to hydrogen, with one lonely proton roaming around in a fifty-room house.

If two of these lonely protons could get together, not only would the resultant nucleus be more stable, but we would have available the energy represented by one empty fifty-room house, considerably more per nucleus than the breaking up at the other end of the periodic table. It's not easy to make it happen, but the fusing of two hydrogen nuclei can release much more energy than the fissioning of a uranium or plutonium nucleus.

Scientists have esoteric names like "binding energy" or "packing fractions" but in essence the difference between fusion and fission is this: The nucleus is most comfortable when it is in the most relaxed, or least energetic, state in the middle of the periodic table; the heavy elements approach this state by fissioning, the light elements by fusing.

Knowledge of the fusion process had been available for a long time. The thermonuclear process in the sun and the stars had been studied for years; in 1938 the ubiquitous Hans Bethe, freshly installed at Cornell University after being driven from his native Germany, had explained the fusion process in the sun, so fusion was understood before fission. But no one expected that fusion could be controlled on earth because of the high temperature required. In 1942 Fermi had suggested to Teller that a fission device might be used to provide the high temperatures for a fusion reaction. From that point on, Teller was hooked. He brought it up at the theoretical physics conference held that summer by Oppenheimer at Berkeley. Teller was not persuaded that work on fusion should take a back seat until fission was developed; he insisted on heading a small group working on fusion all through the war years at Los Alamos. After the war he alternated between a post at the University of Chicago and work on fusion at Los Alamos. He was unhappy with the priority given to fusion. Passionately anti-Russian, he felt that as soon as the Soviets had built a fission weapon, they would move right on to develop a hydrogen device, giving them world leadership in destruction.

Through the summer of 1949 the debate raged on. The technical problems were formidable. Although in principle ordinary hydrogen could be used, in fact it could not. The repelling forces between two positively charged protons were too great to be overcome even in the turbulence of a fission explosion. The best possibility was to fuse together nuclei of deuterium, the hydrogen isotope with one proton and one neutron, and tritium, the isotope with one proton and two neutrons. Deuterium existed in nature in the form of heavy water, deuterium oxide, but tritium, which is radioactive, did not. Tritium could be made in piles, similar to the ones used for making plutonium. But if tritium were manufactured, plutonium production would suffer. This was a critical point. The weapons designs proved at the highly successful Sandstone tests were now going into production. After the invasion of Czechoslovakia and the Berlin embargo, the United States and the nations of Western Europe had set up the North Atlantic Treaty Organization; it was becoming clear that NATO's defense of Western Europe would be based primarily on American nuclear weapons. Plutonium production for the protection of Western Europe was crucial.

A second problem was that all isotopes of hydrogen are gases at room temperature, but gases are not dense enough to sustain a reaction, so the deuterium and tritium would have to be liquefied. That would require cumbersome cryogenic apparatus, which might make the device too large to be airplane portable. A solid compound at room temperature could be conceived, but no one, not even Teller, wanted to consider that big a step. Liquid deuterium-tritium mixtures were technically feasible. The low temperatures required massive vacuum bottles, but they were quite doable. Even then, a bigger and more important matter remained. In order to get the deuterium-tritium mixture to ignite, it not only must be brought to a high temperature, but must be contained for a long enough time for the mixture to burn in a self-sustaining fashion. The time is measured in millionths of a second, but in the center of an exploding fission device that could be an eternity. No one knew how to contain the explosion long enough to ignite it.

Added to the technical problems and the resource allocation question was the practical question of "Why?" Devices with megaton yields were useful only against large areas, which would involve only large cities. Current war plans called for enough weapons for multiple attacks on the few large cities in Russia; it was not at all clear that thermonuclear devices would be more efficient than multiple fission weapons.

Then there was the moral question. There had not been time in the momentum of events of 1945 to properly consider the moral question of nuclear weapons. Now there was. We were all tired of war, tired of weapons. In our own company several of us were planning to devote most of our time to commercial pursuits after the next test series. Wouldn't this be the time to renounce the development of this frightening monster? Couldn't we announce to the world that we would forgo not only the use but also the development of thermonuclear weapons, hoping that the Russians would follow our example? The formidable counterargument was that the Russians might ignore us and develop it first.

As contractors to the Atomic Energy Commission under the technical guidance of the Los Alamos Laboratory, we were completely cleared into the weapons development program. Planning for the test series scheduled in 1951, we were aware of a thermonuclear test proposed for one of the events. There was no doubt in my mind that the program had to go forward, but I, like many others, hoped it wouldn't work — in the sense of being technically unfeasible.

I found that hoping it wouldn't work was only a crutch. It

merely postponed the deeper question: Should I work on it
at all? The morality of thermonuclear weapon development
was a far more difficult question for me than the morality
of the wartime fission decision. I was older; I had a choice;
I understood the consequences; the national security advantage was questionable. But there was a moral question if I
decided to back away. Although I knew nothing about Russian nuclear progress, I was certain that they would soon
have a fission weapon. If fusion worked they would have
that also. The Stalin tyranny was proving to be not much
different from Hitler's. I felt a deeper moral obligation to the
society and the system of government I cherished than to my
personal revulsions. I also knew that I didn't have the information to make a unilateral decision. I finally concluded that
if our government decided to proceed, I would support that
decision unequivocally.

Then the Soviets called the hand. On September 23, 1949,
the President announced that the Russians had fired their first
nuclear weapon. What's more, airborne samples revealed that
it had been a plutonium bomb. I was not surprised — disappointed, but not surprised. It had been a superb feat, starting
with a small program under Kurchatov in 1943 and accelerating after the Potsdam conference. But they had the enormous advantage of knowing it could be done. Our program
didn't really get started until Fermi's pile went critical in
December 1942. We had to build another prototype pile in
1943 to get the data for the large Hanford reactors. We really
hadn't emphasized the implosion technique until data came
out of Hanford that Pu-239 was being poisoned by Pu-240
and would predetonate if used in the gun-type weapon. All
that work had been done for them. They could go to plutonium directly, not having to bother with huge uranium separation plants. Knowing that piles would work, they could
start planning their large production reactors while building
the prototype. In fact, their first pile went critical in December 1946, before the Atomic Energy Commission was a
reality.

The announcement of the Russian test completely changed

the nature of the H-bomb debate. There never was any doubt about continuing the program. The only question was whether a crash program was the proper way to allocate resources. The proponents of a crash program were Edward Teller and Ernest Lawrence, along with Brien McMahon and most of the congressmen on the Joint Committee on Atomic Energy. Most of the scientists at Los Alamos, though they were not in favor of a crash program, were not really opposed. The key advisory committee to the AEC for such policy considerations was the General Advisory Committee, chaired by Robert Oppenheimer and including Enrico Fermi, James Conant, Hartly Rowe, Cyril Smith, Lee Du Bridge, Oliver Buckley, and Glenn Seaborg — all knowledgeable gentlemen, none directly connected with the laboratory. Oppenheimer was opposed to a crash program. I had seen him only once since the war, when he delivered a guest lecture at MIT shortly after the Russian test announcement. Deeply affected by the morality question, he was worried about the hydrogen bomb development, although he did not mention it. In his lecture he used the expression "Scientists have known sin" for the first time.

The General Advisory Committee, on October 29, voted unanimously not to proceed with a crash program. The advice was given on a moral, technical, and cost-effectiveness basis, which is exactly what the committee was supposed to consider.

The political decision went exactly the other way. After the Russian test announcement, Truman had no practical political choice. He disregarded the committee's advice and announced on January 31, 1950, that the thermonuclear feasibility program would be pursued, effectively endorsing the crash program. Could Truman have done differently, even if he had wanted to? Probably not. Public opinion was very strong; the people felt betrayed by the Russian test. The Joint Committee on Atomic Energy was very powerful in the Congress. Veto-proof legislation could have mandated the program. The votes were there. Even had he delayed, it would have been to no avail. Three days after the announcement, the British revealed that Klaus Fuchs had been a Russian spy. The public was outraged. Once again the opportunity to alter the course to catastrophe was lost. Once more events were in the saddle, riding mankind to possible annihilation. In June 1950, the Korean War broke out. A country willing to go to war to save South Korea was in no mood to stop the development of the hydrogen bomb.

The decision changed the direction of activities at our little company. Bradbury put Los Alamos on a six-day week; all the contractors followed. Our plans to balance out the government work with commercial activities had to be scrapped, at least for the time being, while we grappled with plans for the upcoming test program, now advanced to the early months of 1951. Because of the shortage of people and housing at Los Alamos, more work was contracted out. In addition to our timing and firing work, we were asked to do the technical photography on the upcoming tests, of which high-speed photographs of the rate of growth of the fireball were most important. The rate at which the fireball grew in the first thousandths of a second depended on the yield or magnitude of the explosion. Measurement of that rate of growth with high-speed cameras was the primary measurement of yield; thus, it was one of the most important tests performed. This extra work meant doubling the size of the company, now up to fifty people. We were working long hours developing instrumentation and preparing equipment for the voyage to Eniwetok when another load of work hit us from the military. Two series of events brought it about.

One was the development of small low-yield devices. New implosion techniques and better detonators had made possible much smaller diameter devices than the five-foot-wide Fat Man, devices that could be carried by light bomber or fighter planes, or possibly in an artillery piece. Better knowledge of plutonium characteristics and better designs of tamper, which enclosed the plutonium and reflected back escaping neutrons, had made possible designs of lower yields than the Nagasaki weapon, some as low as the equivalent of one kiloton of TNT.

At the same time an interservice dispute had arisen in the military. Atomic strategy, as it had developed at the turn of the decade, called for massive air strikes with high-yield weapons carried out by Air Force bombers. This left no nuclear task for the Army and Navy, who wanted a piece of the action, and fast. A war was going on in Korea; the Army and Navy requested small, low-yield nuclear explosives that could be delivered by carrier planes or fired from an artillery piece, so-called tactical weapons. The Defense Department agreed and laid a requirement on the Atomic Energy Commission for development and testing of such devices.

But the AEC and its laboratories were deeply involved with preparations for the upcoming Pacific tests. A task force had already been organized, this time under the command of Lieutenant General Elwood R. (Pete) Quesada. The Defense Department and the AEC together asked the President for authority to establish a continental test base, which would not have the logistic problems of the Pacific atolls. The President acquiesced; Quesada was directed to locate a site. An Air Force pilot, Quesada knew just the spot. He had flown many times from the Nellis Air Force Base in North Las Vegas, Nevada, to the Las Vegas Gunnery Range, a huge tract of government-owned land a hundred or so miles to the northwest. It was bleak, uninhabited desert with dry lake beds surrounded by mountains, which would cut down the blast effects. The site, 1350 square miles in area, was turned over to the AEC to become the Continental Test Range. In September another crash program was authorized to carry out the first tests before the Greenhouse operation.

As soon as the program, Operation Ranger, was approved, Quesada and Alvin Graves flew to Boston to visit us to describe the program. There would be five shots, with yields ranging from one to twenty kilotons, air-dropped over a dry lake in the new test site, with no firing requirement. They asked Grier and me to coordinate the timing signals and do just enough high-speed photography to determine the yield.

We had no time to design new equipment, borrowing instruments scheduled for the Pacific. For photographic stations

we bought secondhand trucks, installed the cameras, checked
them out in our converted garage, and had them driven to
Nevada.

Grier and I flew to Los Angeles, bought two English Land
Rovers, and drove across the desert to the site. It was a dry
lake bed, called Frenchman's Flat, with nothing but dirt
roads leading down into it from the mountains. We knew
that there would be a good many vehicles driving around the
desert near test time, so we were reluctant to string our
timing cables underground for fear of having them severed.
We asked to have a set of telephone lines strung overhead the
fifteen miles from the control room to ground zero. Reynolds
Electrical and Engineering Company, based in El Paso, Texas,
was hired to do the job.

The test series went smoothly. Everyone in the company
except Edgerton was involved. Grier was in overall charge;
I did the timing work; Germeshausen supervised the photography. We lived in Quonset huts in a place called Indian
Springs, an auxiliary landing field for the Nellis Air Force
Base pilots. The bombs were assembled at the Sandia Laboratory in Albuquerque, New Mexico, and flown to the site.
Although the yields were low, the shock waves were strong
enough to rattle windows in Las Vegas, ninety miles away,
and to blow out all the windows in our Quonset huts in
Indian Springs.

At the completion of the Ranger program in Las Vegas,
the borrowed equipment was air-shipped to Eniwetok. We
went home for a short visit with our families before setting
out again for the Pacific.

The Greenhouse series was much more elaborate than
Sandstone had been. In addition to the weapons development
experiments, there were many military effects tests. The
important test, code named George, was the third in the
series, which involved the crucial deuterium-tritium experiment. The device went off on schedule, but it was late that
day before we could recover the instruments that told
whether the crucial neutrons had been emitted, signifying
that a thermonuclear reaction had taken place. I took a short

nap after being up all night. When I went back to the technical area later in the afternoon, I could tell by the look on Edward Teller's face that it had been a success. I hope the disappointment didn't show on mine.

There was no turning back now. The thermonuclear device would be built, and civilization would be the worse for it.

During the next year fifteen tests were carried out in Nevada. Our company opened a permanent office there and began to build up a staff, relieving some of the pressure for travel on the Boston people.

Work went on at a feverish pace at Los Alamos on the fusion program. The Greenhouse test had been an experiment to see if fusion could take place. There was no thermonuclear yield. The Mike shot, scheduled for the fall of 1952, would be thermonuclear. But it was a monster. Built on the island of Elugelab, it was a massive cryogenic factory, cooling liquid hydrogen to near absolute zero in order to maintain the two heavier isotopes, deuterium and tritium, in the liquid state. The device, weighing sixty-five tons, was surrounded with cryogenic equipment and instrumentation, which used up practically every square inch on the tiny island. Attached to the device was a rectangular wooden container, tall enough for a man to stand in, stretching four miles across the water to the next island. At shot time it would be filled with helium to provide an optical path to special instrumentation that would analyze the emission spectrum at the time of detonation. It looked like a railroad train pulling into a station.

Since the yield of the device was expected to be ten megatons or greater, the atoll was not big enough for the firing party to stay on. We had to fire from a ship located forty miles away, below the horizon.

In order to monitor the various meters and gauges connected to the cryogenic monster, we built a special television station with its antenna on a three-hundred-foot tower so that a TV picture could be sent back to the ship. It was the world's first shore-to-ship television station.

When the device went off, there was the biggest fireball

and mushroom cloud I had ever seen. We could tell from the shock wave forty miles away that the yield was at least as great as had been predicted. As I watched the mushroom cloud grow miles and miles in diameter, I visualized the silhouette of a major city against the horizon, realizing that one explosion of that size would completely wipe out any city in the world with its yield of 10.4 megatons. It completely vaporized the island of Elugelab and blew a hole in the atoll deeper than the height of the Empire State Building.

Two weeks later, while we stood ashore on the island of Parry, the world's most powerful fission weapon, yielding half a million tons, was dropped from an airplane and exploded over Eniwetok lagoon. This weapon had been on the drawing boards during the H-bomb debate. Even if the hydrogen weapon proved undeliverable, there was more than enough potential destruction available in the world.

But it wasn't to stop there. Even before the Greenhouse test, there had been a theoretical breakthrough. Generally credited to Teller, but shared by Stanislaw Ulam, a Los Alamos mathematician, the exact nature of the breakthrough has never been declassified, but it is sufficient to say that it dealt with the distribution of radiation from the fission primary trigger to allow time for the fusion reaction to take place. Further, it permitted the use of a solid deuterium-tritium mixture, eliminating the need for cryogenics and promising an aircraft-deliverable weapon. Instead of using the expensive low-temperature tritium, the trick was to substitute lithium, a very light metal, which forms tritium when bombarded by neutrons. Combined with deuterium in the form of lithium deuteride, all the materials needed for a thermonuclear burn were available in a completely solid form, easy to handle and to fabricate. One final ghastly step was needed to complete this concept of calamity: The whole mixture was surrounded by ordinary, cheap U-238, the abundant isotope of uranium. Although U-238 would not fission by itself, it would burn when stimulated by the energetic neutrons from the fusion reaction. Thus the concept of fission-fusion-fission was established, permitting unlimited destruction in a small convenient package. The first test of the new lithium-deuteride bomb was scheduled for 1954.

In the meanwhile the testing program at Las Vegas continued hot and heavy. Eleven tests were conducted in 1953. Grier and I were involved in all of them. On one the event that we had always feared occurred. The pre-shot checkout had proceeded routinely. We had spent the previous day checking out systems in Yucca Flat, the site to which testing had been moved to be farther away from Las Vegas. By evening all personnel had been evacuated from the test area, about fifteen miles from the control point. Late in the evening a contingent of military passed our control area to a location about ten miles from the bomb tower to witness the explosion through dark glasses from trenches under simulated battlefield conditions. On Newsmen's Knob, a small hill adjacent to our control point, a select group of newsmen and newswomen had been given permission to view a detonation. We had plenty of spectators watching as we started out in the chilly desert darkness to perform the arming function. The headlights on our Jeeps were the only glimmers of light to be seen by the observers as we slowly drove the fifteen miles to the brightly lighted shot tower. The familiar heavily armed guards opened the gate to the barbed-wire enclosure surrounding the tower. They inspected our badges meticulously, although they knew us by sight and certainly knew what we were there for.

The party consisted of Jack Clark, the test director; John Wieneke, a Los Alamos physicist; Herb Grier; and me. We made the usual silly jokes about what would happen if it didn't go off as we rode the elevator to the top of the two-hundred-foot tower. It took about twenty minutes to do the final checkout. When the cables were plugged in to activate the weapon, all the levity stopped. We knew we were dealing with fifteen kilotons' worth of plutonium, one thousand pounds of explosive lenses, and thirty-two supersensitive detonators. We were all very cautious — always a little scared. It's like the old story about airplane pilots — there are old pilots and there are bold pilots, but there are no old, bold pilots. I wouldn't want anyone near me and an atom bomb who is casual or careless; we could never forget for a second the energy that could be released from that innocent-looking piece of metal in the middle of the cab.

Describing each step of the checkout by telephone to the control point where a duplicate checklist was maintained, we received permission to close the final switch and rung off to descend in the elevator, two hundred feet to the ground below. As we stepped out of the elevator a construction crew was ready to dismantle it. We were still very much in the middle of the cold war; the test site was much more difficult to patrol than the Pacific islands. It would be perfectly possible for the Russians to come in after we left, cut the cables, and literally steal the device. They would never be caught if they drove off in the desert darkness and hid in the surrounding mountains. To prevent such an action, security required that the elevators be dismantled and carried away for use at another tower. We on the arming party never liked the idea, but it was impossible to win an argument with security. We waited a few minutes for the truck carrying the elevator to get a head start and filed slowly back to the control room. The final two hours went routinely. The weather was good, the troops were in their trenches, the newspeople on their knob. At minus one hour we turned on heaters for remote instrumentation, allowing time for temperature stabilization in the chill desert air.

As always, the detonation was scheduled for thirty minutes before sunrise. I could see the first faint glow of dawn over the mountains as I took a last glance out the small window in the control room before giving my complete attention to the meters and lights on the control panels.

At minus fifteen minutes we started the automatic timer, which would send signals to actuate oscilloscopes, high speed cameras, and other experimental gear. At minus one minute a small explosive charge was detonated in the tower area to calibrate the atmosphere for blast-measuring instruments. At minus thirty seconds the arming signal was sent to charge the electrical capacitors in the firing set. I watched the needle monitoring the charge come slowly up to the fully charged position at about minus twenty seconds. The countdown went on; no one spoke as we each gave undivided attention to the lights and meters on the panel board. I braced myself for the flash of light that would come in the small window and freeze the image of the control panel on my retinas at time zero.

Ten ... nine ... eight ... seven ... six ... five ... four ... three ... two ... one ... zero.

Nothing happened. I watched the meter monitoring the firing-set capacitors slowly go back to zero as the charge leaked off.

What had gone wrong? No one knew. Everything looked all right. But the bomb had not received a firing signal. Either that or something was wrong inside the device. The most probable cause of the trouble was that some remote instrumentation wasn't working.

This was a weapon development test; certain experimental measurements were crucial. To prevent the device from detonating if the experimental gear was not operating, the readiness condition was monitored and interlocked with the firing signal. But we could not be sure and would have to proceed with the utmost caution. The firing party would have to go back, climb the tower, and disarm the bomb.

Grier and I looked at each other. There were only two cables to be disconnected to make the device safe. We didn't need two of us to disconnect two cables. We flipped a coin to see who would go. I lost. Now I would have to climb that damned tower with the elevator removed. Clark, Wieneke, and I set off to retrace our steps.

We took two Jeeps in case one broke down. It was full daylight as we passed the newspeople, who were wondering what had happened. They looked at us in our roofless Jeeps for all the world as though we were riding in tumbrels on the cobblestones of Paris, wending our way to the guillotine. The troops were out of the trenches, milling about, the officers bewildered about this occurrence, which had not been in their battle plan.

As we arrived at the tower, nothing looked any different. Empty boxes, soft drink cans, and candy bar wrappers littered the tower area. Nobody bothers to clean up on the last day, when the area is going to be vaporized in a few hours. We strapped our instruments onto our backs and started the long climb to the top of the tower, cursing a nameless security all the way up for removing the elevator. The air was still cool, but the sun was high enough to feel warm on my back as I climbed. When we reached the cab, Clark picked up the telephone to establish contact with Al Graves, the test manager, back at the control room.

"Everything looks O.K. here, Al." he said quietly. "Wieneke has inspected the firing rack. Looks fine," Clark continued. "O'Keefe is disconnecting the first cable."

I worked very carefully as I unscrewed the locking ring on the first connector. I felt alternately silly and scared. Silly because I knew there was no danger. I had seen the capacitors discharge and knew the bomb was not armed. Scared because something had gone wrong and we shouldn't take any chances. Maybe two things had gone wrong and my meter reading had been false. In that case I'd better be as cautious as possible.

I pulled out the first plug and handed the cable to Wieneke.

"First plug's out," reported Clark crisply.

I unscrewed the second ring and gingerly worked the connector out of its socket.

"He's taking out the second one."

With a last soft tug the second connector was disconnected.

"Everything's safe, Al," Clark reported. "Have some cold beer ready. We'll be back in half an hour."

Leaving our instruments to be picked up later, we slowly climbed down the tower, got into our Jeeps, and drove back to the control point. We floored the accelerators, driving at top speed, knowing there would be no police out to give us a ticket. By this time everyone knew that the bomb had been disarmed. As we passed the soldiers in the trenches, they cheered. Even the newspeople clapped as we went by. Again, I felt a little sheepish, but, there was always that chance.

Later it was found that an experiment being performed by another group had become inoperative and locked out the firing signal, as designed. I felt good that it wasn't our gear that had caused the delay. The equipment was fixed and the shot went off routinely two days later.

Another event occurred on that test series that I will never forget. The Army, anxious for its piece of the action, had designed a 280-millimeter artillery piece to handle a tactical nuclear weapon for which Los Alamos had designed the warhead. Two hundred eighty millimeters is just a little over eleven inches; implosion lenses had been designed to be much smaller than the original five-foot-diameter Fat Man, but nothing small enough to fit into that diameter had yet been designed. They were forced to use a gun-type design, much improved over the Hiroshima weapon but still not as efficient as the implosion devices. The Army planned a test during 1953, but wanted to do everything themselves. The Yucca Flat site was busy with weapon development tests, so the Army took over the old Frenchman's Flat site used during Operation Ranger in 1951. The artillery piece was set up at one side of the dry lake bed. The projectile was to be fired six miles over to the other side of the lake bed; it would contain a seventeen-kiloton warhead, designed to explode fifteen hundred feet in the air. The test was lightly instrumented; the main objective was to make it "go boom." On the day of the test most of our group was pretty busy; I was supposed to be leaving for Boston. Jack Clark asked me to stay over another day to witness the test as his representative. I had no interest but reluctantly agreed.

I was disconcerted when I arrived at the gun site. A 280-millimeter gun is an enormous piece of machinery. I had never seen anything that big, even in the Navy. Only twenty-five people witnessed the test, all Army artillery officers. For protection they had built a five-foot-deep trench fifty feet on either side of the gun. I expected to see an elaborate electronic control system, but, no, this was being conducted under battlefield operating conditions. Once the device was inserted, the block would be screwed closed and the officer in charge would fire the gun by pulling on a lanyard, as with any other artillery piece.

I couldn't believe it, after all our elaborate safety precautions. I wished that I had turned Clark down and gone home. But fire it with a lanyard they did, and then everyone jumped into the trench for protection. (I was already in the trench.)

This time I had nothing to do, so I put on dark glasses. I had never been this close to an exploding weapon before; we usually kept a wider distance. When it went off it was a sight to behold. Snatching off my dark glasses at the earliest possible moment, I watched the fireball churning its way thousands of feet up into the sky, visible for fifty miles around, the familiar mushroom cloud identifying it to all the world as a nuclear explosion, then the shock wave, very powerful in the trench, rattling windows in Las Vegas, ninety miles away; I was aghast. I had never really believed in tactical nuclear weapons anyhow. I have always felt that if one were used on a battlefield, the war would escalate immediately to full-scale nuclear warfare. Here was proof! I, of course, knew what was coming. My dark glasses protected my eyes against the first flash. What of the soldiers on a battlefield? The first flash would sear the eyeballs of anyone looking in that direction, friend or foe, for miles around. Its intensity cannot be described; it must be experienced to be appreciated. The electromagnetic pulse would knock out all communication systems, the life blood of a battle plan. In addition to its effect on troops in the vicinity, everyone for fifty miles in any direction who lived through it would realize that it was a nuclear explosion. It would seem like the end of the world, and it probably would be, for any man who had a similar weapon under his control, who had a button to push or a lanyard to pull, would do so instinctively.

Never again was a tactical weapon fired into the atmosphere. I wonder if any of the twenty-five people who witnessed that event thirty years ago are alive and active today, listening to the academic arguments about the possibilities of a limited nuclear war.

6

BRAVO

ALTHOUGH THERE HAD BEEN a successful thermonuclear experiment in 1951 and a full-scale thermonuclear explosion on November 1, 1952, Edward Teller and Ernest Lawrence were still not happy with the progress of H-bomb development. They felt it should be given the highest priority. However, Los Alamos had other responsibilities. It had to worry about production problems with the stockpile, the development of the half-megaton fission weapon, and the development of lower-yield tactical devices for the Army and Navy. Tensions built up between Teller and Norris Bradbury to the point where Teller did not attend the 1952 test. There had been considerable agitation in Washington, particularly from the Joint Committee on Atomic Energy and the Air Force, to open a second weapons laboratory. In October 1952 a second lab was established under the aegis of Ernest Lawrence of the University of California's Berkeley Laboratory. The new weapons lab was located in the small town of Livermore, thirty miles east of Berkeley. It was a good compromise. Los Alamos was clearly overworked; the University of California would run both laboratories; Berkeley had been the center of cyclotron research and electromagnetic uranium separation. A cadre of scientists from Berkeley, headed by Herbert F. York, the new Livermore director, had worked at Eniwetok on the Greenhouse tests. Although Teller became chief scientist, the laboratory was not organized soon enough to play a significant part in the first thermonuclear weapon explosion, scheduled for test at Bikini in 1954.

While the opening of a second laboratory calmed down the scientific bickering, it had no effect on a larger battle going on in Washington. As the emphasis on thermonuclear research increased, the importance and power of the Air Force grew with it. If the big bombs were to be used, they would be used by the Air Force, particularly the Strategic Air Command, with its new bomber, the B-36. Although tactical weapons were being developed, they were not yet available, nor was there any means of delivering them. The Army and the Navy were being squeezed out.

The first public indication of this interservice rivalry came in 1949 with the "revolt of the admirals," when the Navy publicly protested overreliance on the B-36 as opposed to the super aircraft carriers they wanted to build.

The admirals' revolt was quickly stifled, but the controversy continued inside the Pentagon. For the most part, hearings and reports were classified and unavailable to the public.

It flared up again in the hydrogen bomb controversy, where the pivotal character became J. Robert Oppenheimer. He was not directly involved in the battle between the services, nor was he in a position to influence the allocation of budgetary resources. But he was able to exert influence over the size and purpose of atomic weapons being designed. He was convinced that atomic weapons with smaller yields could be designed for armed services other than the Strategic Air Command, and for conflicts short of total war. He believed that atomic weapons had a potential tactical as well as strategic role. This conviction by Oppenheimer and others led to the fateful recommendation of the General Advisory Committee, chaired by Oppenheimer, that a crash program for the development of the Super weapon not be pursued. The big bomb men saw Oppenheimer as an enemy.

Within the White House, the new President, Dwight D. Eisenhower, was having budgetary difficulties. He had campaigned on the pledge of a balanced budget; but his Treasury Secretary told him that to balance the budget he must not only end the Korean War, but make drastic cuts in the peacetime services. The quickest and cheapest way to this objective was to emphasize the cheapest and most powerful weapon, the atom bomb. Secretary of State John Foster Dulles conceived the concept of "massive retaliation," where any provocation would lead to a full-scale atomic blitz. It was effective because the Soviets had not yet built up their atomic arsenal, nor did they have delivery capability comparable to our B-36. It was cheap; nuclear weapons cost only a fraction of the cost of a standing army or fully equipped navy. But it was a dangerous doctrine. A simple border clash could bring about total war. Only a man of Eisenhower's reputation could convince the people that massive retaliation made sense. The Air Force had won the battle.

Even though the administration policy seemed solid on the outside, it was not so tranquil in the secret world of military planners and their science advisers. Tempers grew short and tolerance narrowed. Nine days after Truman announced the Russian explosion, Senator Joseph R. McCarthy, in a speech at Wheeling, West Virginia, stated:

> While I cannot take the time to name all of the men in the State Department who have been named as members of the Communist party and members of a spy ring, I have in my hand a list of 205 that were known to the Secretary of State as members of the Communist party who nevertheless are still working and shaping the policy of the State Department.

The witch hunt was on.

As time went on, the internal battle continued; externally, McCarthy's witch hunt widened. A jittery President saw the investigations spread into his beloved Army. Scurrilous articles against Oppenheimer appeared in the press. Finally, William Borden, the former staff director of the Joint Committee on Atomic Energy, composed a letter to J. Edgar Hoover, accusing Oppenheimer of being an espionage agent for the Communists. A copy was sent to the Joint Committee.

The system moved quickly. Hoover brought the letter to Eisenhower, who ordered a "blank wall" between Oppenheimer and classified information. He instructed the Atomic Energy Commission to investigate. A three-man board of inquiry was set up to investigate the charges.

Oppenheimer never had a chance. The opposing attorney, a skilled prosecutor, was given full security clearance, with fifteen years of documentary evidence in the form of classified material, bugged telephone calls, and taped conversations at his command. Oppenheimer's attorney, a courtly labor relations lawyer, had no courtroom experience, no clearance, and no access to data. The data on the old Communist associations were clear and undenied. There was no specific proof on the H-bomb controversy; it was a question of Oppenheimer's veracity.

The inquiry, the closest thing to a trial for heresy ever seen in American politics, was a travesty. Oppenheimer had said: "The very least we can say is that, looking ten years ahead, it is likely to be small comfort that the Soviet Union is four years behind us ... The very least we can conclude is that our twenty thousandth bomb ... will not in any deep strategic sense offset their two thousandth."

This completely contradicted the traditional doctrine that national security lies in the attainment of military superiority. This was heresy, for which the penalty is excommunication. Dozens of witnesses spoke for Oppenheimer, to no avail. The damaging testimony came from the military. Air Force chief scientist David Griggs summed it up: "I have been involved in ... a number of pretty strong controversies in the military, and it is a fair general observation that when you get in a hot enough controversy, it is awfully hard not to question the motives of people who oppose you."

To a lesser extent, Teller's testimony constituted a second element of tragedy at the trial. Teller never questioned Oppenheimer's loyalty; he did question his judgment. Teller was passionately opposed to secrecy, never believing in it, never understanding its purpose, willing to go along because it was the law. His final answer to the chairman of the Personnel Security Board, for which he earned the opprobrium of the scientific community for a decade, was as much an expression of uncertainty of the basis for security clearance as it was an indictment of Oppenheimer.

"I believe," he said ". . . that Dr. Oppenheimer's character is such that he would not knowingly or willingly do anything that is designed to endanger the safety of his country. To the extent, therefore, that your question is directed toward intent, I would say that I do not see any reason to deny clearance." Then he went on, puzzled: "If it is a question of wisdom and judgment, as demonstrated by actions since 1945, then I would say one would be wiser not to grant clearance . . ."

The board chose the latter interpretation. Oppenheimer was excommunicated as a heretic against the dogma of massive retaliation.

With massive retaliation firmly established as policy, the test series at Bikini Atoll scheduled to begin on March 1, 1954, took on added importance. The Greenhouse George test in 1951 had been a "thermonuclear experiment," showing only that a deuterium-tritium reaction could occur. Ivy Mike in 1952 had been a full-scale, ten-megaton thermonuclear explosion, but it was a sixty-five ton monster with liquid tritium and deuterium cooled to a temperature close to absolute zero, certainly not a weapon. Bravo shot, the first in Operation Castle, had two major revisions that made it the prototype of an aircraft-deliverable device. It used lithium deuteride, a solid with the tritium derived by neutron bombardment of the lithium. It also used the "Teller-Ulam" configuration, an assembly scheme that held the weapon together an extra hundred-millionth of a second until the hydrogen isotopes could fuse.

Operations had shifted back to Bikini after the Mike detonation had erased the island of Elugelab in Eniwetok Atoll from the face of the earth. Bikini was large enough to allow twenty miles' separation between the shot island of Namu and the control island of Enyu. The firing party could stay ashore in a heavy, sand-covered concrete bunker, eliminating the need for radio-controlled ship-to-shore firing mechanisms. Once again our company, now employing 150 persons and operating simultaneously at the Continental Test Site in Nevada, was awarded a contract to do the timing and firing and the technical photography.

Because of the complexity of the experimentation, the Joint Task Force carrying out the operation this time numbered over ten thousand men (no women) commanded by a lieutenant general in the Army. Typically, there were four task groups: Army, Navy, Air Force, and scientific. Alvin Graves, veteran nuclear physicist from Los Alamos, was scientific director and deputy task force commander. His deputy, William E. Ogle, also from Los Alamos, commanded the scientific task group. The nucleus of the firing party, now veterans of many tests, included Jack Clark as firing party director, Herb Grier, and me.

This was my fourth journey to the South Pacific in addition to my wartime experience. I expected it to be the last for which I would have a major responsibility. I was training a replacement so that I could devote most of my time in Boston to the company's commercial activities; Grier was preparing to devote his time to the Nevada operations, which now continued year round. The previous Pacific test had been relatively short, with only two shots — the thermonuclear and the high-yield fission tests. We had been able to bring our families to Hawaii, relieving the strain of time away from home. This time the operation would be a long one; we decided to split it up. I came out with the preparation party and had already spent weeks in the field by the time Grier arrived. I was to return home immediately after Bravo, with Grier continuing on. We would overlap only for this experiment.

I was anxious to get it over with. Important though it was, the experiment was routine for us. It was predicted that the yield would be smaller than that of the Mike device, seven megatons rather than ten; also the logistics would be less difficult. Nevertheless, we carried out our preparations with the same meticulous detail as always. Notwithstanding the island base, it was tougher than Nevada, where we could move around in Jeeps or trucks, get into Las Vegas, and go home frequently. At Bikini we were five thousand miles from home, a four-day journey at best; we island-hopped to our timing and photographic stations by small boats in tossing seas, Piper Cub aircraft from postage-stamp runways, or helicopters still in the developmental stage. Instrumentation was difficult to maintain in the tropics; special care had to be taken with our high-speed cameras in the salt-laden air. It was no South Seas paradise.

As we finished our arming preparations that last day of February, I was looking forward to the trip home. Up all night before the predawn firing, we would be "off duty" as soon as the shot went off. We had keys to the meat locker, plenty of gin and vermouth in our tents, and time to take a nap before the fleet arrived back in the lagoon. As soon as the airstrip was cleared, I would take off with early records from the experiments, fly to Eniwetok, then to Kwajalein overnight, on to Hawaii the next day, finally San Francisco and home.

The group in the firing party included five others in addition to Clark, Grier, and me. Dr. Harold Stewart, a Naval Research Laboratory expert in spectroscopic measurements who would be doing some experiments from the control bunker; Lieutenant Douglas Cochrane, a career naval officer assigned to our company as communications officer; an air-conditioner expert from the construction company; and two Air Force sergeants to operate radios.

The morning tasks went smoothly, the late winter tropical sun not too strong, the trade winds a pleasant twenty knots. By noon all construction personnel were evacuated, leaving only the helicopter crew, one scientist from Los Alamos, and the firing party. The fleet steamed out of the lagoon, to be safely out to sea before we made our final connections — no point risking ten thousand lives if we had an accident. We were to arm the device in the early afternoon, then fly to the control island to give the helicopters plenty of daylight to rendezvous with the fleet. We'd have time for a leisurely meal, which we would cook ourselves, then a few hours' sleep.

The first snag hit at noontime. Dr. Gaelen Felt, the Los Alamos scientist, was making some crucial experiments, which required that his instruments be in a helium atmosphere at time zero. He normally had a twenty-four-hour supply, but discovered at the last minute that the pipes from his helium tanks were leaking. We calculated the leak rate and decided that if we delayed opening the valves until 11:00 P.M., there would be sufficient gas left by 7:00 A.M. to conduct the experiment. We radioed for permission to delay the arming. We weren't eager to fly helicopters at night with no landing lights or ground crews, but it was either that or postpone for a day. Al Graves agreed; the helicopter crews, not too happy, flew off to get some food, which had been left by construction workers on another island. We invited Felt to stay with us in the bunker, which he preferred to rejoining the fleet after dark, so our party grew to nine.

It made no difference to me. I found an old cot and took a nap beside the bomb rather than in the bunker on Enyu. At 11:00 P.M. we opened the helium valves and armed the device, then flew the twenty miles to the control island, the pilots using the phosphorescence of the surf breaking on the white coral shoreline to guide us around the lagoon. We arrived at Enyu about midnight. The men who had been checking equipment at the control point took our places in the helicopters, which then scooted off to join their ships, already forty miles offshore.

Everything was ready: Ships in place, aircraft for cloud sampling, submarines for underwater measurement, destroyers and patrol craft alert for possible hostile action or sabotage, all instrumentation checking out perfectly.

The one last question was the weather. On the surface it was perfect: light trade winds, no moon, puffy tropical clouds with less than 10 percent cloud cover, and a beautiful sunny day predicted for the first day of March. The radioactive cloud, however, would rise hundreds of thousands of feet, where wind shears could take it in different directions. Measurement of upper atmosphere winds was difficult because aircraft could not fly high enough. The primary measurement was taken by weather balloons released in the first few hours before dawn, but in this section of the vast Pacific there was little real estate from which to launch balloons, so late measurements were necessarily crude. On the other hand, there was room for a wide margin of error. Bikini was chosen as the site because there were not many people around. Kwajalein was two hundred miles south, Rongelap Atoll with eighty-two natives was one hundred twenty miles to the southeast, and Rongerik Atoll, with a couple of hundred inhabitants, was two hundred miles away, also to the southeast. There was an area about ninety degrees wide where the cloud could move to the north and east with no danger. In the bunker we felt secure. We had three-foot concrete walls, ten feet of dirt on top, a moat surrounding us as protection against water waves, and a watertight door should the wave wash over the moat.

About 3:00 A.M., four hours before zero, the last weather balloons were sent up. At 4:00 A.M. the final weather briefing was held aboard the command ship. At 4:30 we heard from the scientific director.

"We've just had the weather briefing. Everything looks normal. Start the countdown."

Grier was pushing the buttons. I was making the time announcements. "Ten seconds ... five ... four ... three ... two ... one ... Now. The Time is H minus two hours. Next time announcement at H minus one hour. Next time announcement at H minus one hour."

At the exact instant that the clock had registered zero and I had said "now," Grier had deftly pushed the red button marked TWO HOURS, had satisfied himself that all was well, and was back in his chair before I had finished talking.

I rechecked the meters on the control racks, flipped the switch on my radio transmitter, turned and nodded to Jack Clark before reaching for my cup of coffee.

The minutes dragged on in agonizing slowness. We were

a little sleepy now at five o'clock in the morning. The room
didn't help a bit. The concrete walls were bare and ugly with
the damp ugliness of new cement, hardly cured before we
moved in with the tight time schedule of the whole operation. They were ready to drip water at any moment; they
would be dripping now if the massive air conditioner in the
next room were not audibly sucking all moisture from the
windowless walls before it had a chance to appear. The ceil-
ing and floors were also unpainted concrete, rough, with the
marks of the wooden building forms still showing. The
lights, yellowish, with metal poolroom-type reflectors, added
to the gloom. No fancy quarters these.

Along the back wall were workbenches, roughhewn, unpainted. Mixed along the tops of the benches were the standard tools of the electronics trade — soldering irons, radio
tubes, bits and pieces of wire, tape cans used as ash trays.
Two beer cans stood empty and unappetizing, left by technicians enjoying a last drink before evacuating to the forced
prohibition of a day aboard ship. One side wall held a tool
rack; on the other side hung a huge blackboard — the one
symbolic reminder of the scientific and academic backgrounds of the inhabitants. The blackboard was the Aladdin's
lamp that loosened the scientific tongue. Give the shyest,
most inarticulate scientist a blackboard and a piece of chalk
and he immediately transforms himself into an orator of
Churchillian loquacity. Now the blackboard stood dusty and
unused, a few half-erased equations and a notice that there
would be no laundry service this week scrawled across its
face.

In the middle of the floor, in gleaming contrast to the general shabbiness of the room, stood the control cabinets, called
racks — the reason for the presence of these nine men at five
in the morning. There were twelve racks in decorous gray
and shining chrome, pompous, self-assured, and incongruous
as Cadillacs in a blacksmith shop. Ten thousand people
waited in the middle of the Pacific Ocean; manned stations
all over the world were on the alert. The fate of nations hung
in the balance, anticipating the story that these racks with

168 NUCLEAR HOSTAGES

their bewildering complexity of electronics gear would tell. It had taken a year to design and build them, and this building that housed them had been constructed with walls three feet thick, half-buried in the sands of a tropical island as protection against the tremendous power they would control.

The racks were connected by slender, tenuous wires many miles in length to an object capable of releasing the most tremendous forces mankind had ever known, a shapeless, nameless device waiting to expend the energy of millions of tons of TNT within a split second two hours from now. They were connected to hundreds of thousands of other wires sampling the heartbeat of a myriad of experiments to diagnose the operation and measure the effects of this explosion. For the next hour, these racks of inanimate electronic equipment would be the eyes and ears of Joint Task Force Seven, telling the Task Force Command the condition of its fearsome weapon and of the complex equipment waiting to measure its destructive force. Monitored and controlled by the men in the bunker, they would set in motion, with ponderous, deliberate ease, the vast multitude of events necessary to the orderly performance of the experiment in their proper chronological order and, when and if satisfied that all was ready, would send the signal to the object at the other end of the line to unleash its force and send a Pacific island into vaporous oblivion.

An hour passed and the countdown signals were repeated; then the forty-five-minute signal and the thirty. At fifteen minutes Grier would push the button to make everything automatic — no trusting human reactions in the last grueling minutes and seconds.

After the thirty-minute signal, a final check was made on aircraft. One by one the far-flung aircraft reported to air control. For the next fifteen minutes the radio networks belonged to the airplanes. Hours before, while the rest of the people were sleeping, they had taken off, sluggish with fuel, from the woefully short runways allotted to them by the cramped geography of the small islands. They made an awesome sight, with jets flaming and exhausts roaring, using every inch of the runway as they strained for altitude, their fuel loads calculated so closely that they must skim the whitecaps for miles before rising into the pitch-black sky. Now, their load lightened by hours of cruising, they had lost their sluggishness as they settled into the final flight pattern, which would put them at their assigned distance in the split second of detonation.

In the control room we could hear them plainly as all other traffic ceased. Each man betrayed his tension by calling and checking more often than was necessary. On the surface, the betrayal of tension was watched for and welcomed. From now on, no man could afford to be casual. This was no place for the fly-boy or the fifty-mission cap. Each of these pilots was experienced, seasoned. Most wore the scrambled eggs of seniority. They were confident of their ability and proud of their aircraft, but each of them respected the force with which he was soon to come into contact. No man who failed to be awed by the prospect of the explosive force of millions of tons of TNT belonged in a position of responsibility in the air, on the sea, or on the ground. The Task Force Command had seen to it that none were there.

By 6:35 all had reported in with no difficulties. Each plane was running smoothly, gasoline levels were adequate, and ten solid minutes remained before the fateful order to proceed to final flight pattern for the detonation. Everything was going fine.

In the control room, Clark spoke into the radio circuit to headquarters. "How did things go at thirty minutes?" he inquired.

"No complaints, Jack," Ogle's voice replied casually. "Looks like we'll keep going."

This was good news, although not unexpected to the crew in the control room. We knew that there was no trouble or we'd have had an inkling of it by now, but it was good to have someone say so. Everyone relaxed a little. The fat radio sergeant returned from the communications room.

"How about some coffee, sergeant?" I offered.

"No thanks, not right now," he replied.

"What do you mean, not right now. In just a few minutes all hell's going to break loose around this place, and if you don't get coffee now, you'll never get it. After you have your coffee you'd better stand by that radio channel, and if it doesn't work any better than it has been working, the colonel will have twenty pounds off your hide when he gets back." I poured him a cup of coffee.

"Listen, fella, the colonel can have this job right now and my stripes to go with it. I don't know why I ever volunteered for this job in the first place. I must have been nuts. Are you guys sure you know what you're doing here?" he asked distrustfully.

"You'd better know how to swim, sergeant." Someone else took up the cudgel. "The latest reports say its going to knock the island right into the middle of the drink, and this concrete building doesn't float too well."

"I'm with you bastards." The fat sergeant took his ribbing for a while, then grinned to indicate he'd had enough and took his coffee back to the radio room. He was a competent technician, as was his associate. They and the air-conditioner man were not regularly part of a firing party, but they stood up well under the strain and did their jobs.

"Who's cooking the steaks, Jack?" asked Felt. "I'm getting hungry."

"One of you boys, I hope," Clark replied. "After all, I got the keys to the meat locker. Somebody else should do the work."

"We'll cook them." Grier volunteered for both of us. "How did you ever talk those guys into letting you have the keys, Jack?"

"Oh, I told them that we'd paid our ration allowance and were entitled to breakfast. If they didn't leave the keys I told them that they'd have to stay behind and cook for us. That did it!"

Grier cut short the conversation by looking at the clock. "Let's get a little work done or we'll never get anything to eat."

One by one we got up slowly, trying to appear unconcerned as we started our final round of checks. Cochrane left the room to check aircraft radios, and the air-conditioner man went out to make a final check of all air inlets and ports to see that they were secured against the blast. Clark put on his headphones for final instructions from headquarters; Stewart moved over for a last look at his charts.

I picked up the voluminous checklist I had carried for the last twenty-four hours. Since eight o'clock yesterday morning I had been checking meters, lights, and switches against this list. Grier and I had journeyed up and down the whole atoll by helicopter, stopping at each little island, checking the condition of every station in the complex array. Our own engineers and technicians had checked every wire before leaving the island, but just to be sure that no one had deliberately or accidentally touched any adjustment, we revisited every spot after the island had been cleared. Each of the hundreds of points had been checked dozens of times previously on a dozen dry runs, but there was always the possibility that a bulldozer had inadvertently cut a wire before leaving the island, or that water had seeped into a station after the last rainstorm. Now we were on the last sheet, the most important one. We had already gone over every item at least twice in the last hour, and our minds rebelled against the drudgery of repeating the list. Each of us knew, however, that he could no longer afford to trust his own memory or judgment, since our complete familiarity with the equipment might be enough to lull us into a false sense of security.

"Main switch on." . . . "Check."

"DC voltage." . . . "Twenty-eight volts."

"Sequence timer in ready position." . . . "Check."

"All bypass switches off." . . . "Check."

"Bomb arming lights green." . . . "Bomb arming lights green."

"Bomb firing lights green." . . . "Bomb firing lights green."

"Signal switch number one on." . . . "Roger."

"Signal switch number two on." . . . "Roger."

Each of the switches had been checked three times previously, but this was the crucial check. Fifteen minutes was the break-off point, the point beyond which everything became automatic. The whole system was designed to be untouched by human hands from that stage on. Once this last button was pushed, we could leave the room and the operation would proceed to set up all experiments automatically and fire the bomb at the right instant. Furthermore, if anything went wrong after that time, the system would shut itself down and stop the shot.

Aboard the flagship the final weather meeting was coming to an end as we worked. Some felt there might be a shift of the upper winds, but the data to substantiate such a conclusion were meager. Clouds from explosions as large as this one rose a hundred thousand feet into the air and spread for hundreds of square miles before starting to break up. Weather forecasts under these conditions were at best an educated guess, but the meteorologists on the job were tops in the business and their record to date had been excellent. One of the classics of weather forecasting had occurred on a previous operation when the forecast had been for sunny weather at zero time. It had rained with tropical intensity all the night before, and when dawn broke, the skies were still black and heavy with rain. Nothing daunted, the weathermen were found playing horseshoes in the downpour, insisting that it wasn't raining according to their weather charts and that it would be clear as a bell at shot time. Sure enough, thirty minutes before zero the moon broke through, and fifteen minutes later there wasn't a cloud in the sky. With a record like that, who could say them nay. Certainly not the men in the bunker; after two days of preparation and faced with the prospects of a disarming team, we could no longer be considered unprejudiced scientific observers. Right then and there we could have been talked into firing with snow on the palm trees.

But there must be one unprejudiced observer who would weigh all the variables. Would there be a shift in the wind? If so, how bad would it be and what damage would it do? What were the prospects of better weather tomorrow? Not so good, probably. Would airplanes be ready to fly again at a day's notice? All these intangibles must be assessed and the decision made to shoot or not to shoot. The man to make the decision was Al Graves, the scientific director. In order to be as certain as possible, the decision is postponed until the last possible moment and that last possible moment was selected to be the fifteen minutes before zero. At that time instruments were turned on which could only operate for twenty minutes and would need days of reconditioning before they could be reactivated. Graves knew all these facts and the depths of his responsibility. The decision could be postponed no longer. Graves rose from his seat with the simple expression, "Let's go!"

"Al says to let 'er go!" Clark reported. I went to the microphone now to begin my monotonous litany, dull and uninteresting, but today charged with a doomlike destiny. My throat felt dry, as though words wouldn't come, and I had to say something just to get my vocal cords in order. If I missed an announcement now I knew that I could throw the whole timetable off for the people whose lives might depend on hearing my voice.

"In one minute the time will be H minus fifteen minutes ... H minus fifteen minutes."

I looked around me at the faces of the others. The smiles and the nervousness had gone. Here were men trained to do a job and they were intent on it, impervious to all else. Clark and Felt had their eyes glued to the meter that would tell them that the fifteen-minute signal had gone out properly. Douglas Cochrane watched the lights on his radio telemeters for proof of operation, while Harold Stewart puffed thoughtfully on his cigarette.

Grier had eyes for nothing but the clock. The bomb would go off exactly fifteen minutes after he pushed the button, since it would be controlled for the rest of the time by a clock that is much more accurate than any human being's reaction. At the time of the detonation a camera actuated by the bomb burst would record the time to a thousandth of a second; any deviation from the scheduled burst time would be caused by Grier's reaction in pushing the button. Although human reaction times are on the order of tenths of a second, Grier, through long practice, was often able to come within hundredths of a second of the exact time. He and I often took turns in firing, and a friendly rivalry had grown up over who could come the closest. I removed my finger from the microphone button. "Bet you a beer you're off more than a tenth of a second."

"Bet," he replied, refusing to take his eyes off the clock to answer.

"Thirty seconds until H minus fifteen minutes."

I watched the clock closely now. I had only a short time left to concentrate, after which it would become automatic.

"Fifteen seconds ... ten seconds ... five ... four ... three ... two ... one ... NOW!"

As I said *now* I released my finger from the microphone as Grier leaned heavily on the button that started the automatic sequence. It took only seconds for my eyes to sweep the board and see that all was well. Herb had pushed the right button and the ponderous mechanism known as the sequence timer had started its ominous trip toward destruction. The fifteen-minute meters and lights had indicated correctly, and the big reel containing the tape broadcast had started exactly on time.

I stepped back and listened to my own voice emanating from the radio receiver monitoring the time broadcast.

"H minus fifteen minutes ... H minus fifteen minutes."

My own voice spoke to me, for the final fifteen minutes of the broadcast had been recorded on tape and synchronized to the sequence timer. The script had been recorded and played over and over again until planes' crews and ships' companies had every inflection drilled into them and could follow the broadcast with split-second accuracy and no possibility of a missed count or stammered statement throwing them off in the excitement of the last few minutes.

The last fifteen minutes are an eternity. There is nothing to do to relieve the tension except to watch the lights turn from green to red as each portion of the program becomes activated.

Fourteen minutes ... thirteen ... twelve ... eleven ... ten.

Ten minutes to go — six hundred of the longest, hardest, toughest seconds a man could experience. They must be used carefully so there are just enough of them to last until zero time with none left over. Some for checking the panels, some for worrying about mistakes, some to plan emergency action in case of trouble, and some to dwell on that wonderfully different future ten whole minutes from now when this would be all over and steaks and martinis would be the order of the day.

Nine ... eight ... seven ... six ... five.

Ships were in their final positions, having swung around to face the blast head on; aircraft were in their last turn to station themselves properly for the shock. Aboard the flagship, the meeting of blast experts, meteorologists, and radiologists had broken up after everyone had spoken his piece and the decision had been made to shoot. The advisers and VIPs, the visiting congressmen, had gone on deck to see the shot; the overworked Task Force Command could take a short breather. There was nothing that they, or anyone, could do now; everything depended on the men in the bunker and the adequacy of their preparations.

Four ... three ... two ... one.

The one-minute signal went out, the needle of its meter jumping suddenly from its reclining position to stand proudly erect beside her sister signals, looking like chorus girls with legs kicked high in the air.

"All observers having high density goggles put them on ... All observers having high density goggles put them on ... All others face away from the blast ... Do not face blast until fireball dissipates ... Do not face blast until fireball dissipates."

The unhurriedness of my own voice sounded less irritating than it had a short time before. With unhesitating obedience, thousands of soldiers, sailors, airmen, and scientists fitted the dark glasses over their eyes as ordered — a little nervous at the unaccustomed blackness. Others turned duti-

fully away from the blast and braced themselves for the coming shock wave; some, like Lot's wife, could not resist another look and would pay the penalty of temporary blindness
when the shot went.

Fifty seconds. At forty-five the needle on the meter assigned to the bomb arming signal snapped into position, followed immediately by the switch of the first of the big green
lights to red.

"She's armed," said Grier tersely.

"Right." I agreed, unable to restrain myself from speaking.

"Bomb armed," Clark reported into the microphone and
moved a step closer to the guarded panel with the big red
STOP switch, to be ready to push it up to the last second
should the word be passed from headquarters.

"I hope nothing goes wrong now." I spoke to myself,
knowing that the problems of a disarming party would be
multiplied tenfold should something go wrong after the
bomb was armed.

"*Thirty seconds until zero time ... Twenty-five seconds
until zero time ... Twenty seconds until zero time ... Fifteen
second until zero time ...*"

"Fifteen-second signal O.K.," reported Grier. Clark nodded,
but it was too late now for any announcement.

I took one quick sweep of the board with my eyes, my lips
counting and my head nodding to the passing of the seconds;
arming light red, one-hour signal in, forty-five-minute signal
in, all others in down to the fifteen-second signal, which had
just come in, firing light still green, all interlocks still green,
nothing amiss.

"*Ten seconds ... nine ... eight ... seven ... six ...
five ...*"

The five-second meter snapped up and its light went red.

"*Four ... three ... two ...*"

I could see the firing cam on the sequence timer starting
slowly to close.

Not so quickly, I begged it silently. Take your time.

"*One ...*"

Then, as suddenly as a hammer blow, the last light turned

red and the needle on the firing meter started to climb. The two were almost simultaneous, but the merest fraction of a second existed between them, almost imperceptible, but in plenty of time to close the last gate between the firing switch and its receiver at the end of the miles of water under the lagoon. The signal sped quickly along the wire to its destination, and another pair of wires carried back with the speed of light the information that the signal had arrived and had done its job. The firing light flicked red, only a brief flick, as a mighty force pursued the return signal down the wires destroying them as it went, but it was long enough to tell its important tale.

"Zero."

The shot had fired, it had really fired, it was over with, everything had been ready and worked. I began to dance in my excitement as the firing switch began to open as ponderously as it had closed.

I looked around at the others. The air-conditioner man wore the same puzzled look he had worn over the last five minutes, and the two sergeants stood poised, expectant, waiting for something to happen. What's the matter with them? I wondered. Aren't they impressed? Can't they realize what has happened? Suddenly it came to me that they could not. They had seen nothing, felt nothing; they probably didn't realize that anything had happened. The flick of a meter needle, the race between the interlocks and the firing switch, the final victory of the operation as designed was enough to fill me with excitement, to leave me limp with the struggle my mind had gone through, to leave me elated at the result. To the three men who had never seen a test, who were not familiar with the system, the shot was an anticlimax. Buried in this cavern there was no atomic fireball to blind them, no enormous cloud forming in the sky, no shock wave to mark the release of the biggest explosion mankind had ever devised, set off by these men in this bunker.

"Let's get ready for the steaks," Cochrane suggested. "I'm getting hungry." The sergeants smiled and relaxed. This they understood. The job was over, the day was done, it was time

to "knock off." They couldn't imagine what everybody was
so happy about, but who cared if it was all over.
*"The shock wave will arrive shortly. The shock wave will
arrive shortly. Keep firm footing until shock wave passes.
Keep firm footing until shock wave passes . . ."*
Once again the sound of my own voice intruded on my
thoughts. It intruded on my elation as it had on my tension.
I paused, took stock of my surroundings. The clock said that
ten seconds had passed since the detonation. A relay was
chattering in back of the racks as the circuit that controlled
it opened and closed. Lights were flickering on and off, red
and green, with no pattern, indicating violent electrical dis-
turbances up and down the atoll. This was not unusual, but
the explosion must have been a big one to cause that much
electrical commotion.

Clark was listening on the command channel.

"Bill says it looked like a good one to him," he reported
jubilantly. "The shock wave may hit pretty hard. Let's get
ready for it."

I looked at the clock and calculated that the shock wave
wouldn't arrive for another forty-five seconds at least, so I
ignored the warning and turned to talk to Cochrane.

I started to tell him of my plans to go home, but as I talked
his attention wandered. His look of flushed pleasure had
slowly changed to one of puzzlement; then his expression
changed as his face turned white with concern. I felt it too
as I talked, the words coming more and more slowly and
finally stopping as all thoughts of home quickly vanished.

Something was wrong!

Grier spoke the words first, as he reached out to steady
himself at the workbench.

"Is this building moving or am I getting dizzy?" he asked.

"My God, it is. It's moving!"

"The whole building is moving."

Grier reached for the bench to steady himself as I stood
bewildered in the center of the room. The whole building
was moving, definitely now, not shaking or shuddering as it
would from the shock wave that had not arrived yet, but

with a slow, perceptible rolling motion like a ship's roll; I began to feel a nausea akin to seasickness.

I was completely unable to get it through my head that the building could be moving. The building is made of concrete, I told myself. The walls are three feet thick. It's anchored like a rock on this island. Besides, the shock waves can't be here yet.

But it *was* moving! The motion was unmistakable as it built up. Objects were beginning to slide on the workbench. My initial period of astonishment must have lasted about five seconds before I could move over to the bench to hold on and steady myself against the strong rolling motion. Subconsciously, I pushed back a screwdriver, which was rolling back and forth in a narrow arc on the bench. Then I realized what it was.

"It's the ground shock," Clark and I yelled simultaneously.

I had never felt it before, but it was due to the fact that the shock wave from the blast traveled much faster through the ground than it did through the air. Generally, the ground shock was never felt, as it died off more rapidly than did the shock wave through the air; the fact that this one was evident at all was an indication that the explosion had been one of tremendous force. A force that could move this heavy concrete building so many miles away so that it felt like it was resting on a bowl of jelly must be wreaking terrific havoc with this whole Pacific atoll. From the way the building felt at this moment, it might just as well be floating in the middle of the Pacific Ocean. For all I knew, maybe it was!

This was a subject we had joked about for years, that one of these days an explosion would be strong enough to shear the top off the atoll and send it plunging down into the depths of the Pacific Ocean. Norris Bradbury, the Los Alamos director, and Carson Mark, head of the theoretical division, had mentioned that it might "go big" in a conversation in Jack Clark's tent two nights ago. If this one was a mistake, it sure was a beaut, I thought to myself.

The same thoughts must have been running through

everyone else's minds as all stood there in silence. The lights
had dimmed for a second and were flickering occasionally
but were still on. The only sensation was that slow, weird
oscillation as the building rolled back and forth, back and
forth. At any moment I expected the walls to crack and the
ocean to come pouring in or for the whole building to start
sliding, intact, on the two-mile journey to the bottom of the
ocean floor. But the walls didn't crack and the building didn't
slide; it just kept rolling back and forth with the same deliberate motion. The whole thing couldn't have lasted more
than fifteen seconds before it began to subside. Maybe we
will live through this after all, I thought.

Grier was the first to break the silence.

"At least we're on the part of the island with the power
plant," he commented wryly.

I had to smile as I realized that the lights were still on and
the island must still be intact. I took another look at the
clock and realized that the air shock had not arrived yet. We
weren't going to slide into the ocean from the ground shock,
but the danger wasn't over by a long shot!

Crash!

There it was like a thunderclap, the steel door and the concrete walls reverberating like drumheads; next the suction
phase — here it came — a slow sucking *whoosh* as the air
found its way out after the shock wave had passed. I held
on to the bench, ready for it, but it was all over before I
could react; my body waited for the sharp clap, the quick
suction of air, and the soft, gentle return, recognizing the
three phases before my senses could catch up. One of the
men, not quite ready, staggered to his knees before he could
steady himself. In the corner of the room a cloud of vapor
began to rise. I could hear the sputter of the electric batteries
and see sparks from where I stood.

"Water! Water! There's water coming in," someone yelled.

I had been rooted to one spot since the ground shock had
started. The roll of the building had unnerved me, but the
fact that the air shock had not been so bad gave me some reassurance. Here was something I could understand and do

something about. It is only the unknown and unseen that one worries about; if water was coming in on top of the batteries, I wanted to see it. I ran around to the back of the racks, my legs still a little rubbery.

"It's too early for a water wave, unless the whole ocean has erupted," I told myself. "A water wave could not travel fast enough to be here for five or ten minutes yet."

It must be water forced through the electrical conduits by the shock wave. This was not too serious, but it could mean that the air shock had been much stronger than we had realized in the protected building. That's what it was, water that had been in the pipes, blown through by the force of the blast. No permanent damage; the sputtering stopped and we wiped off the tops of the batteries.

The radio was alive with sound. Every circuit was chattering madly as the air shock hit the ships of the task force. Aboard ship the ground shock went unnoticed. Headquarters was clamoring for a report from the control room.

"Where is the water?" Ogle's voice was excited and worried. He had heard the initial cry of water and had heard nothing else for the last sixty seconds.

We nine men in the control room looked at one another, a little dazed and disrupted by the events of the last minute. Clark moved slowly to the radio to take up the order of business again.

"We're all right," Clark reassured him wearily.

Normally we would be anxious to get out to take a look at what had happened, but today we would not be so venturesome. We waited fifteen minutes. Headquarters reported no evidence of a water wave from the sampling aircraft, giving us permission to open the watertight door. The air-conditioner man, custodian of the door, deserved the honor of the first look through the small porthole: no water. After a nod from Clark, I followed him and the air-conditioner man out the door.

The scene outside was a mess. I looked up. By now the sun should be quite high. On other mornings the sky would be sparkling at this time. Birds should be flying, looking for their daylight meal; there should be the hustle and bustle of a construction camp, which came to life with the rising of the sun. Today there were no such things. The cloud stretched heavy and ominous, completely obliterating the puffy white fair-weather clouds that normally dotted the tropical sky. The water, robbed of the play of sunlight on the waves, looked dull and lifeless. Birds, normally active and raucous, were nowhere to be seen.

"Any radiation?" I asked Grier.

"Yeah," the answer came. "Too low for fallout; must be shine from the cloud."

There should be little likelihood of the cloud bothering us. It would take hours for normal particles in the cloud to fall from the twenty-five-mile height to which they had risen, sucked by the tornadolike funnel of the hot fireball as it rushed skyward. With the trade winds, the cloud should be hundreds of miles away and dispersed to a safe level before it settled onto the sea.

"When are we going to eat?" the fat sergeant asked.

"Let's stick around just in case there's any fallout," Clark replied. "We'll have plenty of time to eat after the cloud dissipates."

"That's a good idea, Jack. The level's gone up to five MR," Grier cut in.

"No kidding." I picked up a meter, carefully checked the calibration, and switched to a sensitive scale. "Right you are; it's rising too."

Still nothing to be concerned about. Five MR (milliroentgens) was five thousandths of a roentgen per hour, well within tolerance levels.

I watched the needle climb until it went off the scale at ten MR per hour.

"Ten MR, Jack," said Grier. "We'd better stick fairly close to the building."

"Let's round everyone up," Clark directed.

Twenty MR now and rising rapidly. The level had increased four times in as many minutes. Time to seek shelter.

Suddenly the sky became filled with a whitish chaff. I

stuck out my hand, which was soon covered with a substance like talcum powder.

It all happened in a few seconds, but the reaction was instantaneous. "Let's get inside." It was unanimous as everyone broke for the doorway.

"Hey it's one hundred MR," someone shouted.

No question about it, the stuff was falling on top of us. The particles were bigger now; it began to feel like a hailstorm as larger and larger particles fell from the sky. At first they were finely divided like dust, but quickly small pebbles, then rocks began raining from the sky.

The nine of us ran quickly into the corridor of the blockhouse; the air-conditioner man slammed and bolted the big steel door. The fallout drummed on it like hail as everyone retreated to the safety of the control room.

"Let's all stay in one place. Keep away from the door," ordered Clark.

I looked at my meter: one MR per hour. I walked to the doorway that led to a twenty-foot corridor to the outside door. The level jumped to twenty MR. Cochrane took out his meter and walked slowly down the corridor. Fifty MR, a hundred, two hundred, five hundred. He stopped five feet from the door, turned, and hurried back to the protection of the control room.

"It's one thousand MR five feet from the door. It must be a good five R per hour outside."

Five R per hour meant five thousand milliroentgens per hour. At that rate a man could receive the maximum allowable yearly dose in less than one hour. There go the steaks and martinis.

Clark put on the headphones of the special radio circuit to headquarters.

No one else in the task force was experiencing any fallout. I began to munch on an apple but quickly lost my appetite when the needle of the meter at my feet began to climb, first to five MR, then to ten MR per hour. I looked around, startled.

This was serious. Clark reported the levels to headquarters.

"It can't be," came back Ogle's reply. "You guys have a factor of ten thousand shielding in there."

"Can't be, hell," Clark said angrily. "If we have ten thousand shielding, it must be awfully hot outside."

Suddenly someone shouted, "The air conditioner, it's still running."

"For God's sake, shut it off."

The air-conditioner man, looking hurt and puzzled that anyone should berate his beloved air conditioner, turned for instructions.

"Shut it off," said Clark. "It's probably circulating dust particles from around the door."

It took only a second to cut the switch; within thirty seconds the level began to drop — eight MR, seven, six, five, four. It hung there for a minute, then settled to three and then one MR. I felt so good I kissed the meter.

What a bunch of sharp characters, I thought, circulating air past that doorway. If we hadn't all been out on our feet, we'd have thought of it right away.

One more crisis over, but there was still a big one left.

We checked the outside monitors.

"What's it like outside?" I asked Grier.

"Twenty-five R and rising."

Twenty-five R. The impact of the statement struck me. At this rate, only eight minutes outside were allowable. We were safe behind the massive concrete walls and ten feet of protective sand, but there would be no other living thing left on the island. The fallout had started an hour ago, which meant that any bird or animal that had survived the tremendous blast would already be sick from radiation. Two hours of such exposure would begin to kill humans. How high would it go? Anything up to one hundred R we could live with. We would be trapped for hours or days until the level decayed enough for a rescue. If it crept up over a hundred, we would begin to be in serious trouble. The higher it went, the longer it would be before we were rescued. If it went to one thousand, it would be impossible to rescue the party for many days, perhaps a week; in that time the accumulated exposure, even if we huddled in the farthest corner of the

building, would be enough to make sick people out of most
of us. If it went higher...

Still no sign of radiation elsewhere. "Forty R per hour
outside now," Clark was reporting to an incredulous
headquarters.

"Are you sure, are you sure?" queried Ogle. "We have
practically nothing here."

"Damned right, I'm sure." Clark snorted into the microphone. "If you don't think so, come on in."

"O.K., Jack, it looks like you might have caught quite a
bit. I'll be in as soon as we can get a helicopter to make a
survey."

Thirty minutes went by. We dragged cots into the corner of the building where the level was lowest, moving away
only to answer the radio or check the levels outside. They
kept rising: thirty, forty, fifty, fifty-five, but the increases
were at a slower rate. We took turns reading the levels. It
was my turn now.

Sixty R, but almost steady.

Grier had also noticed the slackening of the radiation rise.
"I'll feel better when it starts going down."

"Me too."

"Sixty-five now and steady. Hasn't changed in almost five
minutes," Clark reported. I listened to the radio. There was
little traffic. The word had gotten around about the men
trapped in the blockhouse; all the normal chitchat had
ceased.

Fifty-nine. It was falling. I felt the same butterfly sensation as I had when the bomb went off. The final danger
hazard had passed; I could relax.

We were still stuck here, still couldn't leave the building
without serious danger, but hope was in sight. The radiation
would decay rapidly at first but more slowly as time went on.
There was a possibility that we could be rescued today; if
not, certainly tomorrow. I'll settle for that, I thought.

I began to peel an orange. The food tasted good. I hadn't
been able to eat for the last hour, but my appetite was coming back with a vengeance.

The radios in the control room began to pick up traffic.

The fallout was hitting the ships now; a note of concern crept into the voices on the radiation monitoring network.

"D.J., D.J., this is Hardtack. Over."

"Ten MR this station, ten MR this station."

I couldn't worry too much about the ships. Although their thin steel plates offered little protection against radiation, they did have wash-down systems with which they could use uncontaminated sea water to keep their decks clean. Most important, they could move, which we couldn't do. On the other hand, with our troubles behind us, we were probably the safest people in the Marshall Islands — provided we didn't leave the building.

There was little to do but wait. Gradually we were able to piece out from the radio reports what had happened. Although accurate measurements of the yield would not be available for days, remote measurements indicated that the yield was at least double that predicted, at least fifteen megatons. The upper winds had shifted in the last few hours before dawn so that the cloud was traveling slightly south of east rather than north as had been predicted. It was traveling in the direction of the inhabited islands of Rongelap and Rongerik, but no readings of radioactivity were reported as yet. The ships retreated to a point fifty miles out to sea and were activating their wash-down systems. We were barely able to continue radio communication at that distance when another disaster struck.

We were preparing a fresh pot of coffee on the hot plate when the lights started to flicker and the coffee stopped boiling. Gradually the lights turned yellow, then into a dull glow.

"Oh, God, there goes the power," yelled Clark.

The generators and main power plant were in a separate building half a mile up the road; placing them at that distance was a standard procedure to cut down noise and radio interference. The two buildings were connected by half a mile of cable; it had been gratifying at shot time to realize that the shock wave had not disrupted the cable lines between the two buildings.

The present trouble might be in the lines or the generators

might be stopping. We knew that they had been refueled just before evacuation and had enough fuel for several days. Fortunately we were well equipped with diagnostic equipment.

We checked the frequency of the generators; it was right on the nose — sixty cycles. We checked the voltage on each of the generator's three phases and found them to be at sixty-five volts. One of the phases inside the generator had failed.

"Let's put the one-ten-volt lines on the two-twenty-volt circuit," Cochrane suggested.

"Good idea," I replied. "If the generator repairs itself, we'll blow out all the equipment, but it's worth the chance."

In the meantime we had lost all contact with the fleet. We could hear them frantically calling on our battery-operated emergency radio, but we didn't have enough power to reach them fifty miles away.

We compromised by putting half our radios on the 220-volt circuit and half on the 110-volt circuit. That way we would have some communication either way. We were out of communication about thirty minutes while we diagnosed the problem and reconnected the lines.

We flipped the switch on the reconnected radio. It warmed up beautifully; we made contact with the fleet right away. Soon the worried voice of Al Graves was heard, relieved that nothing more had happened to us. There was a pause at the other end as our new situation was discussed. Finally, Al's voice came out of the speaker, calm, crisp, and decisive.

"Look, Jack, the feeling here is that if you lose one phase of that power, the whole thing may go at any minute, so we are starting to steam in closer to you. The cloud has passed us, and we can get in quite a bit closer. Come up on your battery-operated circuit; we'll come in close enough to establish good communication by walkie-talkie in case you lose all your power. We want to keep communications open with you. Bill Ogle is now out in a helicopter taking a survey of the atoll. He should be back in half an hour. We'll know then what the radioactivity problem is on the island. What do your meters say now?"

"About thirty R per hour outside," Clark reported.

"At that rate you could stand five or ten minutes' exposure, but we don't know how localized it is so we'd better not make plans until Bill gets back."

Cochrane went to the walkie-talkie and started calling. Nothing to do but wait some more. The inside of the building looked eerie. The bulbs were too dim to read by; they lent an additional air of dinginess to our stuffy surroundings, warming up rapidly as the noonday sun beat down on the unairconditioned building. A feeling of what-can-happen-next? pervaded the building as we sat around waiting word from headquarters.

The fleet apparently hadn't been far out of walkie-talkie range, as Cochrane raised them on the battery circuit within twenty minutes. The ships, after making contact, continued to approach us until good communication was assured. After satisfying himself that all was well, Cochrane shut off the battery switch. No telling how long we'd be here; we needed batteries. Clark and Graves set up a schedule of contact times in case we lost our power. We were to call for five minutes on the hour and half-hour only until contact was reestablished. This would conserve precious battery power.

After ten more minutes of silence, Graves called us back.

"Bill's back and says the atoll's still there," he joked.

"I thought for a while that it wouldn't be, Al," I answered seriously.

"He sees no reason why we can't get you guys out tonight. What do you think?"

"Stand by, Al, until we talk this over, please."

Everyone was anxious to get out, but Clark pointed out that we were safe here; the longer we stayed the easier it would be. On the other hand, even he was not anxious to be left here another night if we could help it.

"We're for it, Al, but we're safe here and would rather stay all night than be rescued if we can't do it right." I reported the sentiments of the others.

Graves explained the plan. The thirty-R-per-hour level read by our meter was representative of the general level of radiation in the atoll, and the admiral was not anxious to re-enter the lagoon that night. Conditions were too hazardous to attempt re-entry or recovery operations for another twenty-four hours. The Task Force Command preferred to retire to their uncontaminated home base at Eniwetok Atoll, but could not go away and leave us stranded at Bikini. Our opinion was unanimous. If the ships were leaving, we wanted to leave.

It was now two o'clock. The rescue would be set up for five o'clock to allow another three hours for the radioactivity to decay, but still giving plenty of time before dark to effect an unhurried rescue. We were to establish radio contact every thirty minutes until 4:30, when the helicopters would leave the aircraft carrier. The helicopters would buzz the building at exactly 4:45 and circle it twice, then hover offshore until we appeared. At 4:55 we were to leave the building and drive to the airstrip, half a mile from the control building. If our vehicles were still operative, the hovering helicopters would time their landing with our arrival. There would be two helicopters. We were to divide into two parties, each in a separate vehicle if we could get two running. The vehicles were to go to opposite sides of the airstrip to prevent confusion. In the event that we could not start any Jeeps or trucks, or the radiation levels were too high, we were to return to the building to await instructions. The reason for driving to the airstrip was that the antennas and poles around the control building would make the rescue more hazardous. Also, the airstrip was tarred and partially paved; the helicopters would stir up less dangerous radioactive dust.

Graves stopped reading his plan to ask us if we knew the condition of our vehicles. We went into a huddle before replying. There were six vehicles outside, three Jeeps and three trucks. Several had been used the night before by the firing party, and others had been left behind the building as blast protection. So far as we knew they were in good condition. We had seen them when we were out that morning after the blast, before the fallout drove us indoors. We were all willing to take the chance that at least one would be operable and decided not to set up an alternate plan.

Clark asked us for any other comments. The plan sounded good to all of us.

"What ship are we going to?" Felt asked.

Clark repeated the question over the radio.

"I don't know. The aircraft carrier, I assume," said Graves in a puzzled tone. "What difference does it make?"

"That ship's so crowded they're sleeping on the decks. We'd rather stay here," Clark joked. "We have good mattresses and plenty of food."

The ship was filled with helicopter crews, radiation safety personnel, and members of recovery parties. An aircraft carrier, a fighting ship, is not designed for comfort under the best conditions; now it was badly overcrowded, and the ship's company fought a game but losing battle to accommodate the influx of visitors. No one would spend a night there if he could help it, and the word had gotten around.

Graves knew what we were talking about and laughed.

"Don't worry. We'll find someplace for you to sleep, and chow will be waiting. Anything else?"

"No. Sounds good to us, Al."

"O.K., we'll call you again at two-thirty."

Everyone beamed as Clark put down the microphone. Rescue in three more hours; the thought of it was wonderful. Everyone's spirits hopped up. The day's experience, the stuffy air, the dim lights were forgotten as plans were made to get out. Clark divided us into two parties — one headed by him and one by Grier. Stewart and Cochrane were designated monitors to check the levels as we went along. The two sergeants were designated as drivers since we had decided to use their vehicles, which were personnel carriers and rode higher off the ground than did the Jeeps.

We decided to eat before leaving. It was an odd meal. The voltage was still low and the lights dim. We managed to coax some lukewarm water out of the hot plate and to take the chill off some cans of meatballs and beans. It wasn't very appetizing, but the prospect of action lent zest to the meal. Graves checked in with us at 2:30 and again at 3:00 P.M. At 3:30 Ogle came on the air, chiding us for not waving to him as he flew over our island.

"It looked pretty peaceful to me down there. The least you could do would be to stick out your head and wave."

"Why didn't you stop in and see us, Bill," Clark chided. "We'd have served you coffee."

We hadn't heard any helicopters all day, so I assumed that they had hovered over water as much as possible on the survey, as a dunk in the lagoon would be safer than a land-based landing in case of trouble.

By 4 00 P.M. we were chomping at the bit, ready to go. Clothes were the big problem. Grier and Clark had long-sleeved shirts and long pants, but the rest of us had only shorts and T-shirts and no caps.

"Let's use bed sheets," someone suggested. We ripped up bed sheets and pillowcases to make leggings, sleeves, booties, and caps. We covered up what clothes we had as much as possible because they would have to be discarded if they picked up contamination, and they were the only clothes we had. Our belongings had been left in our tents, which, if they were still standing, would be unapproachable for days.

What a run on the PX there will be tomorrow morning, I thought.

We ran into a problem — no safety pins. Stewart found two rolls of paper masking tape. It broke easily, but we wound ourselves in tape like mummies.

We made a truly comic sight as we inspected one another for uncovered spots, like monkeys inspecting one another for bugs. The fat sergeant, I thought, would get the prize for the best costume. His feet and ankles were wrapped in one pillowcase each and secured by black electrician's tape. He had made puttees with pieces of rags and paper tape. He had tried to do the same for his arms, but the impromptu sleeves wouldn't stay put and kept sliding down. His body looked like a mummy that had forgotten to reduce. His headpiece, another pillowcase, enveloped his head and draped down his neck, his face peeping out like a cherubic nun's from a habit. We were all a little nervous as we waited, but the outlandish costumes lent a masqueradish air to the dimly lit room.

Grier and I had been on many recovery programs. He cautioned the first-timers: "The important thing is not to rush. If we move carefully, we should be out in the open only eight minutes or so before we get to the helicopters. It should take no more than thirty seconds to get to the automobiles. Keep your feet off the floor as much as possible. You'll be several feet off the ground, which will help considerably. Don't get out of the automobiles until you are ready to go for the helicopter. Trot, but don't run. A fall in this dust can do more harm than the few seconds you will gain by rushing. Do you have any further instructions, Jack?"

Clark instructed the air-conditioner man. "When I give the word, you open the outside door so that we can hear the helicopters. Leave it open and come back to the control room. When I say go, the drivers will leave to go to the personnel carriers. If they do not start immediately, come back in and Grier and O'Keefe will go out to try the Jeeps. If none of the vehicles start, we'll contact headquarters and set up a different plan. Does everyone have film badges?"

All nodded.

"Doug and Harold, do you have meters?"

"All set, Jack."

"O.K., that's it until the choppers come."

Clark went back to check with headquarters.

"We're ready," he reported.

"O.K., Jack." It was Ogle's voice. "The copters are airborne. You should be able to hear them in about ten minutes. We've just raised them on King net."

Although we had most radio circuits in the communications center, there was no provision to talk directly to helicopters, which had their own radio network. Graves and Ogle, however, could talk to both of us.

"What does your level read now, Jack?" Bill asked.

"About twenty-two R per hour," Clark replied.

"You shouldn't have any problem at that level," said Ogle encouragingly.

Clark and Ogle chatted aimlessly to pass the time until we were ready to leave. All other networks had radio silence imposed until we cleared the island.

At 4:35 Clark gave instructions to open the outer door.

The afternoon tropical sunshine poured in; we blinked and rubbed our eyes. I had forgotten how dim the lights were in the windowless building. The sunlight almost blinded us, although we were twenty-five feet or more from the door.

"We're like a bloody bunch of moles," muttered the air-conditioner man in his Scottish burr, but there was no reply. We strained to hear the sound of the helicopters.

At 4:40, on schedule, the faint *flop, flop, flop* of the helicopter blades was heard, softly at first, but soon distinct and unmistakable. Cochrane and I grinned at each other out of our shroudlike garments.

"Here they come," someone said softly to himself, unable to be quiet in his elation.

"O.K., Bill, we hear them," Jack reported.

"Right, Jack. Give them time to buzz the building twice before you come out," Ogle warned.

"Roger, out," said Clark, ready to cut the conversation and be gone.

"Good luck and out here" came the final message from the ship.

The noise grew louder, deafening in the small corridor, as the first helicopter passed low in front of the building, its shadow visible for an instant before the sound subsided to a steady *flop, flop, flop*. Again the noise as the second helicopter passed in front of us, just high enough to be out of sight. There was a thirty-second pause, then both helicopters repeated the maneuver. The sounds grew quiet, barely audible after the second pass, as the copters backed off and hovered over the lagoon.

Thank God for helicopters, I thought as I took a last look at the building. The dinginess and dimness of the lights and the building were more obvious now that we had been staring at the sunlit corridor. The other shrouded figures looked ghostly as they prepared to quit their tomb.

"O.K., start the cars," said Clark.

The two drivers went out, trotting softly and trying not to hurry. I heard the engines whirr and catch almost immediately.

"Let's go."

We moved in unison, needing no instructions. It was only a few steps to the personnel carrier. I had wrapped my hands and shoes in rags just before leaving and was careful not to touch the vehicle with my hands as I climbed into the back. Only seconds had passed before we were driving slowly down the road in first gear, stirring up as little dust as possible for the group that followed. We had all made breathing masks with which we covered our mouths and noses before leaving and were virtually unidentifiable, with only our eyes showing.

I looked out the side window for the choppers. There they were, motionless in space, but with wings whirring like dragonflies poised over a sunlit pool.

I looked at Cochrane to check the radiation level. He nodded his head in reassurance and held the meter where I could see it.

It was wavering a little as we drove along but seemed fairly steady at about ten R per hour. The three-foot separation from the ground did help some, I thought.

The truck lurched as the driver detoured around a fallen tree. The road was a mess, with palm branches, leaves, sticks, and rocks scattered around by the blast; most of the debris was small though, and we had little trouble along the half-mile stretch to the airstrip.

The copters settled closer to the ground as we approached the edge of the strip. We went to the far side and the others came up on the near side, the two vehicles coming up on the paved strip almost simultaneously. The copters were directly overhead now; it was impossible to talk or hear. The driver cut the engine precisely as our copter settled on the strip. We jumped from our vehicle and trotted gingerly about the helicopter to the side door, carefully avoiding the spinning rear propeller and running with our heads down from force of habit. Helicopter blades are set to clear the heads of a basketball team, but I have been never able to resist the temptation to duck. As I made my way the twenty yards to the helicopter door, I could see the pilot in the cockpit, grin-

ning broadly and waving. It was Jerry, the squadron commander who had left us some seventeen hours earlier.

The side door opened as we approached, and a familiar
figure reached down to help us into the copter. It was Major
John Servis, the commander of the Rad-Safe detachment,
looking relaxed and calm, as though he did this every day.
He was dressed in conventional radiation protective clothing
— loose coveralls taped tight at the ankle, snap-on booties
over his shoes, a cloth cap, and cotton disposable gloves. He
had a respirator-type face mask on a strap around his neck
but apparently preferred not to use it. He looked like home
and safety to me. I smiled at him, completely forgetting that
only my eyes were visible through the bed sheets. A big grin
on his face showed his amusement at our clothing, and he
threw up his hands in mock despair as we clambered aboard.
The noise of the engine was too strong for him to be heard,
but he pointed to our feet like a housewife whose children
had dirtied up her nice clean living room.

I understood immediately and removed the rags from my
hands and shoes. The others followed and we tossed them
overboard before fastening our seat belts.

Major Servis reached up behind the pilot and nudged his
legs — the signal to take off. We were airborne immediately,
as Jerry wasted no time getting off the island. The major
passed his survey meter expertly over all of us.

He shook his head negatively and shrugged his shoulders
as if to say, "What's all the excitement about. You guys are
as cool as a cucumber."

Missouri-like, I grabbed Cochrane's meter and checked my
clothes — not more than ten MR per hour. Apparently we
had picked up no contamination to speak of in our journey
along the island and could relax. The back of the plane
looked like a ragpile as we removed makeshift caps, face
masks, and leg and arm shields. I felt cooler and more comfortable as I sat back in my shorts and T-shirt. We spent the
twenty minutes back to the ship grinning at one another
like canary-eating cats.

There were handshakes and backslapping as we debarked

from the helicopter, but the efficient Rad-Safe crew was not to be deprived of its only customers of the day. We were monitored carefully, head to foot, as we disrobed and showered. Our clothes were passed as safe. We dressed, turned in our film badges and were given new ones. Considered clean, we went off to a drink, a meal, and a debriefing.

We were safe. We were lucky. But others were not so lucky. Our film badges showed that we had accumulated only a few hundred milliroentgens, less than half a roentgen — an excessive dose for a single day — but well within tolerance limits if we were careful for the rest of the operation. Similarly, aboard the fleet total accumulations were not outside limits. The wash-down systems, the evasive actions, patrol aircraft to tell the task force commander which way to go, all kept the radiation accumulation within reasonable limits. But we were the experts. We had meters, film badges, we understood what we were doing and for the most part what was happening; we knew how and what precautions to take. We had all the tools and techniques of modern science to protect us.

Others were not so well prepared. An Air Force weather unit about 180 miles from Bikini reported that evening that their dosimeters had gone off scale at five roentgens. They were told how to wash themselves, but serious concern set in. The fallout was far more serious than had been supposed. The next day a full downwind evacuation was undertaken. There were eight-two Marshallese on the island of Rongelap, 120 miles to the east and most directly in the fallout path. They were evacuated to Hawaii by destroyer escorts. No precautions had been taken by the natives nor had anyone thought to advise them. Measurements showed that they had received between one hundred and two hundred roentgens, an amount that could make them sick but not kill them. Within two days of the explosion they all fell ill. They vomited, their skin itched and burned, most developed sores, but none died. They were kept under constant medical care for months; it was three years before they were able to return. Even then they were lucky. The island of Rongelap is thirty miles long. Measurements showed that the northern tip of the island, where they often fished, received one thousand roentgens in two days after the explosion; this would have meant certain death for anyone living there.

We too had been fortunate. The area outside our bunker received eight hundred R. Unprotected exposure in this region would certainly have been fatal. A few miles up the atoll, however, the total dose was more than five thousand R, a level that would have made rescue difficult. The atoll was uninhabitable for the remainder of the test series. Barges were used for detonation sites; heavy radiation protection clothing in the hot tropical sun made operations very uncomfortable; control operations were transferred to a ship; all further devices were detonated by radio from the open sea.

But the operation was still not out of trouble. Unknown to anyone, a Japanese fishing vessel, the *Fukuryu Maru*, or *Lucky Dragon*, with twenty-three crewmen on board, was seventy-five miles east of Bikini, trawling for tuna on the morning of March 1. A tiny speck in the vast Pacific, it had been unnoticed by the planes and ships sweeping the area before the test. Just before dawn one of the crewmen standing watch on the bobbing deck stared out at the calm sea. Suddenly the whole western horizon lit up with a whitish yellow glow that gradually turned to orange. He rushed down to the cabin shouting, "The sun's rising in the west." Incredulously, the others rolled out of their bunks and up to the deck just in time to feel the shock wave, which had taken six minutes to travel the seventy-five miles.

A few hours later, a whitish ash settled on the deck and into their hair and clothes. By evening they had lost appetite, and the next morning most were vomiting. On the third day they decided to head for home; in the two weeks it took them to reach their home port all became seriously ill. Taken to a hospital, they were found to have low blood count and to be contaminated with radioactive material.

In Japan, the disclosure was electric.

Nine years had passed since Hiroshima and Nagasaki, but

the memories were strong. Reporters came from all over the world to interview the seamen; anti-American demonstrations were set off in Tokyo. Some of the fish was found to be radioactive and was dumped, which set off a panic in Japan, a country where fish is the main staple in the diet. People refused to buy fish in stores all over the islands. It was weeks before confidence could be restored and the fishing industry returned to normal. Six months later some of the seamen were still in the hospital; on September 23, Aiticki Kuboyama, the radio operator, was the first postwar casualty from a nuclear weapon. He died in a hospital only eighty miles from Hiroshima.

On the international scale the result of the Bravo test was that the United States now had a deliverable thermonuclear weapon. But had we won the race for the hydrogen bomb? No, we had not.

Early in 1951, before our Greenhouse experiment, Air Force planes picked up a sample of radioactive debris from a Russian test, which indicated that a tritium-deuterium reaction had taken place. Robert LeBaron, chairman of the Military Liaison Committee, the link between the Pentagon and the Atomic Energy Commission, was informed, but no one in the AEC or the Joint Committee was told about it. Only six Air Force officers, Secretary of State Dean Acheson, and President Truman were given the information. It is likely that the evidence was marginal, since there would be no reason to hold back from people like Teller or Oppenheimer. It is also likely that neither Acheson nor Truman understood the significance of the information. Subsequent intelligence indicated that Andrei Sakharov's breakthrough in 1950 led to this first thermonuclear experiment. Although there is some question about the 1951 test, there is no question that the Soviets exploded the first deliverable bomb on August 12, 1953, six months before the Bravo test. The true father of the H-bomb is not Edward Teller, but Andrei Sakharov of the Soviet Union.

The American public was told nothing about either Russian test. The public believed that the Russians had set off their first fission test so soon because of information obtained by espionage. It is true that their program was expedited by espionage, but again the main reason was simply the knowledge that it could be done. Who would tell the spy-conscious American public that not only had the Soviets caught up to us, they had surpassed us? Certainly no administration hoping for reelection.

No single event better exemplifies the inevitability, the inexorability of the nuclear and thermonuclear development. While Americans searched their souls about continuing after Hiroshima and Nagasaki, the Soviets plunged ahead without a twinge of conscience. While we labored over the Acheson-Lilienthal Report and tried vainly at the United Nations with the Baruch plan, they marched resolutely ahead. While we agonized over the role of the military and civilians and took a year and a half to activate our Atomic Energy Commission, they were building their first self-sustaining chain-reacting pile. While our nuclear research capability eroded in 1945 and 1946, they managed to achieve criticality with their first pile before our Atomic Energy Commission became operational. Within two weeks after their first 1949 fission test, they were hard at work on fusion. While the great debate raged in secret over thermonuclear research, Andrei Sakharov and Igor Tomm were preparing their first thermonuclear test. Nothing we could have said or done would have dissuaded them.

In the first place, they never believed that we would turn any secrets over to them. It simply was not in their ken that any sovereign nation would voluntarily relinquish a military advantage to a potential enemy.

Second, there was their firm and unshakable belief in the superiority of the Marxist philosophy. They did not, could not believe that a capitalist nation could maintain an advantage for very long.

Third, they had good people. Perhaps "they couldn't make a saucepan," as one U.S. official put it, but they could make a fission weapon and a fusion weapon. The quality of their economic system was inferior, not the quality of their science.

Does their system have advantages? It certainly does. Policy is decided at the top. Objectives are pursued rigorously and relentlessly. To a totalitarian state, secrecy is an asset. Only those who need to know are told; no one else can object. Resources can be allocated with complete disregard for alternatives, with complete disregard for disruptions and inefficiencies in other programs, with complete disregard for the general welfare of the populace.

In our society, secrecy is anathema. Policy is decided not from the top but by a consensus emanating from the people. To establish policy there must be debate. To have meaningful and productive debate, information must be widely disseminated — to the public, to the press, to the political opposition. Secrecy in the nuclear and thermonuclear programs hindered our progress, hindered our ability to set rational priorities, hindered our ability to assess fully the dangers or advantages to our national security of alternate courses of action.

Although the Soviets had caught up to us and for a time surpassed us, they did no thermonuclear saber-rattling. They knew we had a larger stockpile, that we had superior delivery systems, that any boasting of superiority would rally the American public to greater efforts. So the Soviet thermonuclear progress was not divulged to the American public by either the Soviets or our own government, each for its own reasons.

Another startling revelation came out of the Bravo explosion. Dr. K. Kimura of the Japanese Institute of Scientific Research examined the ash from the *Lucky Dragon* and was surprised to find traces of uranium 237, a rare isotope of uranium, which he had created in 1938 by bombarding natural uranium with neutrons. But a thermonuclear weapon was not supposed to contain U-238, the abundant natural isotope of uranium. Gradually, from this observation, the next secret came out. The enormous yield from the Bravo shot had come not just from the thermonuclear reaction, but from a blanket of U-238 wrapped around the fusion bomb. The first stage was a plutonium fission bomb trigger igniting a fusion reaction in the lithium-deuteride. Neutrons from the fusion reaction ignited a third stage by causing fission in the surrounding U-238 blanket. The device came to be known as a three-stage bomb, a fission-fusion-fission device in which most of the yield came from the highly radioactive third stage. It was a weapon whose radius of destruction would be measured not in miles but in hundreds of miles, rendering any civil defense by evacuation useless. As we had found out in the bunker at Bikini, the area of destruction depends on which way the wind blows, and that is impossible to determine in advance. The Atomic Energy Commission summed it up in a terse report published in 1955: "On the basis of our data from this and other tests it is estimated that, following the test explosion of March 1, 1954, there was sufficient radioactivity in a downwind belt about 140 miles in length and of varying width up to 20 miles to have seriously threatened the lives of nearly all persons in the area."

Returning home from the Pacific, I found little comprehension of the enormous amount of destruction possible from an explosion of the magnitude of the Bravo test. Even the furor from the Japanese fishing trawler was treated as an isolated incident, a freak that happened because the vessel was someplace it shouldn't have been. The experience of the Rongelap natives was played down in the tight security atmosphere of the times. Again, as I found when I returned from Japan at the end of the war, the public was unable to grasp the great scope of the destruction, unable to comprehend that a single explosion could wipe out an area of twenty-eight hundred square miles, unwilling to believe that there was no place to run to and no place to hide.

After the Castle operation, there was almost a year's respite from testing while the two weapons laboratories digested the information from the Pacific and prepared a variety of tactical weapon devices for testing in Nevada the following year. Grier moved to Nevada to devote himself full time to continental weapons test activities. Germeshausen and I devoted more of our time to nonweapon activities. Our first work was for the government, with improved ceramic designs of hydrogen thyratrons for radars, which Germeshausen had developed at the MIT Radiation Lab during the war. The second project was development and production of an instrument for the Air Force, which I had played a principal part in conceiving. It was a welcome change from the years of concentration on nuclear weapons to return to what had been my first love, the development and growth of a modern corporation. In 1954 our sales grew to $2.3 million and we earned $40,000 profit. The number of employees had grown from six to two hundred. By 1955 sales exceeded $3.5 million and the number of employees reached 390. By 1956 we reached $5.7 million in sales, employed 480 people, and broke into six figures with our earnings at $111,000. It was a thrill to convert an organization of scientific researchers into a cohesive, competitive, efficient performer in the marketplace.

In the flush of the initial formation of the corporation, when we plunged full time into preparation for the Sandstone test series in 1948, we didn't even have an accountant. We packed up our bills in a large envelope and sent them to the New York office of the Manhattan District for payment. We didn't have facilities of our own, operating out of MIT as we did when working for the university. We did our budgeting on the blackboard and then erased it. Later in the year, government auditors pointed out to us that this was not quite acceptable financial practice. After Sandstone, we acquired our own facilities in a converted garage on Brookline Avenue in Boston. We hired accountants, clerks, secretaries, and telephone operators. At one point, as our numbers approached one hundred people, we seriously debated whether we should stop there and not get any larger because we would begin to lose quality. Grier's logic was simple: "When we get that big, we'll have to start writing memos to each other. If we have to start writing memos, we should quit."

But we burst through that barrier in 1952 and kept growing. Our budgeting technique took a quantum jump. Instead of budgeting on the blackboard and erasing it, we budgeted on the blackboard and took a Polaroid picture before erasing it. We thought certainly that would satisfy the auditors, but for some reason it didn't. We set up an accounting system to pay our own bills and send invoices. We hired a personnel man to set salary grades and monitor performance against wages. We set up our own machine shop and chemical laboratories. We developed our own networks of suppliers and converted some of our aging electronic technicians into buyers and purchasing agents.

Everything did not go smoothly or without protest. After we had grown to the size of several hundred employees, the business needed more and more accountability. It is the practice in small laboratories to have an open stockroom where engineers and technicians can go in and take the supplies they need. When a box gets empty, somebody orders more. There comes a point in growth when a stock clerk is needed to maintain continuity of supply and to account for distribution to various tasks and product lines. Edgerton objected to this. He maintained his own laboratory at MIT, where he was now a full professor. He felt that accounting for supplies was a nuisance and hindered his research. But progress marches on. I finally had to hire a stock clerk and lock up the stockroom, but I forgot to tell Edgerton. I arrived one Monday morning to hear the stock clerk reporting a burglary over the weekend. I soon found the culprit. It was Edgerton. He had come in to do some work on a Sunday, a normal workday for him, found the stockroom locked, went to his car for a pair of wire cutters, and calmly cut the screen out of the stockroom wall. A free spirit!

Although we were moving ahead nicely with commercial diversification in Boston and had moved all of the continental test work to Las Vegas, the testing program was still our prime responsibility. In 1955 Grier had his hands full with a test program calling for fifteen detonations in Nevada, where our work on timing and firing and high-speed photography had been expanded to include measurement of the rate of multiplication of the neutrons in the reaction.

I still had responsibility for weapon tests in the Pacific. During the Nevada test series, the Navy had a requirement for an underwater weapons effects test. We were asked only to do the timing and firing; all of the experimental work would be done by the Navy. Grier was too busy to go, so I had to take time from my other activities to supervise our group. It was like no test ever performed before — a deep-water weapons effects test for naval vessels. The idea was to tow a five-mile cable, with a tow ship on one end and a thirty-kiloton device on the other, five hundred miles out to the quietest spot in the Pacific Ocean, the Pacific equivalent of the Sargasso Sea. At intervals along the cable would be secured a variety of small naval vessels, landing craft, amphibious vehicles, and the like, all fully instrumented by the Navy. When the detonation point was reached, the weapon would be lowered two thousand feet into the deep ocean and set off.

There had been an underwater test at Bikini in 1946, but the lagoon was too shallow; the explosion broke through the surface of the lagoon and contaminated the test vessels so badly that much of the test data was lost. At two thousand feet down in mile-deep water, the explosion would be contained and deep-water effects tests could be performed. The operation was staged out of the San Diego naval base. We had plenty of experienced people to prepare the equipment, so I didn't have to be there until departure time. I hoped to keep my time away from Boston to a minimum, probably about twelve days. It would take five days to get to the zero point because the tow could only travel at eight knots, then a few days at zero point, and two or three days to get home. It was a thrilling sight to see the fleet leaving San Diego harbor. The flagship was an aircraft carrier to provide patrol planes and helicopters. There were destroyers for protection and patrolling; submarines for remote underwater measurements; the tow tug pulling its five-mile cable with test vessels strung along its length like beads on a string; and finally, the device barge, squat and ungainly, with a large, makeshift, unpainted plywood container holding the weapon and its lowering equipment. There was also a postage-stamp-sized helicopter platform for the firing party to use in the final arming mission.

We moved along in fairly good weather to start, but the seas, instead of getting smoother, became rougher as we went farther along. When we arrived at the detonation point, the waves were eight feet high and the wind was at twenty-five knots. It was extremely difficult to get on and off small boats. We flew back to the barge and landed on the helicopter platform. It took three tries before the pilot could put down; even then it was pretty hairy. We managed to check out the weapon and lower it two thousand feet into the ocean, but every thirty seconds there was a terrific jolt as the barge snapped at the end of the five-mile-long cable. In the heavy seas the cable was so long that it was virtually fixed in space, with the ships and boats attached to it not able to roll with the seas as usual. As we flew in the helicopter, I could see crews being knocked off their feet on the smaller vessels as the cables slackened and then went taut as the seas moved the boats toward and away from the rigid tow cable. Veteran Navy petty officers who had spent a lifetime at sea became so seasick that they were unable to carry out their preparations for the test.

About the time we left San Diego there had been a significant earthquake in the Aleutian Islands, which formed a large tsunami or tidal wave, causing heavy seas and strong winds as far away as Hawaii. The disturbance reached our location just about the time we did, turning the normally placid ocean into a storm center. Worse still, it was not expected to abate for another two days. By morning of D-day, boats were snapping off the tow as cables and stanchions gave way under the relentless beating, which they had not been designed to take. It was clear that the tow would not survive another twenty-four hours. There could be no postponement. It had to go that day or the whole operation would be canceled.

With no aerial photography to worry about, it was not necessary to fire in the usual predawn darkness; zero time was set for noon. We had planned to fly to the shot barge by helicopter, arm the weapon, and fly back to the control ship. But the barge was pitching and weaving so badly that a helicopter landing was too dangerous. We could take a small boat downwind to the barge, but it would be difficult to beat back up against the wind and the waves. We decided to split the firing party. I remained on the control ship to oversee the actual firing; two of our people and the Navy firing party commander went by small boat to the barge, armed the weapon, and continued downwind another ten miles, where they were met and picked up by a destroyer escort. I had it pretty easy this time since the control ship was reasonably steady even in the high seas and strong winds. The arming went smoothly considering the circumstances; by eleven o'clock I had checked all the circuits and was ready to relax. The arming party had been picked up and was safe. I had no instrumentation to worry about; once the weapon detonated I was finished and ready to go home.

I fixed myself a big ham and cheese sandwich and poured a cup of coffee, then sat down to wait out the last hour, confident that our equipment would work properly. I was sorry for the Navy people who had gotten such a bad break in the weather, but there was nothing I could do about it.

Just as I bit into my sandwich, the admiral in charge of the task force came into the control room. He was a nervous wreck. His whole experiment, his whole career depended on us in this final hour. He started asking me questions about what might go wrong. I told him to relax, everything would work perfectly. He was still worried. I said to him, "Admiral, I'll make a deal with you. If I get this thing off on time, will you get me back to San Diego as soon as you can?"

He grinned nervously.

"You have a deal," he said, and we shook hands.

Everything worked perfectly. The device was detonated at noon to the second. The shock wave arrived quickly, as it traveled rapidly through the water. There was the familiar sharp crack as it hit the ship, but no damage was done. I checked out our control racks; everything was in good shape and could be left as is until it could be dismantled back in San Diego. I didn't see the admiral again. He was busy supervising post-detonation activities, but at one o'clock I was paged to come to the helicopter platform. Sure enough, a helicopter was waiting to fly me to the aircraft carrier. When I arrived on the aircraft carrier, I was told that a destroyer was leaving for San Diego with some water samples right away and that I could go on it. I looked down from the stable flight deck of the carrier on to the destroyer bobbing in the high seas.

"How do I board her?" I asked.

"Breeches buoy" came the laconic reply. "We're rigging it now."

A line was thrown to the destroyer about fifty feet down and forty yards away. The breeches buoy was rigged, stable at the carrier end but moving in circles at the other as the destroyer pitched and rolled in the heavy seas. I stuck my legs into the two holes in the buoy. I was off. The weight of my body pulled down the line and I dropped about ten feet before the line caught with a jolt. I was wishing I hadn't been in such a hurry as I bobbed up and down, almost touching the water one time, and then high in the air as the skilled crew worked me on to the deck of the destroyer. I looked around the deck; it felt familiar. When I asked the name, I realized that it was one of the destroyers I had worked on in Bath, Maine, during the war before I joined the Navy. When I told the skipper, he was pleased to have "an old destroyer man" aboard. I had a good dinner in the wardroom, a good night's sleep in a private cabin as the destroyer sped toward the coast at twenty-five knots, and the next morning I called my wife from the San Diego Navy Yard. The admiral had been true to his word.

Although the location picked for Operation Wigwam was not in a fishing ground, word soon spread that a bomb had been detonated underwater in the Pacific; the fishing industry went into a panic. The public reaction was similar to the Japanese experience a year earlier with the *Lucky Dragon*. Fish stores were unable to sell anything; whole boatloads of tuna were dumped although no radioactive fish were ever found. Jittery housewives threw out canned tuna fish that had been sitting on their shelves for weeks. There was a congressional investigation, and the press had a heyday. After a week or so, the furor settled down, but there were heavy losses in the fishing industry, as there had been in Japan. The people were getting fed up with indiscriminate weapons testing.

7

THE TEST BAN TREATY

THE BRAVO SHOT had awakened the world to the dangers of fallout. A wave of protests followed. Highly respected world leaders, including Pope Pius XII, Albert Einstein, Prime Minister Jawaharlal Nehru, and Albert Schweitzer, joined in the call to end nuclear tests. Negotiations on disarmament began again with the Soviet Union, but there was a basic difference in the approaches of the two countries. The United States wanted to agree on a set of controls and inspection procedures, then proceed to disarmament. The Soviets wanted it the other way around: disarmament, then controls. The negotiations dragged on for years with no resolution. Adlai Stevenson made testing and fallout an issue in the 1956 presidential campaign and was getting a lot of attention until Soviet Premier Nikolai Bulganin made the mistake of agreeing with him. This closed the issue for the American public. Through 1957 negotiations dragged on, with the main stumbling block centering on the question of inspection stations inside the various countries. It was clear that the Russians wanted no inspection stations inside the Soviet Union.

On March 22, 1958, the Soviets successfully pulled off a major diplomatic ploy. The Supreme Soviet issued a decree prohibiting further nuclear testing by the Soviet Union provided other nations did not test. We knew and they knew that they had just finished a major testing program and we were just about to start one, but the rest of the world did not. When we refused to stop immediately, there was strong worldwide opinion against the United States. President Dwight D. Eisenhower backpedaled by recommending a technical conference on the requirements for verification of a nuclear test ban. The Soviets reluctantly agreed; Eisenhower was able to buy enough time to get our test series under way.

Of course, the likelihood of a test ban was well understood by our company. We were able to diversify into a number of other government and commercial programs to ease the possible effects of a test ban. We obtained a significant position in Project Rover, a program to develop a nuclear rocket engine for interplanetary travel. We also became involved with Project Plowshare, a program to develop peacetime uses for nuclear explosives, particularly nuclear excavation and mineral exploration. On the commercial side, we were able to expand our hydrogen thyratron production and introduce a fast traveling-wave oscilloscope for research laboratories.

After the Wigwam test in the Pacific, I had trained replacements for myself in the field, although I spent a good amount of time on instrumentation development. By the time the 1958 Pacific series came along, we had sufficient depth that I had planned not to go into field operations at all. The pressure for a test ban was also well perceived by the weapons laboratories. They stepped up their designs for antiballistic missile warheads, tactical weapons, and for "clean" thermonuclear weapons, which were designed to eliminate the third stage of the fission-fusion-fission devices and to reduce the size of the first fission stage. Since it was the fission portion that caused most of the radioactivity, these designs were expected to reduce fallout greatly.

The Nevada program was expected to run throughout the year. In the Pacific, both Bikini and Eniwetok atolls would be used. This meant three simultaneous full-scale programs. The laboratories began to run short of test managers. When they heard that I did not intend to participate in field operations, I was approached to accept an assignment in the scientific task group for the Pacific operation, Hardtack.

Although I was reluctant to accept, I took a leave of absence from the company and became scientific commander for the Bikini operations. During Hardtack the United States carried out fifty-four tests at Nevada, Eniwetok, Bikini, and Johnston Island. Eleven primarily high-yield weapon development tests were carried out at Bikini. The pace was frenetic. As I sat evening after evening in the senior officers' mess, I was struck by the siege mentality of the senior military and of the civilian scientists. I had been away from direct involvement in field operations for almost two years; I understood the worldwide concern about fallout, the sincere desire of the President to do something tangible about stopping the headlong race to oblivion. To me a test ban treaty, or at least a temporary moratorium, was inevitable. Not so to the people at Bikini. They were inculcated with a spirit of the importance of nuclear superiority to the national security. They were strongly anti-Communist, deeply suspicious of the Soviets, convinced that the Russians would find some way to cheat. They dismissed the fallout question as media-inspired; they felt betrayed by the politicians and duped by the Soviets. Having no one to talk to but one another, they became more and more convinced of the validity of their position, more and more eager to complete as many tests as possible before they were put out of business.

The best example of their frustrations had to do with high-altitude explosions. Intercontinental ballistic missiles were going into production in the United States and the Soviet Union. Conventional defense against such missiles was impossible because of the difficulty of searching out a missile traveling at fourteen thousand miles per hour in outer space; intercepting it and destroying it was outside the capability of any conceivable non-nuclear air-to-air defensive missiles or aircraft. If, however, a rocket with a nuclear warhead were exploded outside the atmosphere, X-rays, unabsorbed by air, could incapacitate guidance systems of incoming missiles, providing a blanket over a large city or military installation.

My feelings about such antiballistic missiles were negative, although I never let personal opinions interfere with the aggressive performance of my duties. The idea of exploding a multimegaton missile over my head to protect me never quite made sense, but I agreed that an assessment of the feasibility of such a defense was the appropriate thing to do.

We had scheduled two rocket tests in the Bikini Hardtack series. The first, code named Teak, was a megaton-range warhead on a rocket to be detonated at an altitude of 252,000 feet, nearly forty-eight miles. The second, code named Orange, also in the megaton range, was scheduled for 141,000 feet, about twenty-seven miles. It is characteristic of explosions in the low-density atmosphere at altitudes between twenty and fifty miles to have an extremely bright fireball capable of producing injury to the eyes at great distances. For the Teak and Orange experiments severe retinal burn would result to anyone looking in that direction for a radius of fifty miles. Task force personnel would be directed to look away or wear dark glasses, but what to do for natives on neighboring atolls? The task force commander recommended evacuation or warnings to remain indoors at zero time. The White House, sensitive to the plight of the Rongerik natives after the Bravo shot, vetoed both recommendations. Frustrated, the Task Force Command decided to move the two launch points to Johnston Island, a tiny spit of land just large enough for a runway, about seven hundred miles west of Hawaii. This was the only piece of real estate governed by the United States in the whole Pacific Ocean that did not have inhabited islands in its line of sight at the designated altitude. The move caused extreme disruption of the Bikini test schedule since it meant setting up a complete new operating site fifteen hundred miles away.

When Teak was detonated, it was a frightening sight. Because of the long range of the X-rays in the low density of the atmosphere, the fireball grew very rapidly. In 0.3 second its diameter was eleven miles; in 3.5 seconds it increased to eighteen miles. The fireball also ascended at a high rate of speed, initially at one mile per second. Surrounding the fireball was a very large red luminous spherical wave. About a minute or so after the detonation, the Teak fireball had risen to a height of ninety miles, clearly visible by line of sight all the way to Hawaii, seven hundred miles away. In addition to blocking radio communications over a radius of several thousand miles, the Teak shot created an "artificial aurora," which was observed in the Samoan Islands, two thousand miles from the point of burst.

It didn't seem like a very good defensive weapon concept to me.

Similar observations were made from the Orange shot, though they were not as spectacular because of the lower detonation altitude.

By the end of August, shortly after the Teak and Orange shots, the technical analysis of the feasibility of a moratorium was completed with affirmative conclusions. Two days later President Eisenhower proposed that England, the United States, and the Soviet Union meet to negotiate a permanent end to nuclear tests. He announced further that, to create a favorable atmosphere, the United States would abstain from testing for a year from the date negotiations began. Both sides rushed to complete testing programs before the October 31 deadline. The United States completed the last test on October 30. The Soviets tested twice after the conference began, but the violation was ignored in the spirit of the negotiations.

True to the spirit of the moratorium, both President Eisenhower and President John F. Kennedy refused to prepare for resumption of testing; the United States capability for test resumption atrophied while delegation after delegation of United States, British, and Russian negotiators wrangled over the terms of a comprehensive test ban treaty. The main point of contention was the number and type of inspections to be allowed by the several countries within their borders. There was no problem in the United States or Great Britain. We were open societies; inspection teams could come and go freely. The Soviet Union was a police state; it could not tolerate other nationals moving within its borders. Although from time to time they seemed ready to allow inspections, the target kept shifting and they always backed off. I don't believe they ever intended to allow inspections.

The Soviets stalled for almost three years. On August 30, 1961, while a disarmament conference was in session in Geneva, the Soviet Union did it again, announcing, with no prior warning, that they had decided to resume testing.

This was an act of perfidy and the United States was caught flat-footed. The Soviets conducted their first test, at 150 kilotons, the day after the announcement. In the next sixty days the United States monitored fifty Soviet atmospheric tests. It was the most intense sustained test series the world had seen, exceeding in megatonnage the totals reached by all preceding tests of all nuclear nations. Since it takes years to prepare for a large-scale test program of this magnitude, it was clear that the Soviets had never stopped test preparations. From the day the moratorium started in 1958, they must have been getting ready for this operation. With their typical single-mindedness of purpose, they prepared, and when they were ready, they resumed testing.

The United States was caught unprepared, technically, militarily, and politically. The weapons laboratories, without the deadlines of a scheduled test program, had delayed settling on the final designs of most of their new devices. The military, with restricted budgets and limited technical personnel, had allowed their task forces to atrophy. Politically it was embarrassing not to be able to resume testing immediately as the Soviets had done.

Fortunately, we and the laboratory test organizations had small field crews in Nevada conducting chemical explosive experiments and very low-power nuclear simulations. A field organization was conducting nuclear rocket experiments. With this cadre the United States was able to begin a series of low-yield tests underground at Nevada within two weeks. The first tests were sparsely instrumented and carried out primarily for the political effect. We were able to staff our Las Vegas operation fairly rapidly and soon had a full-scale, low-yield underground test program under way.

High-yield atmospheric tests were a horse of another color.

These were needed to develop high-yield weapons, particularly since the Soviets had already tested a sixty-megaton device, and hardening capability for intercontinental ballistic missile sites, to study electromagnetic effects, and to develop antimissile defense weapons, none of which could be accomplished underground. Not only did we not have a test organization, we didn't even have a testing site. Eniwetok and Bikini atolls, where we had carried out most of the high-yield tests prior to 1958, were part of the Marshall Islands Trust Territory, which the United States administered for the United Nations. The State Department predicted that strenuous objections would be raised in the United Nations to test resumption in the territory. We did have Johnston Island, where we had carried out rocket tests, but it was too small for a full-scale program. The best location was Christmas Island, a British territory about one thousand miles south of Hawaii, which the British had used for their own tests.

There was a great deal of secret debate between our government and the British as to whether we should resume atmospheric testing at all. Nikita Khrushchev was already clamoring for a new treaty now that his own test series was substantially complete. In the curious twists of reasoning, which seem always to accompany nuclear weapon decisions, both the British and we decided that we must deal with the Soviets from a position of strength, so that our chances of achieving a comprehensive test ban would be better if we resumed atmospheric testing. The British agreed to the use of Christmas Island, and a full-scale test program was scheduled to begin in April.

Again there were two full-scale test programs, one in Nevada and one in the Pacific. Because of the three-year moratorium, there was a severe lack of trained testing personnel, particularly in the military and in the nonweapons government laboratories. The commander of the task force for the Pacific operation, code named Dominic, was badly in need of help. Contrary to what had happened in other organizations, we at EG&G had not lost any experienced people. In accordance with our fundamental diversification strategy they had been transferred to other, nonweapons programs.

When asked to take on a heavy test load, we were reluctant to do so since it would delay many of the commercial developments into which we had put so much time, effort, and money; furthermore, the President had ordered that the atmospheric tests be completed in six months, after which there would be an atmospheric test moratorium. But the appeals to patriotism on the importance of the tests could not be ignored. We reluctantly put aside many of our most promising developments and took up a full-scale, seven-month program in the Pacific. The extent of the effort can be gauged from our sales, which more than doubled, from $19 million in 1961 to $38 million in 1962.

The test series was a rigorous one, with many of the failures and disappointments that follow poorly planned and hastily conceived programs. Only four months were available for the kind of planning that normally takes three years. It was particularly galling because we knew that the Soviet Union had carefully used the whole three years of the moratorium to get ready for their tests. Forty tests were carried out at Christmas and Johnston islands. One of them, Starfish, was to examine the effects of a nuclear explosion on the Van Allen radiation belt, an immense cluster of high-intensity charged particles held in space by the earth's magnetic field at altitudes between five hundred and twenty thousand miles. After numerous delays and one aborted mission, the device — a 1.4-megaton explosion at 270 miles altitude — was detonated on July 9 over Johnston Island. It lit up the sky from Hawaii to Australia and, contrary to predictions, added significantly to the electrons in the Van Allen belt. This test brought into serious question the viability of a high-altitude antiballistic missile; it also indicated how little we know about the earth's outer environment and gave a hint of its fragility in the event of a full nuclear exchange.

Although we seriously disrupted our commercial programs to field a full-scale test program from Boston, I did not participate in the field operations, which always bring out management problems in the strangest places. I was preparing to leave with Grier for a short inspection trip at the beginning of the series when I received a call from an assistant secretary of the Interior who wanted to know what we were doing in Samoa.

"We are making some measurements of an aurora effect from high-altitude nuclear detonations on Christmas Island," I replied.

"Well," he said, "you have the natives all stirred up. Two of the villages are about to go to war about some disputed land."

"I'm sorry," I said. "Hold them off for a couple of days. I'm on my way to the Pacific now. I'll see if we can solve the problem."

Grier and I flew first to American Samoa, landing at Pago Pago, then driving through jungle roads twenty-five miles to the western tip of the island, where our photographic installation was located. We had found a promontory about fifty feet high, which was ideal for our cameras; to help us with the installation we hired two chiefs from the village to the east at the going rate of $28 per week each. There we found the source of the friction. None of the natives had ever paid attention to ownership of the high ground because it was useless to them. Their main livelihood was fishing, so everyone lived by the beach. When the chiefs of the village to the west of the promontory heard that the chiefs to the east were making $56 per week, however, they claimed ownership of the promontory, starting a dispute that filtered all the way back to Washington.

We solved the problem in typical American style, by hiring the other two chiefs for $28 per week each; since there was now nothing to do but wait for the test, we had four employees watching two plywood shacks.

The natives were delighted. They decided to have a big feast for the two chiefs from Boston who had brought peace to their villages. Held in a large thatched hut it was magnificent, with roast pig, delicious tuna, and all sorts of luscious fruits and vegetables. Children waved palm fronds as fans; everyone was dressed in their most festive native costume. It would have done justice to a Bing Crosby–Bob Hope movie. I expected to see Dorothy Lamour come walking in at any time. At the conclusion of the meal, the chiefs held up their hands; something more was coming. In came the prettiest young lady in the village, proudly holding dessert in a platter over her head. She had been dispatched to the commissary at Pago Pago to pick up the pièce de résistance — a Betty Crocker chocolate cake — the appropriate conclusion to the festive meal. Thus did we solve tribal wars.

The Dominic series lasted until November, when the final atmospheric test was conducted on the fourth. Meanwhile negotiations continued on a comprehensive test ban treaty in Moscow, Geneva, and Washington. They dragged on for a year, sometimes showing progress, but on every occasion eventually running into the blank wall of Soviet refusal to permit inspections. Kennedy became increasingly pessimistic about a comprehensive treaty, but refused to back off to consideration of a limited treaty prohibiting tests only in those environments — the atmosphere, oceans, and outer space — where on-site inspections would not be necessary. During May 1963 a poll was taken in the Senate, confirming that a comprehensive test ban treaty would fall ten votes short of the two-thirds needed for ratification but that a limited treaty would be ratified easily.

On July 2 Khrushchev made a speech accusing the West of demanding inspections for military purposes and stating that there could be no bargaining on this matter. The Soviet Union would never "open its doors to NATO spies." He went on to say, however, that the Soviet Union "expresses its readiness to conclude an agreement on the cessation of nuclear tests in the atmosphere, in outer space, and underwater."

From then on events moved with lightning speed. A new conference was arranged to convene in Moscow. By August 5 a treaty had been agreed to and initialed by the three nations. Hearings were held in the Senate beginning August 12. After a month of bitter debate, the limited test ban treaty was ratified by a vote of 79 to 9 on September 23, 1963.

8

THE NUCLEAR HOSTAGES

THE 1963 test ban treaty effectively removed nuclear weapons development and testing from the consciousness and conscience of the world. For eighteen years the superpowers had struggled to formulate a strategic approach to the nuclear problem that would maximize each country's internal security, minimize the chances for future nuclear conflagrations, and satisfy the fears of the rest of the world. As in all things nuclear, the search for a strategy brought out a number of paradoxes, contradictions, and incongruous political solutions.

President Harry Truman's problems had seemed simple. He had the bomb; the Soviets didn't. With such overwhelming military superiority, temporary or not, his advisers sought to obtain concessions from the Stalinist police state on human rights, territorial expansion, and disarmament, but it didn't work out that way. From the day Truman announced the existence of the bomb to Stalin at Potsdam, the Soviets had a single, unequivocal objective — parity — and, if possible, superiority. They would not be cowed by the threat of annihilation or seduced by the blandishments of a Baruch plan. In the four years before their first test detonation they were as belligerent as if the bomb had not existed. The United States learned its first strategic and diplomatic lesson: As a threat, the bomb didn't work. It was too big a club to be credible.

As the United States debated security, international control, and the morality of the development of the thermonuclear weapons, the Soviets sailed right by our state of the art to develop and test the first thermonuclear device. The Eisenhower administration, headed by the most experienced and respected military man in the free world, paradoxically chose its strategy for economic rather than military reasons, completely unappreciative of the rapid development of Soviet science. President Dwight Eisenhower wanted a balanced budget; to get it he had to cut down on military spending. Nuclear weapons were much cheaper than standing armies. Ignoring the lessons of the Truman administration, Eisenhower chose the bomb as the solution for all military problems. John Foster Dulles was the spokesman for the strategic concept of massive retaliation. Any aggressor, any instigator of brush-fire conflicts anywhere in the world must face the prospect of nuclear annihilation.

Operating navies and standing armies became secondary; the Air Force was king, the Strategic Air Command its shining knight, the big bomber its gleaming steed. Robert Oppenheimer, spokesman for the scientists who urged thermonuclear restraint, allocation of resources for air defense, and development of smaller tactical weapons for limited war, was excommunicated for his heresy. The strategy of massive retaliation produced a balanced budget, but it also produced a badly unstable world political and military situation.

The 1957 orbiting of Sputnik finally awakened the American public from its delusions of invincibility. The early Russian lead in thermonuclear research had not been disclosed to the people, but there was no hiding a satellite spinning ominously over their heads. U.S. citizens, shattered by the event, went from the smugness of superiority to concern over the specter of inferiority. The issue of a missile gap became dominant in the 1960 campaign; the strategy of massive retaliation was obsolete.

When the Kennedy administration examined its military position, it uncovered a basic flaw in the capabilities of a totalitarian state. Such an organization can and does concentrate on developments such as a thermonuclear weapon, a ballistic missile, or a satellite, but it has great difficulty commanding the cooperative resources for large-scale quality production. Examination of satellite photographs and monitoring of missile tests revealed that the Soviets were far behind in quantity and quality of propulsion equipment and missile bases. There was still time to formulate a new strategy.

The strategy President John Kennedy devised with Robert S. McNamara, his Secretary of Defense, was known as flexible response. It allocated resources to conventional armies and fleets to conduct non-nuclear warfare and paid greater attention to defense and development of tactical weapons for limited nuclear warfare. The concept was rational, but it soon ran into its own set of difficulties. Surprisingly, the first objection came from our European allies in the North Atlantic Treaty Organization (NATO). Flexible response meant building up armies to face the superior land forces of the Warsaw pact nations, which was too expensive for the limited resources of a rebuilding Western Europe whose people preferred to live under the American nuclear umbrella. The American solution was to supply NATO with tactical weapons for battlefield use in limited nuclear wars. It was the strong opinion of virtually all nuclear strategists that using tactical nuclear weapons on the battlefield would lead to escalation into full-scale strategic nuclear exchanges between the superpowers. Shortsightedly, NATO insisted on tactical weapons, reasoning that the high probability of escalation would require the continued protection of the American nuclear umbrella. The United States succumbed to the pressure; the weapons were deployed, and we were right back where we started. Flexible response in Europe had effectively reverted to massive retaliation.

The administration did not have much more luck when it looked at the prospects for defense. For a time, fallout shelters were considered as a possible solution to limit the carnage, but it didn't take long to prove that these were impractical solutions against megaton blasts that give thirty-minute warnings. It was impossible to build structures strong enough or in large enough numbers to provide protection for millions of people in large cities. Besides, the American people did not want to think about thermonuclear warfare. They were willing to be taxed for bombers or missiles or submarines or whatever was needed; but these things were out of their sight, out of their minds. Fallout shelters reached into their daily lives, but that solution faded away in the early sixties.

What about active defense? A great deal of time, effort, and deliberation went into the prospects for antiballistic missile devices. But they wouldn't work; it was like trying to hit a bullet with a bullet. Intercontinental ballistic missiles could come in with practically no warning. A single warhead could have a dozen non-nuclear decoys to confuse the defense; little was known of what would occur when the upper atmosphere was hit with defensive explosions. Several systems were designed: Nike, Safeguard, and Sentinel; none was ever deployed.

Faced with the impracticality of limited nuclear warfare and the futility of defensive systems, the Kennedy administration was forced back to reliance on high-yield thermonuclear weapons. Morally, instinctively, they rebelled against the indiscriminate destruction of metropolitan areas. First they studied the concept of counterforce or a no-cities strategy. They analyzed the practicability of aiming their weapons at military installations only: missile silos, air bases, supply depots.

This concept also failed. The accuracy of guidance systems against hardened concrete missile silos was not good enough, the growing nuclear submarine fleets were unreachable, and the certainty of radioactive fallout over thousands of square miles would kill millions of people no matter how pinpointed the targets. There would be no way to limit the casualties.

Then there is the question of a first strike: Should a nation, faced with the high probability of a nuclear war, strike first to destroy the enemy's ability to retaliate? Here again comes an eerie twist to the macabre mating dance of the sparring superpowers. The Russians have announced that they will not strike first, but we don't believe them. The American people are satisfied that we will never initiate a thermonuclear war, but our government cannot renounce the first-strike option out of deference to our NATO allies should Europe be overrun by conventional armies. In other words, we won't strike first but can't say so. Neither side can take the chance that the other will not strike first. Crowded into a strategic corner, the only viable strategic concept available was mutual assured destruction, appropriately acronymned MAD.

This was the strategy the Kennedy administration chose, a large enough and diversified enough strategic nuclear force that could survive a first strike and still destroy the enemy. It was a reversion to the Middle Age hostage concept: If you shoot at me, I'll kill your hostages. With the wonders of modern science the hostages don't even have to leave home. For the most part, they don't know that they are hostages. But in fact, each nation holds the populace of the other hostage against the initiation of hostilities. The polite name for the strategy was "deterrence."

But how large is large enough and how diversified is diversified enough? Both sides went into a race for size and diversity. The Soviets detonated a sixty-megaton bomb. The Americans developed and tested bombs for new aircraft, warheads for advanced ballistic missiles, and warheads for launch from submarines. But there was outrage and protest all over the world — not at the development of new weapons, which nobody understood, but at the orgy of weapons testing to prove them. The 1954 Bravo test, resulting in the radiated Rongerik natives and the Japanese fisherman fatality, followed by the losses to the fishing industry, was the first event to wake the public's outcry. The tuna fish scare after announcement of the Wigwam deep-underwater test in the mid-Pacific showed again that radiation hit where it hurt, in the pocketbook. Radiation from fallout from the Nevada tests began to concern the people, most demonstrably when it showed up in the milk from cows who had eaten irradiated hay.

Adlai Stevenson made it a major campaign issue in 1956;

a moratorium on testing was declared in 1958 after the Teak shot on Hardtack had lit up the skies from Hawaii to Samoa. After the moratorium had been broken by the Soviets and U.S. testing was resumed, the Starfish Prime shot had been visible all the way from Hawaii to Australia. The Cuban missile crisis of 1962 forged a bond between Khrushchev and Kennedy; both desperately wanted a comprehensive test ban, for humanitarian as well as political reasons. They had to settle for a partial ban, ostensibly because the Russians would not accept inspections, but probably deep down because military and weapons developers on both sides genuinely believed that they had to continue some testing in the interest of their national security. To assure the strategy of deterrence, or mutually assured destruction, more and better weapons were needed, they felt.

The treaty was hailed as the first step toward a comprehensive test ban and, better still, a first step toward disarmament. I applauded it, even though I thought it would adversely affect our company, which it did not. Company or no company, I, as much as anyone in the world, understood the full implications of unrestricted nuclear warfare; I ached for disarmament.

It was not to be. Sadly, the treaty solved one problem only, that of fallout. By literally taking testing underground, the pact hid its implications from the world. True, effects tests were difficult and expensive to perform, but they were carried out nonetheless. Elaborate underground vacuum chambers were required to simulate outer space, but the simulation was adequate for the accuracy required. True, weapons with yields over one megaton could not easily be contained. It was dimly understood at the time, but high-yield tests were no longer necessary. In a fission-fusion-fission device, most of the yield comes from the third stage, the heavy natural uranium casing, which fissions from the fusion neutrons. This was the simplest part of the whole reaction chain. If you want more yield, make the casing thicker. The Soviets had tested a sixty-megaton monster; we didn't bother because we knew it would work and it had no practical value. It was the fission trigger and the fusion secondary, the low-yield stage of the reaction, that needed improvement, so the underground restriction had little practical effect. Testing at Nevada went on year round while the public's attention turned to Vietnam and Watergate.

After 1963 the strategy of deterrence or MAD remained central to the superpowers, as it does to this day. Improvements in propulsion and guidance systems went on all over the country. Better bombers with cruise missiles were developed for manned delivery systems; the solid propellant Minuteman, with hardened silos, was manufactured for ICBMs; Polaris rockets were developed for submarine launched ballistic missiles (SLBMs). Gradually, the operational concept of the triad developed: manned bombers with cruise missiles, Minuteman ICBMs with hardened silos, and Polaris submarines with SLBMs. Each had advantages and disadvantages, but they filled the purpose of diversity in systems designed to retaliate after a first strike. The manned bombers were slow, but they were mobile and could be recalled if the President changed his mind; the Minuteman ICBMs were powerful, swift, and accurate, but they were immobile and vulnerable; the submarines were expensive and not accurate enough for counterforce use but were virtually invulnerable to a first strike. The Soviets also developed a triad but with different characteristics; they had fewer and lower-quality bombers and submarines, but a greater number of more powerful missiles.

The 1963 treaty, although not intended to do so, allowed the two nations to pursue their MAD strategy without the opprobrium of world opinion brought on by atmospheric testing. More tests have been carried out since the treaty was signed than were done before 1963, but the world has taken little notice. Other signed treaties give the impression of achieving progress toward disarmament, but they are mere tokens. An Outer Space Treaty became effective in 1967 and a Treaty for the Prohibition of Nuclear Weapons in Latin America in 1968. A Seabed Treaty, similar to the Outer Space Treaty, became effective in 1972, but neither power had any nuclear interest in outer space, the seabed, or in Latin America.

The Nuclear Non-Proliferation Treaty of 1968, under which nuclear nations undertook not to transfer nuclear weapons to non-nuclear states, was a worthwhile step forward. As of now over one hundred nations have signed the treaty, but it is disturbing to note that those which have not signed include France, Israel, Pakistan, India, Brazil, China, Cuba, South Africa, and a number of the Arab countries.

In the seventies attention turned from testing to arms limitation. Under the deterrence concept meaningful disarmament was out of the question, but it was desirable to put a limit to the buildup of arms as a first step. The main impetus to a strategic arms limitation treaty, or SALT, as it came to be known, was the development of multiple warhead capability for a single missile. As propulsion systems became more advanced and weapons more powerful and smaller, it became practical to mount a number of nuclear warheads on a single launch vehicle. As guidance systems improved, the warheads could be directed to different targets after leaving the rocket. The inevitable acronym is MIRV, for multiple independently targeted re-entry vehicles. This one development increased the firepower of existing launch systems by an order of magnitude and put the number of deliverable warheads into the tens of thousands on each side, far beyond any conceivable number needed for first-strike retaliation.

The first agreements, SALT I, were signed by President Richard M. Nixon and U.S.S.R. General Secretary Leonid Brezhnev in 1972. They provided that neither side would deploy a larger number of missile launchers than were already deployed or under construction when the treaty was signed. It took seven years to negotiate the SALT II treaty, which set limits on the total number of delivery systems each side could have and on the number of individual warheads each "MIRVed" delivery vehicle could carry. In addition, the treaty called for reducing the number of delivery systems in the future. Signed by Jimmy Carter and Brezhnev on June 18, 1979, it was never ratified by the United States Senate.

Carter withdrew the treaty after the Russians invaded Afghanistan later that year.

Before attempting to terminate this tale of terror I should discuss two other weapons, the neutron bomb and the MX missile. The neutron bomb, or radiation enhanced warhead, is the most impractical weapon yet conceived. It originated in the old problem of defending Western Europe. The use of standard fission-fusion-fission weapons would kill millions of noncombatants and destroy buildings to the degree that there would be nothing left to protect. If, however, the third stage of a three-stage warhead were eliminated and the yield built up by increasing the second stage, most of the yield would be in the form of neutrons rather than blast. It was first conceived as an antitank device that would kill the crew without requiring enough yield to destroy the tank.

The media have had a field day with the idea, calling it the capitalist bomb that kills people and saves property. But the whole concept is ridiculous. Soviet tanks in an invasion would number in the thousands; to destroy them many thousands of guns would have to be fired. Since the tanks would be deployed into heavily crowded areas, millions of people would be killed. What good would it do to have houses standing if no one was left to occupy them? The guns themselves are enormously large howitzers, unsuitable for camouflage. They would be the natural first target in the event of an invasion.

What utterly destroys the concept, however, is that the Soviets will not play by the same rules. They have hundreds of nuclear missiles deployed in Eastern Europe and would certainly use them should we initiate a first tactical nuclear weapon strike. Theirs are not "clean" warheads; the Soviets have announced that they will have nothing to do with the enhanced radiation concept. If, then, NATO officials did decide to use such weapons, not only would they be ineffective, but they would provoke a Soviet response that would completely destroy Western Europe and almost certainly set off a chain of escalation that would end in world annihilation.

The latest element in the nuclear debate is the MX missile.

It comes about because of a possible flaw in the triad concept. As the Soviets build up their missile capability and improve guidance systems within the limits of the SALT II
agreements, it is calculated that sometime in the late eighties
they will have the capability to destroy our immobile Minuteman missiles in their silos on a first strike. This is known
as the "window of vulnerability." It is not at all clear that
this is so, nor is it likely that the Soviets would risk the gamble of a first strike. Even if it were, we still have the two
other legs of the triad to assure destruction of the Soviet
homeland. Although the SALT II treaty has not yet been
ratified, both sides seem to be conforming to its provisions.
We cannot then close the window of vulnerability by building more ICBM missiles. A concept evolved under which a
new missile, Missile X or MX, would be designed. It would
be mobile and could evade a first strike by random movement among a large number of silos. The trouble is that the
plan to disperse the missile silos widely enough to survive a
multimegaton first strike would have chewed up a good part
of the states of Nevada and Utah, to which the inhabitants
of those states objected strenuously. President Ronald Reagan
canceled the mobility scheme in 1981; the question of how
to deploy MX is still open. One wag suggested that they be
put aboard an Amtrak train and that the Soviets be sent the
schedule. That way they'd never find them.

I object to the mobility concept for another reason. These
missiles are mammoth devices; they cannot be randomly
moved. Someone has to decide at least a day in advance
which ones are going to be moved and where they are going.
Soviet missiles can be reprogrammed in less than an hour;
the flight time is only thirty minutes. Then would come the
question, Can the Soviets steal the schedule and reprogram
their guidance systems so as to negate the whole idea? It is
not very likely, but in the weird world of nuclear strategy,
anything that is at all possible has to be considered. I have
been around nuclear strategists for many years and I know
how they think. I am certain that if the MX missiles are deployed in a mobile configuration, someone will write a paper

suggesting that the Soviets could break the scheduling code. Someone else would write a paper suggesting that since we don't know whether the Soviets could break the code or not, we should, for maximum security, assume that they could. This would open a new window of vulnerability, and off we would go to a new level of escalation.

Now a new proposal has been put forward by President Reagan. It is known as dense pack. It is the exact opposite of the mobility concept; all the missiles would be packed closely together. Enemy missiles, exploding in close proximity over the deployment, would create an environment of high radioactivity, shock, and missile debris strong enough to prevent penetration by succeeding waves of missiles. The buzz word is *fratricide.*

It won't work. There are a wide variety of countermeasures available. Missiles that burrow into the earth, missiles with time-delayed detonators, missiles designed to explode with microsecond simultaneity, a host of other countermeasures will surface. Almost certainly a requirement for an antiballistic missile will be brought up again, a concept that also does not work. Most important, the concept of fratricide cannot be adequately tested, since these effects cannot be simulated without atmospheric testing. Far better that our efforts be concentrated on our economy, the true bulwark of our strength against the Soviets.

The most striking characteristic of the development of nuclear weapons was the inexorability of the process. From the day Roentgen first discovered that his X-rays could penetrate solid matter, the curiosity of the scientist predestined that man would search out first the composition of the atom, then of its nucleus until all was revealed, the stupendous energy that nucleus contained, and the mechanism by which it could be extracted. With that curiosity and the developing knowledge went the misgivings and the fear that the energy of the nucleus would be used to the detriment of mankind. Pierre Curie's statement in 1903, Rutherford's warnings in 1911, the extraordinary prescience of H. G. Wells in *The World Set Free* in 1914, all indicated that concern went with curiosity but could not arrest the relentless search for the secrets of the nucleus.

Roentgen, Becquerel, Curie, Thomson, Rutherford, Planck, Einstein, and Bohr all made their magnificent contributions until Chadwick discovered the final analytic tool, the neutron, and Fermi became the master craftsman of the art of slow neutron measurement. Then an astounding thing happened. After forty years of steady, persistent progress, everything stopped. Fermi had achieved fission in 1934, but didn't know it. It was five long years, the "five-year miracle," before Meitner and Frisch in January 1939 correctly interpreted Hahn's and Strassman's results as nuclear fission. It then took only ten days for Bohr to bring the message to the United States, where Fermi was waiting for him on the dock ready to regain scientific leadership. Fermi's first pile in 1942 closed the gap between knowledge and application; there was no turning back. Most remarkably, the first two nuclear weapons were ready less than ninety days before the scheduled invasion of Japan.

Truman's announcement to Stalin at Potsdam was the start of the postwar arms race. Through all the soul-searching, the politicking, the efforts at international control, the Soviets moved single-mindedly, determinedly toward nuclear parity and possible superiority. Nothing we did with the Acheson-Lilienthal Report, the Baruch plan, Atoms for Peace, Open Skies, the hydrogen bomb debate, seems to have had one iota of effect on their nuclear development program. Nuclear weapons were going to be developed, whatever the United States said or did.

Recognizing that the world would be better off if nothing had been discovered, and at the risk of sounding like an apologia, it is probably best that it happened as it did. If the development had happened five years earlier, Hitler would have had the bomb. If it had happened five years later, Stalin would have had it. If we had not developed the device during the war, our postwar mentality would have renounced it. Stalin's would not.

We are a unique generation. Others have said it before,

but if we survive, future generations will look back on our actions as the single most important turning point in the history of mankind. If we do not . . .

What is this capacity we have to destroy ourselves, and what can we do about it? I do not propose to chant a tale of horrors. I can only tell what it was like for me in 1954 in a concrete bunker twenty miles from ground zero. Draw your own twenty-mile radius. I can only tell you what happened to the Japanese fisherman seventy-five miles away and the Rongerik natives 125 miles away. Draw your own 125-mile radius. Will a single bomb destroy a large city? I can only tell you that the Mike shot in 1952 blew a hole in Eniwetok Atoll deeper than the height of the Empire State Building. Will a large-scale thermonuclear exchange pierce the ozone layer and destroy all life above the ground? I don't know. Nobody knows. I can only tell you that the Starfish test in 1962 (1.4 megatons, 400 kilometers high) lit the skies from Hawaii to Australia, knocked out the communications capability of three satellites, and seriously disrupted the Van Allen radiation belt in a manner completely unanticipated. This does not prove anything about the ozone layer, but it does tell us how little we know about the earth's outer environment. The ozone layer is very fragile, numbered in parts per million. It protects us from the sun's ultraviolet radiation, which would make the earth uninhabitable, at least above ground, if it reached the surface of the earth. Nitrogen oxides rising from nuclear detonations are concentrated and powerful. Theoretical calculations say they will disperse the ozone layer. Experiments so far have shown no effect, but the scale has been very small. What is the probability that the ozone layer will be pierced? I can only rely on my own knowledge and experience. It's an apples and oranges comparison, but I would put it as more probable than a full-scale nuclear power plant disaster. In many respects, we worry about the wrong things.

But what difference does it make? Civilization as we know it in this country would be destroyed. This threat of instant annihilation is the most horrible legacy we can pass on to

our children and to our children's children. It requires that
we take a radically new look at nuclear politics, that we do
some things which we can do unilaterally, that we do some
things which the Soviets should be willing to cooperate on,
and most important, that we do some things which can lead
to cooperation in the more distant future.

The first thing we can do unilaterally is get rid of the concept of population dispersal for civil defense. It is so ridiculous that it is embarrassing. I believe in simple precautions:
radiation meters, staying indoors, storing up water supplies,
or even, if one is so inclined, preparing fallout shelters. But
population dispersal is impossible for many reasons, some of
which are lack of food supply, shelter, and transportation.
But the basic reason is that no one would know which way
to go. A first strike would be aimed at military targets initially, not large cities. But even so, with so many thousands
of bombs and missiles an enemy would pattern bombs over
a wide area to ensure against inaccuracies. For fallout protection, you have to know which way the upper winds are
going to blow. They can change in half an hour, so you
might be going the wrong way. I thought we were safe in the
bunker. As Joe Louis used to say to his opponents in the ring,
"You can run, but you can't hide." My own survival plan is
to stay home, take two aspirins, and hope for the best.

The next thing we can do unilaterally is refuse to deploy
any more tactical nuclear missiles in Europe. The several
types deployed by NATO are aging and becoming obsolete.
In 1979 NATO ministers voted to ask the United States to
station several hundred new radiation-enhanced tactical missiles in the European theater. The United States has agreed
to build the devices but has not yet agreed to deploy them.
NATO ministers refuse to build up conventional forces adequate to defend against a Soviet invasion. They claim they
must have a nuclear defense. The scenario, as the nuclear
strategists describe it, is that when the Russians advance, a
few tactical missiles will be fired. This act will bring them
to their senses and they will stop. But what sensible person
would bet civilization on such a strategy? This is an armchair

strategy, a war-game strategy, a think-tank strategy. It is not a real-life strategy.

In 1953 I participated in a field test of a tactical nuclear weapon fired from an artillery piece under simulated battlefield conditions. It scared the hell out of me to see seventeen kilotons explode fifteen hundred feet in the air six miles away. The shock could be felt ninety miles away in Las Vegas, the fireball observed for fifty miles, and the cloud for seventy-five miles. This was the only test of its kind ever performed in the free world. Four years later there was a moratorium on nuclear weapons testing; since then all testing has been underground. Of the twenty-five people in attendance almost thirty years ago, all except me have probably retired.

I doubt that there is another person active in military or political affairs in the free world who has seen a tactical weapon explode in the atmosphere under even simulated battle conditions. This includes the United States Army, the British Army, the German Army, the French Army, and all the NATO allies. It probably even includes the Russian Army. Furthermore, no one in the Soviet Union, the United States, or the NATO countries has seen a nuclear explosion of any kind in the atmosphere for more than twenty years. You can't sit at a desk or in an armchair and predict what will happen when the first device explodes under conditions of complete surprise. A nuclear explosion wreaks massive, unpredictable havoc on radio communications, the nerve centers of battlefields. There would be chaos in command posts, and when the second one went off, any commander with a nuclear button to push or a nuclear lanyard to pull would probably do so. The odds are heavily in favor of this scenario. The Soviets have hundreds of medium-range, medium-yield "dirty" thermonuclear weapons in Eastern Europe; it would be folly to anticipate that they would not use them. Under the tactical theory, as in the Vietnam village, it will be necessary to destroy Europe in order to save it.

But there is a more subtle reason to resist additional deployment. As present weapons age and become obsolete, the citizens of European countries will no longer be nuclear hostages. The peoples of the United States and the Soviet Union may gradually come to realize that in a thermonuclear exchange it will only be their countries which will be wiped out. The rest of the world may survive, conceivably even unscathed, with only the citizens of the two superpowers annihilated. What kind of superpower is that?

The third step can partially be taken unilaterally but would best be done in cooperation with the Soviets, since it is in their interests to cooperate. I firmly believe that the most likely nuclear event to occur is the explosion of a weapon by a terrorist organization. Knowledge of how to build a nuclear device is universal; it would not be difficult to steal one from a security-lax European nation. Either way, in the next few years a well-organized terrorist group will certainly be able to obtain a simple fission weapon. To obtain the maximum effect, the logical place to explode such a device would be the governmental nerve center of the country, Washington, D.C. It could easily be assembled on a boat in the Potomac River. Controlled by a time clock set days ahead of time, it could explode when the President was in the White House and the Congress and Supreme Court were in session. Washington would be demolished. This single, easily accomplished terrorist act could wipe out government. There would be no President, no Congress, no Supreme Court, no Pentagon, no newspapers, no radio or television antennas left standing to inform the world of what had happened. As in the shallow underwater test at Bikini in 1946, the radioactive waters of the river would render the area uninhabitable, even for rescue crews. What would happen next? Would a panicky silo commander or submarine captain assume that it was an act of war and unleash a salvo at the Soviet Union? Who knows?

There is, I assume, a secret mechanism for passing on the authority of the President if he is assassinated, and there are constitutional provisions for the succession of the Vice President and the Speaker of the House. But who would know who was alive and who was dead? And who would make the decision? The panic at the White House after John Hinckley's assassination attempt on President Reagan, when Secretary of State Alexander Haig assumed authority he did not have, is a small example of the kind of confusion that might occur in even the simplest of circumstances. There is probably an understanding with the various military field commanders; if so, it should be made public. There is no point in the commander of the Strategic Air Force, for example, assuming authority for firing ballistic missiles if the people have not been informed in advance that he has been granted such authority. This is a complex problem that should be analyzed by the Congress in hearings open to the public. One possible solution would be a constitutional amendment delegating powers to a council of state governors, who could be expected to be dispersed around the country at the time of a catastrophe. There should also be provisions for the rapid election or appointment by the respective state governors of a new Congress and to replace the Supreme Court. However distasteful the problems, they should be addressed, and promptly.

Since one terrorist action could start an accidental full-scale thermonuclear event, the powers of our intelligence agencies and our law enforcement agencies should be strengthened commensurate with the severity of the threat. This would certainly put some constraints on our civil liberties; libertarians will howl, but the people have a civic responsibility to protect their right to survive.

The same thing could happen in Russia. As dissent within the country and in Eastern Europe grows, the probability of a terrorist action in Moscow increases. Although the tight security in Russia lowers the odds of its happening there, the confusion in a rigidly controlled police state would be much greater and more dangerous. Would the Soviet equivalent of our SAC commander or a submarine skipper, his chain of command destroyed, be more likely to assume that the event was directed by the United States? I think so.

The Russians will talk if it is to their advantage to do so. Against this terrorist threat, we should be allies. They should

be willing to sit down and talk with us about respective
chains of command should such an action take place. The
danger is mutual. Perhaps there should be a "hot line" between the SAC commander and his Soviet equivalent. Maybe
there already is. If so, the public should be informed. There
is no point to secrecy in these matters.

We should be able to work with the Russians to curb international terrorism. Granted that Soviet agents are disrup-
tive throughout the world, they are as aware of the dangers
of nuclear terrorism as we are. It is our two peoples who are
held hostage to the mutual strategies of deterrence or mutually assured destruction. Superpowers held in hostage to each
other, we share a common bond.

Let us suppose that terrorism escalates a little bit, to the
nationalistic level. Six countries are known to have nuclear
weapons: the United States, the Soviet Union, China, France,
Great Britain, and India. Israel almost certainly has them but
won't admit it. Such countries as Argentina, Brazil, Pakistan,
Saudi Arabia, and South Africa have refused to sign the nuclear nonproliferation treaty, for whatever reason. Any modern industrial nation, acting within the security of its own
borders, has the capacity to fabricate a quantity of nuclear
warheads. I have heard it said that fissionable material sells
on the international black market for about the same price
per kilogram as cocaine.

What happens if nuclear weapons are used in a local war,
perhaps in the Middle East? The first nation to break the
thirty-seven-year-old nuclear truce should be dealt with
promptly and decisively by the superpowers. There is no
point to soul-searching or moralizing about our being the
only nation to have used them previously; the situation is
different now. We should negotiate an agreement with the
Russians to take whatever action is appropriate against such a
highly destabilizing act. Whatever form the agreement takes,
it should be specific and widely disseminated. This is not a
matter for the United Nations. The rest of the world does
not have the same problems we do. We and the Soviet Union,
united in our common bond of mutual hostage, must act in
conjunction with our own national interests.

But what of the biggest problem of all, the one that faces mankind — the tens of thousands of nuclear weapons held by the superpowers? The first rule of innovation or invention is to understand the problem before looking for solutions. The first thing to understand is that it has been building inexorably, relentlessly, for almost a hundred years. Many have seen it coming and have tried resolutely to hold it off, but to no avail. H. G. Wells predicted atomic weapons by 1956 and a nuclear holocaust shortly thereafter, followed by a world government rebuilt from the ashes. Wells's holocaust was not as complete as ours would be, so it's not a solution.

It is fatuous to pontificate that what we need is world government. That's easy to say, but the question is how to get there. We must understand that the problem was not caused by the present administration nor can it be solved instantaneously. Neither nuclear freezes nor neutron bombs will solve our problems. They make good news stories but are dangerously "destabilizing," the term the nuclear strategists use for the imbalance of power. To understand why nuclear freezes won't work, we must look anew at the delicate definition of "deterrence." It means that each side must have sufficient nuclear firepower to survive a first strike and to counter with assurance that the aggressor will be annihilated. This means nuclear parity — not too much and not too little.

If one side has too much firepower, it might be tempted to make a first strike in the hopes that it could wipe out the deterrent. If it has too little, it might be tempted to strike first before the superior firepower of the other could overwhelm it. It sounds insane as a strategy, but sane or not, it is the strategy that has held the world together for the last twenty years. A nuclear freeze would upset this delicate balance, unless the Soviets decided to obey a United States law forbidding them and us to make any more nuclear weapons. (It might be simpler for us to pass a law directing them to get out of Afghanistan and Poland.) A nuclear freeze is unilateral disarmament because the Soviets obviously would pay no attention to it. To propose such a solution to an unsophisticated American public is demagoguery of the most despicable sort. It purports to provide a simple solution, which will lull the public into a complacency that can only make matters worse. The Soviet Union would be delighted if we enacted nuclear freeze legislation.

The strategic doctrine of deterrence, although it has worked for twenty years, cannot be expected to work indefinitely because it violates one of the most fundamental concepts of combat. The whole history of evolution has infixed into the genes of all living creatures the doctrine of the survival of the fittest. To tell ourselves that superior firepower is disadvantageous runs counter to every basic biological instinct in each human being. It is the reason that both sides, recognizing and abiding by the concept of parity, are constantly negotiating and maneuvering to be primus inter pares, the first among equals. It is the reason that think tanks and strategists on both sides argue about backfire bombers and cruise missiles and MX and MIRV, constantly shuffling and wriggling concepts in a bewildering variety of strategic studies, much like, to mix two metaphors, rearranging angels on the head of a pin.

How do we work ourselves out of this delicate doctrine of deterrence? If we are fortunate, we can do it in a generation, maybe two, if we can borrow that much time.

The first step is to educate our own citizens about the nature of the problem, beginning in the schools. Each of our high schools should have a compulsory course in the history of nuclear development, with enough science to break down the problem of Snow's two cultures, enough history to understand the inevitability of the development, to be aware that Hiroshima and Nagasaki were not random acts of violence, to realize that the United States tried valiantly to stem the tide, to recognize that it is not in the Soviet culture to consider moral values in the pursuit of their national interests.

We can teach the science; that's easy. A high school student today already knows more physics than Isaac Newton did. We can teach the history to a rapidly changing student body. More women than men are entering college, women in whom the concept of superiority in combat is not as deeply ingrained as in males.

But recognition of the Soviet culture, there's the rub. All of our moral and ethical training is repugnant to an understanding of what makes the Soviets tick. We need a relativity theory of geopolitics. The Soviet concepts of space time are different from ours; their concept of required territory is larger than ours; their clocks run slower. The way they view us is different from the way we view them, since we view each other from different geopolitical space time platforms. Our impressions of each other will always be relative; there will be no agreement on absolutes.

But times are changing and herein lies our solution. We have never understood the motivations of a Stalin, a Khrushchev, a Brezhnev, but a new generation is coming into Soviet politics. Not quickly — Brezhnev's successor Yari V. Andropov, looks very much like him — but gradually over the next twenty-five or thirty years. The change must come because the Soviet system is morally and economically bankrupt. Although outwardly the Soviet philosophical message remains the same, it is true that there are no more Marxists in Moscow. Modern communications are reaching the Soviet people and will continue to penetrate as the needs of our increasingly complex technological societies require more complete education and, with it, more inquiry. Agriculturally, the Soviet Union is in its sixty-fifth consecutive year of bad weather; that message won't sell much longer. Eastern Europe has already learned that the concept of the planned economy is both intellectually and financially obsolete. All over the world, democratic capitalism has proved superior to the planned economy. Who would have dreamed in 1941 that Japan and West Germany could be what they are today? True, they lost a war and the change was more rapid, but it will come eventually to the Soviets. At the moment they are in a state of transition, lashing out militarily to insulate themselves from their domestic economic problems. Provided we too do not neglect the doctrine that the best national defense is a strong economy, our present military buildup is an appropriate countertactic. In the long run, however, matching Soviet bellicosity is the wrong thing to do.

I have spent most of my adult life in two worlds, those of
nuclear weapons and of business and commerce. I look on
my weapons activities with a sense of pride and satisfaction
in having done well a job that needed to be done. I look on
my business career with not only pride and satisfaction for
gains accomplished, but a sense of exhilaration at the prospects for our democratic capitalistic system for the future of
mankind.

The nuclear arms race is over. There will be pushings and
haulings with MX missiles and backfire bombers, but both
sides are aware that the deadly doctrine of deterrence domi-
nates the delicate balance of terror in the world today. Nuclear strategists have known it for twenty years. The last several administrations have gradually come to appreciate it —
Carter's by pulling away from it, Reagan's perhaps pushing
too hard against it. But it is there, and it will be there for as
many generations as will exist before we blow the world
apart. There will be SALT talks and START talks, but they
won't do much good. It is a desirable goal to limit production
or to cut back a thousand warheads on either side. It will look
good politically and may even lull us into some sense of ac-
complishment, but we will still be left with the ability to
destroy each other many times over. Meaningful arms reduc-
tion can only come after mutual understanding.

Mutual understanding with the Soviets will come only
after we have reconciled our political systems. That's going
to be tough. Einstein was once asked why the human mind
could conjure up concepts like quantum mechanics and relativity theory without being able to reconcile the most fundamental of political theories. His answer was, "Politics is more
difficult than physics." That is true. The world would be better off if we could think up political solutions as easily as we
think up physical solutions to our problems.

Before we can reconcile our political systems we must reconcile our economic systems. You can't have political freedom without economic freedom. That is where our system
comes in. The concept of free markets, the concept of the
"invisible hand," the notion that individuals working in en-

lightened self-interest also work for the common good is
proving over and over again to be superior to planned eco-
nomics as the world becomes more complex and nations realize that their planned economies cannot extrapolate into
the economies of other nations. Our economic system, open
and market-oriented, preserves an open and individually oriented political system. Now, through the work of Michael
Novak in his book *The Spirit of Democratic Capitalism*, we
are developing the third leg of our triad — not a nuclear triad
but an intellectual triad in which a free and open economy
preserves a free and open government with a moral-cultural
stabilizing leg that satisfies the need for a complete philosophical model of our democratic capitalistic system. It
works. I've seen it work, from a small two-man partnership
struggling to pay the rent in a Boston attic to the chairman-
ship of a Fortune 500 company. Our economic-political-
cultural system has its warts and its wrinkles, but it's better
than anything else that has been thought up in the world
to date.

It is this system we must sell to the Soviets. It will not be
as difficult as it seems if we go about it in the right way. We
must not move at all until we can convince ourselves through
open national debate that this is the way to go. We must not
move too rapidly lest we frighten them away. They were suspicious when we tried to give them the bomb in 1945 and
wouldn't take it. If we try to force anything on them, for example, through sanctions, the results will be negative. We
must first be convinced that a healthy Soviet economy is in
our national interest. If we can make them happy and prosperous, we will be better off. The seeds are there. Twenty percent of the Soviet market is a black market, a "left hand"
capitalist economy. Every collective farm, every factory,
every store has its illegal underground, a capitalist component. Western ideas proliferate as do Western clothes and
cultures. I have been in the Soviet Union, learned some of
their language, and done "booth duty" in industrial exhibi-
tions. I have seen it in their faces and heard it in the innu-
endos behind our Russian-English conversations. They rec-

ognize that their centralized system can do great things in space and rocketry and weaponry when they concentrate their resources, but they also realize that they accomplish these ends at the expense of the common good.

But we have tried détente and it doesn't work. At least so far. When we arm, they arm. When we stop, they keep arming. That has been past experience but need not be the future. The nuclear arms buildup is at a stalemate; the conventional arms buildup will be stalemated soon. They have already built up to the limit of their resources; we will match them, and unfortunately, match them we must, in a few years. When that happens, we will have both a nuclear and conventional weapons stalemate. That is the time to push for mutual economic cooperation. There are risks. If we agree to assist in a gas pipeline construction, it may be used as an economic weapon against Europe. True, but that threat is insignificant against the background of the nuclear threat. We should reinstitute the concept of most-favored-nation status. The last time we tried, we attempted to trade it for human rights progress. It didn't work; such trade-offs will never work. We must make economic progress first, then political progress. Unfortunately, moral progress will come last, and certainly not in this generation.

It's a tough job but we can do it. I see no alternative. We are passing on to the next generation the worst possible legacy of all, the threat of instant annihilation. We say we can't trust the Russians. But we trust them every day, every hour. We trust that they have the good sense and the instincts of self-preservation deeply enough ingrained in their single-minded, self-serving souls to resist the urge to push the button that will finish us all.

We, the citizens of the United States, must realize that we and the citizens of the Soviet Union are held together in mutual bondage, as hostages to the nuclear threat. We are not superpowers, we are superpawns.

It took us a long time to get into this position. It will take a long time to get out. There are no instant solutions, no easy avenues. We must loosen the chains that bind us one link at a time. The first link to be broken is economic, and it is we who must make the moves since their system will not permit it. We should be as willing to give up some trade secrets today as we were to give up the bomb. What's the incremental risk? Minuscule!

Only when we get economic cooperation can we hope to get political reconciliation. Only when a prosperous economy permits it will the barriers to human rights of the police state begin to fall. Only when these things happen can mutual understanding and mutual trust emerge. Only then can come meaningful disarmament. Only then, and generations away, can we realize the hopes for world government, the ultimate solution to the nuclear threat.

We have time.

We have until the end of the world.

INDEX

INDEX